The
EVERYTHING.
Quilting Book

Dear Reader:

I started my first quilt when I was twenty and expecting my first child. With the arrogance of youth, I sought almost no help and made that first baby quilt the way I wanted to. I made plenty of mistakes, too, with it and with the two that followed. My stitches were too large. My quilting lines were too far apart. The colors I chose were too pale for a baby's eyes to even see! But the biggest mistake I made was putting all three of them away too soon.

In order to ensure that the quilts were in good condition to pass on, I prevented the one thing that would have made them desirable: memories. Don't make the same mistake. A quilt that's hidden away is a wealth of energy and time buried instead of invested. Use your quilt. Or give it away. Looking forward to one or the other will make the quilting that much more fun.

Sandra Detrixhe

The EVERYTHING® Series

Editorial

Publishing Director	Gary M. Krebs
Managing Editor	Kate McBride
Copy Chief	Laura MacLaughlin
Acquisitions Editor	Eric M. Hall
Development Editors	Lesley Bolton
	Michael Paydos
Production Editor	Khrysti Nazzaro

Production

Production Director	Susan Beale
Production Manager	Michelle Roy Kelly
Series Designers	Daria Perreault
	Colleen Cunningham
Cover Design	Paul Beatrice
	Frank Rivera
Layout and Graphics	Colleen Cunningham
	Rachael Eiben
	Michelle Roy Kelly
	Daria Perreault
	Erin Ring
Series Cover Artist	Barry Littmann
Interior Illustrator	Eric Andrews
Photography	Scott Watrous

Visit the entire Everything® Series at everything.com

THE
EVERYTHING®
QUILTING
BOOK

Simple instructions for creating
the perfect family heirloom

Sandra Detrixhe

Adams Media Corporation
Avon, Massachusetts

For Eden, with love, from Mom.

An Everything® Series Book.
Everything® and everything.com® are registered trademarks of Adams Media Corporation.

Published by Adams Media Corporation
57 Littlefield Street, Avon, MA 02322 U.S.A.
www.adamsmedia.com

ISBN: 1-58062-872-9
Printed in the United States of America.

J I H G F E D C B A

Library of Congress Cataloging-in-Publication Data
Detrixhe, Sandra.
The everything quilting book / Sandra Detrixhe.
p.   cm.
(An Everything series book)
ISBN 1-58062-872-9
1. Patchwork–Patterns. 2. Quilting. 3. Appliqué.
I. Title. II. Series: Everything series.
TT835.D487   2003
746.46–dc21   2003003536

This book is available at quantity discounts for bulk purchases.
For information, call 1-800-872-5627.

Contents

Acknowledgments

Special thanks to Eden Detrixhe, an aspiring quilter,
for all her questions, comments, suggestions,
and support while serving as this book's first reader.

Top Ten Reasons
to Learn to Quilt

1. You can create unique gifts with a personal touch.
2. Instead of relying on store-bought brands to do it for you, you can use your own designs and create a quilt to fit your needs.
3. Quilting is an absorbing hobby that helps relieve stress.
4. You can make new friends at quilting bees and community groups.
5. You'll be joining in a longstanding American tradition and learning the same techniques used by generations past.
6. Quilting is a great way to recycle leftover fabric.
7. You can make something special to pass on to your grandchildren.
8. Your house can be decorated with a homemade touch.
9. You can express yourself creatively with color and texture.
10. Quilting is a hobby you can take with you anywhere—in front of the TV, in the car, or waiting in line.

Introduction

▶ WHAT DOES THE WORD *QUILT* BRING TO MIND? A faded heirloom tucked away in a trunk with a note telling which beloved relative took each tiny stitch? Or a huge masterpiece raffled off at a church bazaar, the laborious work of many selfless and probably aged hands? Something you have a better chance of winning than making?

Antique quilts are heirlooms to the family, certainly, and social commentary to the historian. But quilts are much more than that. The modern quilt is functional art. It is an expression of the quilter's creativity that keeps her warm at night. What could be better than that?

In spite of what some might think, quilting is not a dying art. A trip to a magazine stand will reveal some six or seven different quilting magazines available. Fabric shops cater to quilters with specialized supplies and fabric swatches cut in convenient sizes.

If you look, you will notice quilts and their influence all around you. A vinyl tablecloth is printed with designs taken directly from old quilt patterns. A greeting card features a Double Wedding Ring Quilt. Crocheted afghans mimic quilt designs. Is this a resurgence? More likely, your own budding interest has revealed things that have always been there.

A trip to a library will uncover books on quilting published in the 1960s, 1940s, or even 1920s. Most will mention the renewed popularity of quilting. Has it enjoyed many little revivals or has it always been in the background, strong but quiet, not unlike those tiny, almost invisible stitches that give quilts their charm?

Since you're reading this book, chances are you've considered the possibility of making a quilt yourself. You might know exactly what kind you would make if you only knew how or if you only had time. You might even have saved fabric for that ever-distant someday.

Admittedly, a quilt isn't a project for one Sunday afternoon. But what does it matter? A quilt begun today will be as beautiful when it's finished whether that day is this summer, in five years, or even in ten years. "Ten years! But I'll be sixty (or forty or eighty) in ten years!" you say. How old will you be in ten years if you *don't* start a quilt? And who knows, you might find quilting so much fun you finish your first in a few months and begin another.

For many, the hesitation to begin that first quilt is caused by a fear of messing it up and wasting time and material. In this book you will find smaller projects that demonstrate the various techniques of quilting. As well as being fun projects in themselves, they will serve as practice pieces and confidence builders. If you can make them, you can make a quilt.

Only you will know when you are ready to begin that full-sized quilt you've always wanted. And when you finish it, whether it's a once-in-a-lifetime experience or the first of many quilts, you will have the satisfaction of knowing you created something beautiful and useful, which just might turn out to be an heirloom someday. (E)

Chapter 1

The Art of Quilting

Quilting is an ancient craft that was born of necessity and continues into the modern age as a popular hobby. The secret of its survival lies in part in the beauty of the quilts themselves, but also in people's fascination with the process.

What Is a Quilt?

At first thought, a quilt is a colorful homemade bedspread. However, as a verb, the word *quilt* means to sew layers of cloth together. Anything made in this way is referred to as quilted, such as the quilted lining of a coat. Quilting, then, refers both to the entire process of making a quilt and to that one defining step in the process, the quilting stitch itself.

The Components of a Quilt

Although there are exceptions, the basic quilt consists of three layers. The backing, or bottom layer, is generally made of a plain fabric and is sometimes called a lining. The term *backing* is less confusing because no other part of a quilt or quilted project is likely to be referred to as such, while *lining* might refer to other things.

The middle layer is the batting. This gives the quilt its insulation properties. The thickness of the batting combined with the style of stitching determines how heavy or puffy the quilt will be. This middle layer is sometimes called the filling or padding, but these terms bring to mind more old-fashioned products than the commercial quilt batting used in modern quilts.

The final layer is the cover. This is the decorated layer often called a quilt top or, more rarely, the face. Since *top* might refer to the headboard end of the finished quilt and *face* can be confused with *facing,* the term *cover* is somewhat preferable and will be used here.

Types of Quilts

There are two primary types of quilts: the pieced and the appliquéd. *Pieced* refers to a quilt cover made up of many, sometimes hundreds, of small pieces of cloth stitched together. These pieces might go together to create one large pattern such as a star on the cover. More often, the pieces are arranged in repeating geometric patterns. Sometimes these patterns are alternately turned to one side or another or dark and light colors are used to create diamond or stripe effects on the overall cover.

Appliquéd quilts are made of cutout shapes stitched onto a contrasting background. If the design consists of one large picture, it is said to have an all-over pattern. Often the appliquéd picture is repeated, much like the pieced pattern, and sewn onto blocks, which are then sewn together.

A comforter, or comfortable as it was called some hundred years ago, is a tied quilt, which means instead of rows of stitching joining the layers together, threads are caught through the layers at even intervals and tied in knots. It's a quilt that isn't quilted. A plain quilt, on the other hand, is exceedingly quilted. The cover is made from one solid-colored piece, often white, and this is where it gets its name. It is then quilted all over in the most intricate of patterns, often very detailed garlands of flowers, feathered wreaths, or figures of animals, people, houses, or ships.

Quilts as Art

Perhaps because quilts are no longer necessities, they are being recognized more and more as works of art. Quilts are often hung on walls to show them off, but even if they are spread across a bed, they are often the focal point of the entire room. Antique quilts and even finely made modern ones sell for hundreds of dollars.

A quilt's value goes beyond a monetary one. Quilts are expressions of the quilter's artistic vision, and no two will be alike. Even following the same pattern, one quilter will stray a little, modifying the pattern to suit herself. Another less adventurous quilter might follow the pattern exactly, but her tastes will show in her choice of fabrics and their arrangement.

FACT

Feminists have suggested that if quilts had been made primarily by men instead of women, they would have been considered art from the very beginning, and more of the really early ones might have been preserved. But then again, the kids would still have needed blankets, so it might not have made a difference.

The Quilter's Language

As with any new skill, there is some specialized language that must be learned for quilting. Quilting language may be more confusing than some because there are terms that have more than one meaning and objects or processes that are referred to by many names. Perhaps this is because so many cultures contributed to the craft, which flourished in small isolated communities. However, it becomes less confusing as the process is better understood.

Construction Terms

Pattern refers to the guide you will follow to make your quilt but also to the design itself. The pattern (guide) will show you how to cut the pieces that will make up a particular pattern (design). Sometimes a template, a cardboard or plastic cutout, is used to cut the pieces. Sewing these pieces together along a seam line is called piecing. Sewing one piece on top of another is called appliquéing.

If the pattern repeats across the cover of the quilt, each of these repeats is called a block. Sometimes the blocks are sewn directly together, but sometimes they are separated by a strip of fabric called a panel. When the blocks and panels are sewn together, it is referred to as setting the quilt. When the layers of the quilt are put together, it is called assembling the quilt.

Details

Often there are strips of cloth sewn around the outside edges of the set blocks. These are called borders. The size of the borders can be easily changed, which is handy if the pattern you are using isn't going to make your quilt quite the size you want. Borders can be plain, designed to frame a fancy quilt, or they can be very intricately pieced, appliquéd, or stitched.

Sometimes they are intended to be the part of the quilt that hangs over the edge of the bed and therefore are present only on the sides and bottom of the quilt. The top, the headboard end, is finished with the top row of blocks or with a narrow border. The process of finishing the raw edges around the quilt is called binding. The material used for this purpose is called binding as well.

Stitching that is used to hold pieces or layers together temporarily until more thorough stitching can be completed is called basting. The tiny decorative stitching that holds the layers together and gives the quilt its distinctive beauty is the quilting stitch.

The History of Quilting

Quilting goes back nearly as far as weaving does. Evidence of quilting has been found in settlements along the Nile and in the Tigris-Euphrates Valley. By the Middle Ages, it was used extensively in Asia, not in bed coverings, but in garments.

QUESTION?

What does the word *quilt* mean?
The word comes from *cuilte,* the Old French word for "mattress." The first quilted fabrics more closely resembled a sleeping pallet or a modern futon mattress than they did a quilt as we know it.

First Appearance in Europe

Knights returning to Europe after the Crusades brought quilted garments among the plunder from the Holy Land. They quickly discovered that these garments made excellent padding to wear under their armor. Recognizing the advantages of quilted cloth, tailors and seamstresses of the day adapted it to other uses, including bed coverings.

Early quilts were padded with combed cotton or flax that tended to bunch after washing. Early craftsmen, or more probably craftswomen, discovered that more and tinier stitches kept the padding in place and increased the durability of the quilt. The large frames used for tapestry making were converted to the first quilt frames.

European Influences on Quilting

Because of the cold, damp winters in England, quilted coverlets became much in demand and produced an early cottage industry. Peasant women made simple quilts for their families and finely decorated ones for the wealthy. Embroidery was already commonplace among the gentry in England. They began combining embroidery with quilting, producing coverlets with finely stitched coats-of-arms and hunting and wildlife scenes.

In France, during the Middle Ages, everything from architecture to clothing to furniture was highly decorated. French quilts reflected this sense of beauty as well. It was the French seamstresses who invented appliqué, which means "to put on."

FACT

With the expulsion of the Moors at the end of the fifteenth century, Spain became one of the most devoutly Catholic countries in Europe. It's not surprising that it was the first to use quilting on ecclesiastical vestments.

Because of the sultrier climate in southern Italy, most quilting there was done with two layers of fabric with no padding between them. The Italian seamstresses developed a type of quilting now called trapunto. *Trapunto* is the Italian word for "embroider," but it is more closely related to quilting. Parallel lines are stitched in a design through both layers of cloth. A cord is then drawn between the threads of one layer of cloth and run between the two layers and between the parallel lines, substituting for the batting. Other shapes are carefully stuffed with bits of cotton, giving the quilt a raised or embossed look.

Quilting in Early America

Early European colonists in America brought their quilts with them, of course. In a land far from any textile mills, all fabric was precious. As quilts became worn, they were patched with bits of cloth saved from garments that had also worn out. The much-patched quilts probably gave inspiration to the notion of making a quilt cover entirely of scraps of cloth.

Shortages

Quilts have always been affected by the availability of fabric. In 1721 the flax and wool industry in England managed to ban the import or production of cotton in England, and hence in the colonies. The relatively new cotton textile industry and cotton production in the colonies were both slowed by the ban.

In 1736 the law was repealed and replaced with a tax on cotton that angered both English and American women who had been managing fine with contraband cotton from India. The tax drove American women back to their looms, and homespun became common. Some women sent their fabric out to be dyed and stamped, but most dyed their own.

England guarded its patents on the spinning frame and power loom and other inventions. Samuel Slater and others memorized the plans and brought them to America. By the 1790s, Slater's cotton mill was in operation and cotton became the favored fabric for quilts.

New England

The northern colonies were settled primarily by religious groups that valued hard work and frugality. The economy represented by producing a quilt cover out of salvaged cloth was very appealing. Patterns of squares became patterns of triangles, then stars and hexagons and curved pieces.

The medallions, sometimes called hex signs, that the Pennsylvania Dutch farmers painted on their barns as good luck symbols may have inspired their wives to develop some new quilt patterns. More than a few of the old quilts bear at least a passing resemblance to the stars in circles and other geometric designs of the hex signs.

Southern Colonies

The settlements to the south became quite prosperous, at least for a segment of the population. The women of the plantations weren't as hesitant to use whole cloth for their quilts, and the appliqué designs became more popular there. Also, these women had more leisure time to devote to this more difficult technique. In the warmer climate, the covers weren't needed in as great a quantity, and more of their handiwork were used as decorative throws.

Wealthy women of the South had the added advantage of slave labor to pick the seeds out of the combed cotton used for padding in their quilts. Therefore, quilts made in the South before 1793 have fewer seeds than do quilts made at the same time in the North, helping antique dealers and historians determine the origins of these very old quilts.

FACT

In 1793, Eli Whitney received a patent on the cotton gin, which removed the seeds from cotton. This invention improved quilting everywhere. The machine may have been invented by his landlady, who later became his wife, but women were not legally able to obtain patents at that time.

Slave women became very skilled at quilting for their masters but had little time or resources for quilting for their own families. Scraps, discarded clothing, and feed sacks were gathered, sewn into strips, then cut into blocks and made into quilts.

Victorian Age

The period between 1832 and 1901, when Victoria ruled England, is known as the Victorian Age. It is characterized by very fancy, highly decorated furniture, architecture, and clothing. The style spilled over into quilts as well. Quilts became more ornate, with more intricate quilting patterns and stitches.

The crazy quilt with its multitude of fabrics and stitches became popular. Quilt clubs and church ladies would write to celebrities for scraps of their clothing, embroider the donor's name on the piece, and put them together into quilts. These would be raffled off as fund raisers for their organization or for a charity.

During the Civil War, Northern women gathered to make quilts for their soldiers. The military requested quilts be made only 7' long and 4' wide. Some 250,000 were made and donated to the Union soldiers.

Don't worry that your first quilt won't be perfect. Some early quilters deliberately made an error in their quilt. To be perfect was to compete with God and was considered bad luck.

Westward Migration

Guidebooks recommended that settlers heading west bring at least three blankets per person. A vast majority of these would have been everyday quilts. The good quilts were packed into trunks and used to protect the china.

Friendship quilts were popular and often given to a woman who was moving west. Each of her friends would make a block on which she would embroider her name. The recipient would finish the quilt herself, perhaps piecing the blocks in the evenings by the campfire.

Away from the textile mills again, the pioneer women had a great deal in common with their colonial foremothers. The family quilts were once again highly valued, not just for their usefulness and beauty, but also as symbols of the family and friends who were left behind.

Missionaries introduced quilting to the Native Americans along with other European skills. They quickly incorporated their religious symbols and designs into their quilts. The Morning Star quilt is a good example of a Plains Indian quilt design. An eight-pointed star made of tiny diamonds fills most of the quilt cover, generally in radiating reds, yellows, and oranges.

Bees and Brides—Quilting Traditions

Quilting was an essential part of a pioneer woman's life, offering a restful activity for her evenings. Names of some of the quilt patterns reflect the settlers' surroundings: Log Cabin, Fence Rail, and Kansas Dugout to name a few. Because of quilting's importance in women's everyday lives, some traditions grew up around quilting.

While the pieced quilts inspired by the "patched" quilts of the early settlers make us think of patchwork, *patchwork quilt* originally referred to appliqué quilts because the pieces were patched onto the fabric. Now it refers to both pieced and appliquéd quilts. Garments made of different fabrics are called patchwork even when they are not quilted.

Quilting Bees

Bee in this usage comes from the Old English *ben* meaning "prayer" or "help given by neighbors." In colonial days it came to mean a gathering for a specific purpose. There were threshing bees and husking bees, during which the farmers would work together to harvest everyone's crops, and there were quilting bees. The word has lost its use in our language today because we more often hire professionals instead of coming together to accomplish tasks.

For the women living on the prairie, the quilting bee was a greatly anticipated social event. In a day when there simply wasn't free time and they absolutely had to be accomplishing something virtually every waking moment, a quilting bee gave women an excuse to socialize. Gossip was shared faster than quilt patterns as the women sat around a quilt frame helping each other with their quilts. Because fabric scraps were exchanged, everyone had bits of each other's cloth in her quilt, symbolizing their shared lives.

Quilts hung out on the line were used as signals for the Underground Railroad. A prearranged code involving the color of the quilt or whether the cover or backing side was hung on the outside indicated if it was safe to bring in the fleeing slaves. Quilts were used in a similar fashion by spies during the Revolutionary War.

Quilting became more refined as each woman shared what she had learned from experience, and difficulties were solved together. These women perfected the techniques used today in traditional quilt making.

Young women joined their mothers and grandmothers around the frame and learned the skills from the experts. If Mother were her only teacher, a young girl might not have been as receptive, but in this setting, Mother could turn the lessons over to someone else. What other life lessons were passed on during the conversation can only be guessed at.

Brides' Quilts

If quilts were an important part of pioneer families' lives, who would be more in need of them than a new bride? She would probably receive the blocks for a friendship quilt, but they would do her no good until her quilt was finished. She would have to start sooner than that.

Girls were expected to learn to sew at an early age. This was a life skill she would need as a wife and mother. Quilting was naturally a part of the sewing lessons. A young woman was expected to have made a "baker's dozen," or thirteen, quilts before she married.

A wedding quilt, one that commemorated the day, often with the date and names stitched in a heart of flowers, was a quilt she was expected to make for herself between her engagement and the wedding. Her mother and close friends were allowed to help, of course.

The names of many quilts bear witness to the popularity of the wedding quilt and to quilts as wedding gifts:

- Bridal Stairway
- Double Wedding Ring
- Honey-Moon Cottage
- Love Knot
- Lover's Link

- Love Ring
- True-Lover's Buggy Wheel
- True-Lover's Knot
- Wedding Bouquet

Superstitions

It was considered bad luck for a girl to begin the bridal quilt before she had been proposed to and bad luck to sew any heart shapes in her quilts before she was engaged. Once she was married, she wouldn't think of letting her husband sleep under a Wandering Foot quilt for fear he would leave her. It was better to keep the quilt away from teenage sons as well.

Later, when the same pattern became renamed Turkey Tracks, it was safe to use.

Rose of Sharon quilts were often used for a bridal quilt. This pattern gets its name from a book of the Bible: "I am the rose of sharon" (Song of Solomon 2:1). Victorian girls might have made the quilts, but they weren't allowed to read that book of the Bible because it was considered too racy for unmarried women.

ALERT!

Don't be confused if you discover two identical quilt patterns bearing different names or quite different patterns with the same name. Quilters modified patterns without changing the name or named a quilt they thought was original that was already popular somewhere else. For example, there are probably a dozen distinctly different quilts called Rose of Sharon.

Machine-Age Changes

The invention of the sewing machine and its availability to families had an enormous effect on quilting. Besides speeding up the process, piecing could be done more accurately. At the same time, machines made commercially manufactured blankets readily available, decreasing the need for the homemade quilt. Yet the tradition held on. Amish, Mennonite, and other mostly rural communities deserve much credit for preserving the craft.

Amish Quilting

Amish communities are known today for their quilts, but they came into the craft relatively late. The communities were intended to keep the Amish people insulated from the temptations of secular society. For decades they continued to make and use the German-style coverlets.

Toward the end of the nineteenth century, they began making quilts. These early Amish quilts were plain quilts in brown, blue, or black, reflecting their conservative lifestyle. Pieced quilting was done later, and gradually more and brighter colors were accepted. Black is still used often as a contrast fabric with very striking results.

Depression-Era Resurgence

During the Depression, quilting became a necessity again for many homemakers. The quilt is something bright and beautiful to decorate a home, and quilting is a cheery activity in a dreary and sometimes desperate situation. Magazines discovered that printing quilt patterns sold issues, and patterns were shared across the whole country instead of from individual to individual.

FACT

The Persian Pickle Club by Sandra Dallas (New York: St. Martin's Press, 1995) is a novel set among the members of a quilting club in Kansas during the Depression. One member had asked her husband for a yard of paisley fabric, also called Persian pickle. He bought the whole bolt instead. Now, every quilt the members make has some of the Persian pickle fabric in it, hence the name of the club.

Today's Quilting

The relatively recent invention of zigzag-stitching machines makes it possible to appliqué in practically no time at all. The appearance of the quilt is quite different, but many of the new patterns lend themselves to this easy way of appliquéing. More recently still, some sewing machines have been designed specifically for quilting. It is quite possible to construct an entire quilt without taking a single stitch by hand.

It is also possible to make a quilt with a minimum of investment. All one needs are a few simple supplies. The traditional techniques are as good as they ever were. How much a quilter borrows from the past and how much she utilizes the more modern techniques is completely up to her.

Chapter 2

Tools and Supplies

Quilting shops and catalogs offer many marvelous gadgets for the quilter that can simplify part of the process or make cutting or sewing more accurate. Yet you can begin quilting with very little expense. Your foremothers did without these modern "necessities." Consider getting a few of those gadgets as your hobby expands, but we'll start with the essentials.

Pins and Needles

Needles and pins are the most basic of quilting tools, and everyone, even a nonsewer, will most likely have a few somewhere in the home. Needles come in numbered sizes. The larger the number, the smaller the diameter of the needle. To quilt, you will need two distinct kinds of needles, each for a separate type of sewing: sharps and betweens.

Sharps

Sharps are the most common type of needle. They are called sharps because they begin tapering right below the eye, becoming narrower all the way to the sharp point. You will be using sharps for basting, piecing, and any other hand sewing that you do besides the quilting itself. Sizes 7 or 8 are your best choices for this work.

Discard bent needles as they will affect the accuracy of your stitching. Dull needles will increase your work, so discard them as well. The tiny strawberry that hangs from the old-fashioned tomato pin cushion is a needle sharpener. It is filled with emery, which works like a file to sharpen needles and pins. It works best for needles that have gotten a little rough; it will not actually bring a really dull needle back to a point. It might be worth a try if you're frugal, but don't be too disappointed in the results.

ESSENTIAL

The more slender needles have tinier eyes. If you find yourself threading needles on faith because that eye has disappeared, use a needle threader. The stiff wire is easier to poke through the needle's eye than the thread is. It's no problem at all to run your thread through the wire loop and pull it back through the eye.

Betweens

The needles you should use for quilting are called betweens. The most common theory is that they get their name because they are somewhere between the sharp and the darning needle in characteristics. They do not taper like the sharps but come to a sudden point very close to the end.

Betweens are the same thickness as the sharps of the same number size, but a $1/4$" shorter. The shorter length makes it easier to make the tiny stitches though the layers of your quilt. Your thumb can reach past the tip to push the fabric down as you quilt. There is that much less needle to draw through the fabric each time, too.

Size 7 or 8 is recommended. The finer the needle, the smaller the holes left in the fabric and the easier it will glide through the layers. Some experienced quilters even prefer size 9 needles.

Pins

Extrafine pins are best for quilting because they leave smaller holes in your fabric. Some quilters recommend ballpoint pins because they are forced to slip between the threads of the fabric and therefore there is no danger of even the slightest fraying. Sharp pins are easier to insert, however, and are used by a great many quilters.

Pins with ball heads, as opposed to the standard flathead pins, are desirable because they are less likely to catch the threads as you sew. The colored glass–headed pins are better still because they are easy to find in your work, unless, of course, you accidentally match a pin to a piece of fabric.

Thoughts on Thread

The thread is what holds your quilt together. If a thread breaks in your finished quilt, you'll have a hole that is difficult to mend effectively. Part of a seam's strength comes from the stitch you use, but the rest comes from the thread itself. This is why it is important to consider the type of thread you will use for your quilts.

All-Purpose Thread

The basic all-purpose thread is what you will use for piecing, appliqué, and all other stitching with the exception of the quilting itself. Most thread will be labeled "Cotton Wrapped Polyester." You might find all-cotton thread, which may appeal to a traditionalist—and may be less likely to tangle while hand sewing—but isn't necessarily a better choice for you.

Generally, use a color of thread that matches the fabric you are sewing. If an exact match isn't possible, a shade lighter is less noticeable than a shade darker. When piecing—that is, stitching two pieces of fabric together—the thread will be hidden within the seam and will not show from the outside unless it is vastly different from the fabric. If you are working with many different colors of fabric, there is no need to switch threads with each pair of pieces. A light shade similar to the lightest fabric or an appropriate hue of gray or tan should blend with all of them.

The color of your thread becomes especially important with appliqué because the thread will be visible. Try to match the fabric exactly and switch colors with each piece unless you want the stitching to accent the pieces. There are caddies available that are intended to keep several threaded needles in order and the threads tangle-free.

Basting Thread

Basting should be done with a contrasting color for ease in finding the threads that need to be removed. Avoid very dark colors as they may leave behind tiny specks of the cotton coating that are difficult to brush away. Some quilters enjoy using their ugliest thread for basting, making it all the more fun to remove as the quilting progresses.

FACT

If your thread has a tendency to tangle, try running a piece of beeswax along it before you begin stitching. Don't worry about getting stung collecting it—beeswax is sold in most sewing accessory departments. Use on washable projects only, though, because the wax will collect dust if it isn't washed out.

If you have inherited a box of threads that appear to be really old, basting is probably the best use for them. Old thread tends to break and shouldn't be used for piecing or appliqué.

Quilting Thread

For the actual quilting you will need a stronger thread especially made for quilting. Besides being more durable, you will find that the stiffer thread is less prone to tangling. Quilting thread is sold in most sewing departments and comes in colors as well as the standard white. Whether your quilting stitches blend or contrast with the fabric is a matter of choice. Remember, it is the three-dimensional effect produced by stitching through the fabric layers, not the stitching itself, that gives a quilt its beauty.

You will also find special thread made for machine quilting. If you decide you will be doing a great deal of machine quilting, you might want to give this a try. Otherwise what little machine quilting you'll be doing can be done with all-purpose thread.

Scissors for Sewing Only

While everyone has scissors in their homes, getting the appropriate scissors for quilting might be worth the investment. Trying to cut fabric with dull scissors will not only frustrate you but will make your pieces fray and will interfere with the accuracy of your cutting. It could easily affect the appearance of the finished quilt.

ESSENTIAL

You will need a second pair of scissors to cut your patterns. You will be making templates of cardboard or vinyl and you don't want to use your fabric shears. An old pair of sewing scissors will probably do nicely.

Fabric Shears

Any good-quality shears will do fine. Buy a new pair, if possible, and mark them in some way as your fabric shears. Never use them for anything else. Cutting cardboard, or even paper, is going to dull them. If you share your house with nonsewers, impress on them the importance of keeping these scissors for sewing only.

Thread Scissors

A handy addition to your sewing basket, but not a necessity, is a pair of small scissors for clipping threads. You will find them so much easier to handle for the quick snip either at the sewing machine or at the quilt frame.

If you plan to do most of your quilt construction by hand, you may find yourself taking your work along to waiting rooms or on vacation. The little scissors are lighter, space saving, and handier to use when you're sewing in less than ideal settings.

Curved-tipped nail scissors are an excellent, though more expensive, choice for this purpose. The curve allows you to snip your threads close to the fabric without any danger of the tip accidentally cutting it. The curve also allows you to get under stitches if you need to remove them. Bend the point upward before cutting and your fabric is safe.

Rotary Cutter

One of the new gadgets that can be worth the investment is the rotary cutter. A rotary cutter has a circular blade that works much like a pizza cutter. It is always used with a cutting mat and often with a clear ruler. If you are cutting out straight-sided pieces, it is much more accurate than the scissors-and-template method and also much quicker. As with your fabric scissors, it is important that the blade be very sharp, so buy extra blades when you purchase your cutter. As soon as the cutter starts to skip areas you are cutting, change the blade.

ESSENTIAL

You will also find a seam ripper very valuable. Though you may dread even the thought of ripping out those seams you worked so hard on, if you are going to be happy with your finished quilt, you need to be willing to rip out crooked or misplaced seams and redo them.

Because rotary cutters are sharp, treat them with respect. They are designed in such a way that there is very little danger of cutting yourself during proper use. However, if you share a house with children, keep your rotary cutter out of reach. Most cutters have a sliding lock that keeps the cover from retracting to expose the blade, but don't count on your child leaving the lock alone.

Don't Rule out Rulers

You will need at the very least a 6" ruler with $1/16$" markings and something longer for measuring the larger pieces. Cloth measuring tapes are not very accurate because they tend to stretch. The plastic ones are better but difficult to keep straight and will not work as a straight edge when marking a large quilt top. A yardstick works better for this purpose.

There are acrylic rulers that are extremely handy for cutting quilting pieces. They come in a variety of sizes. A 6" by 6" square one and another 18" long are recommended if you are able to invest in them.

Protect Yourself with Thimbles

Thimbles are intended to protect the finger that pushes the thread through the fabric from becoming sore or even punctured by the eye end of the needle. Most thimbles have dimples to keep the needle from sliding. Thimbles can seem awkward at first, hampering your ability to guide the needle where it needs to go. They take some getting used to but are well worth the effort.

Wearing a Thimble

Thimbles are generally worn on the middle finger. Some seamstresses prefer the fourth finger (the one next to the pinky) for regular sewing or embroidery. In these types of sewing, the finger with the thimble is fairly useless except for pushing the needle through the fabric once it is in place. The thumb and forefinger (pointer finger) guide the needle through the fabric with the help of the next unthimbled finger. However, for actual quilting, the thimbled finger pushes the needle down through the layers of fabric and rocks it back up through the layers again, and down and up and so forth. The middle finger will control this much better than the fourth finger.

Sometimes a second thimble is worn on the hand under the quilt. This hand helps push the needle back up through the quilt and might need the protection of a thimble as well. Many experienced quilters say they need to feel the needle under the fabric. They've long since developed a protective callus where the needle bumps their finger.

ALERT!

By the time the thimble pushes the needle all the way through the quilting stitch and out, it could be going through as many as twelve layers of fabric and six layers of batting. You absolutely must use a thimble.

Choosing a Thimble

While thimbles all serve the same purpose, there is a wide variety to choose from. The basic types are as follows:

- The standard metal thimble is the most readily available and probably the best choice for a beginner.
- The porcelain thimble is the favorite of some quilters, especially for the hand working under the quilt.
- The leather thimble is more flexible and may be the solution for someone having trouble getting used to a thimble. Look for one with a metal insert.

Once you have settled on the type of thimble to start with, check it for a correct fit. It should not squeeze the fingertip but should not fall off easily either. Some quilters find that they need a slightly larger size in the summer than they do in the winter. Don't expect the same size thimble to fit both your right and left hand. If you switch the thimble from your middle to fourth finger, you will probably need a different size as well.

If your fingernails are keeping your thimble from fitting comfortably, don't cut them off yet. There are special thimbles designed to accommodate long fingernails. Look for them in quilt shops and catalogs.

Pattern Materials

In order to translate a picture of a pattern into something you can use to cut and sew your quilt, you will need a few basic supplies. Pencils, paper, cardboard, and rulers are probably already available to you. Patterns can be made with no more specialized equipment than these. However there are a few things that will make the process easier.

Graph Paper

Most patterns are pictured on a grid. The chore of translating that to the size you want for your quilt is much easier with commercial graph paper. Marking a grid yourself can be tedious, and if you are not accurate, your pattern won't be, either.

If you are designing your own quilt, graph paper can be helpful. Shading light and dark squares to try different variations of a geometric design can save you time later. Designing even nongeometric shapes is easier with the help of the grid lines.

If you are into computers, you might try computer software for painting and drawing. You can scan in pictures and place grids over the images to create your own patterns.

Plastic Template Material

You can make templates out of cardboard, but there are a few advantages to the commercial plastic templates. If you are cutting several pieces from the same pattern, the cardboard will begin to wear down and your last pieces will be slightly smaller than the first. This is not a problem with the plastic template. The best advantage of the plastic template, however, is that it is clear. When you lay it on your fabric to mark it, you can see exactly what your cut piece will look like. This is especially helpful when you are cutting prints with large pictures or motifs that you want to center on the quilt piece.

Cardboard can shrink slightly with the steam of the iron if you use your template as a pressing guide to turn under seam allowances. This, however, is preferable to plastic, which will melt if put to the same use. The shrinking is not going to be enough to matter unless you are making a great many identical pieces. The solution is to make several cardboard templates of each size.

Marking Tools

At several points in the process of making your quilt, you will need to mark lines or designs on your fabric. You will not want any of these marks to show on the finished quilt, yet they need to remain long enough for you to use them effectively.

Marking the Pieces

Unlike dressmaking, where you pin your pattern to the fabric and then cut around it, when you cut your quilt pieces, you will be drawing around your pattern, then cutting them out. A hard lead pencil is often used for this purpose. A soft lead pencil will smear and make your thread dirty. It is recommended that you use an art gum eraser or an eraser made especially for fabric to get rid of any lines that show after stitching rather than counting on them to come out in the wash.

ALERT!

Never use ink to mark a pattern, even if you are marking on the wrong side of the fabric. When the quilt is washed, the ink can bleed through to the right side.

There are special quilt pencils that may be a little safer. They also come in different colors to ensure that one will show up on any type of fabric. Many quilters love architects' silver pencils because the mark shows up on nearly everything. Just don't iron over the marks, as this will set them onto the fabric.

Tailor's chalk can also be used, but it doesn't make a very fine line, and it often rubs off before you are ready. It is handy, however, for quick-fix marking while you are quilting if a line isn't showing up sufficiently or if you've decided to add an additional line. Keep it sharp with an emery board.

Marking the Quilting Design

Once all the pieces of your quilt are cut and sewn together, you will need to mark out a quilting design. This is your guide to the quilting itself. The techniques for doing this will be discussed in a later chapter, but since they require special supplies, they will be mentioned here.

The simplest method is to use commercial stencils. They are available in quilt shops and catalogs. Draw the design onto your quilt cover through the slits in the stencil with your quilting pencils or a regular hard lead pencil.

Another method is to use dressmakers' tracing paper as if it were carbon and draw over the design. Tracing paper comes in a variety of colors to show up on different colors of fabric. It *should* wash out of any fabric you would be using in quilts. If you are tracing the same design several times, be sure to make more than one copy as continual tracing will eventually wear through the paper.

Before these supplies were available, tailor's chalk was rubbed over a paper pattern that had been pricked at intervals with a pin. The chalk would be brushed off when the quilt was done. Unfortunately, with all the handling and rolling of the quilt as it is stitched, the chalk might brush off too soon.

Hoops or Frames

You will need to be able to hold your quilt in place while you stitch the layers together. While it is possible to quilt a small project without any kind of hoop or frame, your stitches will be more even and the result smoother if you use something. Since it takes both hands to do the quilting, something that holds the quilt for you is helpful for even the smallest project, but it is a necessity for a large one.

Hoops

Embroidery hoops come in many sizes, and the heavier ones can accommodate the layers of a quilt. A small project might be worked on one of these. There are sturdier quilting hoops the size of embroidery hoops that have an interlocking feature. This keeps the thickness of your quilt layers from causing the outside hoop to pop off.

There are laptop hoops that are designed to free both your hands for stitching. If your hoop is designed for embroidery, it might not be sturdy enough for a quilt project. Look for the interlocking feature.

Freestanding quilting hoops are larger yet and adjust to several heights. The hoop itself might be oval or round and average about 24" across. Freestanding hoops generally cost between $40 and $150 depending on their features and strength. Wonderfully fancy freestanding hoops that adjust for height and swivel in all directions can cost as much as $500.

An iron is a necessity. Fabric must be pressed to ensure accurate cutting. Seams must be pressed flat before another seam crosses them. Steam is often helpful but not an absolute necessity.

The advantage of freestanding hoops over the traditional frames is that they don't take up as much space. The disadvantage is that the part of the quilt you are not stitching hangs to the floor and will be in the way.

A wall hanging, baby quilt, or even a twin-bed size quilt can be worked conveniently in any of these.

Frames

The standard quilt frame is designed to accommodate any size quilt. The whole width of the quilt is available to the quilter at once and the ends that are finished or waiting to be worked are rolled out of the way.

Modern quilting frames can be tipped for more comfortable sewing or set level for group quilting. Their biggest disadvantage is they take up about as much room as a piano (though they are easier to move), and not every home can accommodate one. Not every budget can accommodate one either. They range in price from $150 to $350 for standard designs and a few hundred more for those with ratchet-type rollers and built-in lights.

Sewing Machines

While not absolutely necessary, the modern sewing machine can be a very useful tool for quilting. Piecing is not only faster and straighter when done on a machine, but it is also stronger. While not always recommended, the quilting itself can be done on a machine, especially if the pattern calls for straight quilting stitches.

Sewing machine prices vary dramatically. Just be clear on what types of sewing you anticipate doing before you shop for one. If you already have a sewing machine, be sure it is clean and in good working order before attempting to quilt with it. Replace the needle with a new one to avoid skipped stitches. A feeder foot or walking foot would be a good investment to ensure all three layers move along under the needle at the same rate.

The traditionalist may want to make a quilt just the way the early quilters made theirs. That is quite possible. But remember that the neighbors probably helped those early quilters. Our modern society makes quilting together difficult. A few convenient tools can help make up for that loss.

Chapter 3

Quilting Fabrics

The fabric will be a major factor in the appearance and durability of your finished quilt. The wrong fabric can cause frustration during construction and even disappointment when the sewing is done. Knowing what to look for and what to avoid at the fabric store can make all the difference.

Fabric Terms

Don't be confused by the terms you hear tossed about in the fabric store. Here are a few of the most common ones to help you start speaking the language. *Yard goods* refers to fabrics sold by the yard or fraction of a yard. The tightly woven finished sides of a length of fabric are called the selvage. The threads that run from selvage to selvage are called the crosswise threads, with the lengthwise threads running, of course, the length of the fabric. Bias refers to an imaginary line in the fabric on the diagonal with these threads.

The seemingly miles of fabric wrapped around a cardboard core and displayed in the store is called a bolt. Fabric can be anywhere from 36" to 60" wide (measured selvage to selvage), but most cotton fabrics suitable for quilting are between 42 and 45.

A fat quarter, a quilter's favorite, is ½ yard of fabric, cut in half lengthwise. In other words, it is a piece approximately 18" by 22". A normal (skinny) quarter would be 9" by around 44". Fabric stores cut them and fold them into attractive little squares for quilters because they are a handy size.

Broadcloth refers to a plain-weave fabric with a semiglossy finish. Most quilting fabric is broadcloth or broadcloth weight.

FACT

Novelty quilts, not intended for actual use except as wall hangings or table covers, can be made of unusual materials. Promotional printed silk and flannel inserted in cigarette packages from 1880 to 1920, silk ribbons that came wrapped around cigars, college pendants, and fair ribbons have all been used in quilts.

Cottons and Blends

Cotton has been the preferred fabric for quilt making for around three hundred years. It is colorfast, washable, easy to work with, and durable. Its only close rivals are today's cotton-polyester blends.

Advantages of Each

An old-fashioned quilt pattern done all in cotton resembles an antique quilt because of the traditional fabric. Cotton is softer to the touch and preferred for baby quilts. Pure cotton creases easily. This can mean a great deal when you are turning under a raw edge on a small piece for appliqué. It makes it possible to flatten a seam allowance after piecing by pressing it with your thumb or finger and get almost as sharp a crease as you would with an iron.

On the other hand, cotton-polyester quilts will keep that brand-new look longer. It's the polyester that gives the blended fabrics their permanent press quality, making them look smooth and crisp. The colors will be a bit brighter and slower to fade than those in 100 percent cotton. Some quilters say 30 percent polyester should be the maximum, but 60/40 cotton-polyester blends are common and often used.

ALERT!

Be aware of the difference between leftover fabric and used fabric. Pioneers might have put used fabrics in their quilts, but to use a piece in your quilt that has already been worn and washed a number of times will shorten the life of your quilt.

Mixing Blends with Pure Cotton

A quilt should probably be made from only one type of fabric: all cotton or all blends that have as close to the same percentage of cotton as possible. This is especially true if the quilt is made up of large pieces. However, it won't be disastrous to do a little mixing. The smaller the pieces in the quilt, the less the differences in the fabrics will show.

Fabric bought in remnant bins, at garage sales, and even scraps left over from your own sewing may keep their exact content a secret. A clue will be how wrinkled they are after being washed. The more they wrinkle, the higher the cotton content. If you must know if two or more fabrics are of similar content, carefully burn small equal-size pieces in heat-proof dishes and compare the ash. Polyester will melt, rather than burn, and leave tiny beads behind.

Velvets and Satins

Nineteenth-century women made quilts from what they had. Everyday dresses were cotton, linen, or wool. Best dresses were silk, which is a type of satin. Wealthy women had dresses of velvet. Victorian crazy quilts were made of velvet or satin or even a combination of both. These were not intended for use but rather as decoration on the back of the sofa in the parlor. Today's crazy quilts often copy the Victorian style and can be incredibly beautiful because of their rich colors and textures.

Velvet is a napped fabric. *Nap* refers to a texture on the surface of the fabric, usually only on one side. You cannot iron velvet without a needle pressboard. The velvet is placed right-side down on the tiny "needles" and pressed from the back. This prevents the nap from being permanently crushed.

Satin fabrics are easily damaged by needles and pins as you sew. If you remove a seam, there will be needle holes left behind that will show if they aren't covered by another seam.

Working with velvets and satins can be a bit tricky because they both tend to fray. However, these are traditional quilt fabrics, and with patience, these difficulties can be overcome if your heart is set on this particular type of fabric. The new velvet-look fabrics or washable silks might be good alternatives, although neither is recommended for most quilt making.

Other Possibilities

Before you limit yourself to the traditional quilt fabrics, consider the project itself. There might be other worthy choices that will make your quilt stand out. Remember that the quilt benefits from the quilter's creativity.

Wool

The first manufactured blankets were primarily wool. Wool is warm and perhaps the most durable of fabrics. A pieced block quilt of wool would certainly be welcome on a cold winter night.

Bear in mind how often this particular quilt will need to be laundered. Wool can be washed in cold water but hanging a full-sized quilt to dry could be a challenge. It would be heavy enough to try the supports of even the sturdiest clothesline. The dryer is absolutely out of the question. Dry cleaning is an option, though an expensive one.

Also consider the weight and weave of your wools. A little difference in texture can add to the charm, but too much contrast can make the lighter-weight pieces tear away from the heavier ones. Too loose a weave will fray too easily and be next to impossible to work with.

Because of the heavy weight of most wool and the difficulty of making a sharp crease, the patterns that call for small pieces should be avoided. Use perhaps 5" or 6" squares or rectangles and allow extra-wide seam allowances. Plan on tying the quilt instead of quilting it.

Almost no examples of antique quilts made of silk exist today because the metal used in the silk fabrics to make the dresses rustle caused them to deteriorate. Consider carefully any fabrics that you might want in your own quilt that contain metallic threads.

Flannel

Flannel is a napped fabric generally made of cotton. The nap in flannel is just a soft fuzz and not the problem it is in velvet. Flannel should not be mixed with broadcloth-weight cotton and blends in the same quilt unless a sharp contrast in the appearance of the pieces is desired. However, an all-flannel quilt, especially for a baby, can be very effective, not to mention snuggly warm and soft. And consider the fun of choosing from all the cute pajama prints available in flannel.

Flannel comes in a variety of weights. Be sure that the fabrics you choose are comparable. Since flannel sometimes has a looser weave than broadcloth, it tends to fray. Planning a wider seam allowance might solve the problem. The looser weave allows flannel to stretch a little more on the bias than other cottons and can cause difficulties with any diagonal seam. Avoid triangles and stay with squares and rectangles if piecing with flannel.

FACT

Since babies outgrow their clothes faster than they wear them out, you might find like-new baby and toddler pajamas at garage sales that could be used in baby quilts. Check carefully for stains before you cut your pieces.

Double Knits

Some years ago double knits were very popular for both men's and women's clothing. Broadcloth fabrics became somewhat difficult to find. Because quilters always want to use what they have, patchwork quilts began to be made of leftover double knits.

Double knits are usually too heavy to quilt and are tied instead. They won't take a sharp crease and are too bulky for quilts requiring small pieces. They also come primarily in solid colors, which somewhat limits their appeal. However, double knits do not fray at all and can be appliquéd without turning under the raw edge. Double knits will run but not without considerable abuse.

Denim

You would need protection on all your fingers and a pair of pliers besides if you tried to hand quilt through denim. However, patchwork projects that aren't quilted can be very effective with this fabric. Overlapping the pieces and zigzag stitching the raw edges might solve the problem of the bulky seams. With denim, a little fraying will add to the charm.

Be sure to use a heavy-duty needle if you do any machine stitching on denim, and don't be surprised if the needle needs to be discarded when you're done.

Fabrics to Avoid

While you shouldn't be limited by tradition, there are some fabrics that will cause you more trouble than they're worth. If you can't resist, at least be aware of the difficulties.

One-Way Fabrics

One-way fabrics look different when they are turned 180 degrees. Fabrics with a shiny surface are often one-way fabrics, though that might not be noticeable until the quilt is finished and one or two pieces reflect light differently than the rest.

Fabrics with nap such as corduroy will cause the same problem. You can test nap to see if it is one-way by petting it in two different directions and seeing if the effect is the same.

Fabrics with one-way prints become more difficult to piece, but with care you can keep the pictures right side up. Be aware that you will need more fabric as panels and borders will all need to be cut one way as well.

Loose-Weave or Stretchy Fabrics

The difficulties of loose-weave fabrics have already been mentioned, but fabrics with exceedingly loose weave should be avoided entirely. If you hold the raw edge of the fabric between your thumbnail and the side of your finger and scratch outward, you should have no more than two or three threads come loose. If more come loose or if repeated scratching pulls more and more threads away, the weave is too loose to quilt with. The seam allowances will fray away, allowing the seam to open.

All fabrics are going to stretch on the bias, but avoid any fabric that stretches horizontally or vertically. These fabrics will be impossible to piece properly and will lose their shape in the finished quilt.

Uneven Surfaces

Seersucker has stripes of loose weave between stripes of tighter weave. If the seam allowance of a piece happens to fall in this looser weave, it would be impossible to stitch it to another piece without puckering. Even if this problem could be avoided, the uneven weave would be impossible to quilt over.

Dotted-swiss and other fabrics with raised designs or flocking on the surface will cause uneven quilting because the raised dot or design will be too hard for the quilting needle. Tiny dotted-swiss is sometimes hard to resist, however. It's all right to use in small amounts as long as you realize that you are sacrificing even quilting by using the fabric.

ALERT!

Striped and checked fabrics should be avoided whenever possible. If your cutting or piecing is less than perfect, the stripes will give it away.

Solids and Prints

Now that you know what types of fabrics to look for and what to avoid, you are ready to make your selections. As far as color choices go, there are two basic types of quilts: the scrap quilts that use up lots of leftover fabric and the quilts in which all the fabric pieces coordinate with one another.

For scrap quilts, the more variety in color and texture the better. In fact, in charm quilts, no two pieces should be from the same fabric. All you have to consider is the placement of the pieces, trying not to put pieces of similar color or similar size prints next to each other.

For the color-coordinated quilt, your tastes will be your best guide, but consider a few suggestions. Before you go shopping, cut a window in a piece of cardboard the size and shape of the primary pieces of your quilt. As you look at fabrics, test how the print appears in the window. You don't want a fabric where the motif is too large for the piece or one where the pictures are so far apart it would be possible to cut a piece and miss the picture entirely.

Once you have chosen your primary print, choose the coordinating fabrics. Using at least one solid will keep your quilt from looking too busy. Tone-on-tone prints will give the appearance of solids from a distance but add more interest and texture than solids. You might be lucky enough to find coordinating prints by the same manufacturer. Usually one is a smaller, simplified version of the other.

Be sure to cut out the pieces for your quilt as soon as possible after purchasing your fabric. If you haven't gotten enough, your best chance of matching the fabric is with the same bolt of cloth—before it's sold out.

When you have picked out the fabrics you need, lay them side by side or unroll the bolts enough that you can overlap the fabrics to more closely simulate the size of your pieces. Then step back. A fabric that doesn't quite fit with the others might be more noticeable from a distance. Squinting can sometimes help you see how they will blend together. Last, don't second-guess your own tastes. If you like it, it's perfect.

Fabric for Backing

The fabric for the quilt backing is as important as the cover. Most of the same rules apply, because it will be quilted along with the cover and will ultimately receive the same care.

Unbleached muslin is a traditional quilt backing. It is often sold in widths up to 108". Special quilt backing, sometimes called sheeting, is sold in some fabric stores. It can be as wide as 112" and can eliminate the necessity of piecing the back to fit even a king-sized bed.

Don't confuse this fabric with actual bed sheets. Quilt backing has a slightly looser weave than broadcloth-weight fabrics, which makes quilting easier. Percale sheets, on the other hand, while tempting because of their width, have a very high thread count that will result in a tight fit for the quilting needle and more work for the quilter.

An alternative is to choose one of the fabrics used in the quilt cover. This will make the quilt reversible. This fabric, however, will almost surely need to be pieced. Consider splitting one length of fabric and stitching it to either side of the other length, thus moving the seam away from the center of the quilt where the added bulk would be most likely to be visible.

Preparing New Fabric

Once you have chosen the fabric to use in your quilt, the hard part is over, but you aren't quite ready for quilting. New fabric needs some preparation before it is ready to be cut for your quilt. A little extra work now can save considerable grief later.

Testing for Colorfastness

The label on one end of the bolt of fabric will say if it is colorfast. You can probably trust that your fabric is labeled correctly and not worry about it unless your fabric is very dark. If your dark pieces bleed onto the pieces next to them the first time your finished quilt is washed, it would be disastrous. Because of what's at stake, very dark fabrics should be tested for colorfastness regardless of what the label says.

Soak the fabric in very warm water for several minutes. If the water remains clear, the fabric is colorfast. If the fabric has left color behind, you might try to "set" the color. Boil the fabric in a solution of one gallon of water and one cup of vinegar for ten or fifteen minutes if you can stand the smell. Rinse it and test again. If it's still leaving color behind, keep it for some other purpose, but don't use it in your quilt.

Preshrinking Your Fabric

Cotton shrinks more than cotton-polyester blends do, and some cottons shrink more than others. You want the fabrics you've chosen for your quilt to do all their shrinking before they are pieced together. To do this, simply launder them the way you would the quilt. The gentle cycle and cold water is probably fine for most quilts, but a baby quilt might need a hot water wash at some point in its life. If your fabric can't handle that, it's better to find out now.

FACT

If a fabric frays excessively in the wash, it isn't a good candidate for quilting. The polyester content may be too high or the weave looser than was originally apparent. Discard it and be glad you discovered its defect before you put it into your quilt.

Because all new fabric is going to fray in the wash, a load made up entirely of new fabric pieces can become a tangled mess. Therefore it's better to toss a length or two in with a regular load of wash. Clipping the selvage corners will also help minimize tangling but will put more loose threads in your washer. Untangle the pieces and cut away the loose threads before you put the pieces in the dryer.

Straightening Your Fabric

Most fabric is not exactly straight with the grain when you buy it, meaning that the lengthwise threads are not exactly perpendicular to the crosswise threads. If you do not correct this, your quilt will not be straight, either.

To see if your fabric is straight with the grain, pull a thread near one raw edge until it breaks and cut along the line you've created. Repeat this until you've cut from one selvaged edge to the other. Fold this newly cut edge in half and hold the fabric up to see if the selvages hang in a straight line. If they do not, your fabric should be straightened.

Fabric is straightened by pulling on the bias to force the lengthwise and crosswise threads into alignment. To determine which direction to pull, consider which side is hanging closer to the fold than the other. That is the corner that will need to be stretched outward.

Stretch the entire surface of the fabric, not just across the center. And remember, unless the fabric is the same length as the width, corner to corner is not the true bias. Stretch several places along the bias and test again.

Types of Batting

The last component of your quilt is the batting. Commercial batting is generally polyester, but you might find cotton batting available in some specialty stores. Cotton batting may shift after a few washings and will need to be quilted more densely.

Batting comes in a variety of weights or thicknesses. Consider how heavy you want your finished product to be when deciding on the weight.

Take into account the added challenge of quilting through a thicker layer and reserve the very thickest batting for tied quilts.

Quilt batting is folded and rolled very tightly to fit into the plastic bag it comes in. A day or so before you are ready to assemble your quilt, it should be unrolled and laid flat. Smooth the wrinkles gently with your hand. A light misting with water will help the worst of the wrinkles disappear.

Chapter 4

Getting Started with a Simple Project

The quilting stitch, while time consuming, is not particularly difficult. It does take some practice, however. If you practice on a small wall hanging, you'll have fun and something worth keeping when you're done. This simple wall hanging uses picture print fabric so there is no piecing or appliqué to do. An inexpensive embroidery hoop serves as the frame and hides the raw edges at the same time.

Supplies You Will Need

How much you spend on this project will depend on how large you want your miniquilt to be. Remember, the larger you make it, the more practice you'll get on the quilting stitch. The most important thing to remember when learning the quilting stitch is to relax both hands as you stitch. Relax your mind as well and have some fun.

Picture Print Fabric

You will need a piece of printed fabric with a picture at least 3" or 4" across. An equal radius of neutral color surrounding the picture would be ideal. Fabrics printed to look like patchwork quilts, sometimes called cheater's quilting, often have large picture "blocks" that work well for this project.

Embroidery and Quilting Hoops

You will need an inexpensive embroidery hoop to use as a permanent frame for your miniquilt. Embroidery hoops can easily be found in sizes anywhere from 3" to 14" in diameter. Choose one of appropriate size to frame the picture you've chosen. The best way to do this is to have your fabric with you when you pick out the hoop.

You will also need a good quality quilting hoop for the actual stitching. For lap quilting—that is, quilting without a freestanding frame or hoop—a hoop of about 8" in diameter is a convenient size. If your picture is to be smaller than that, you may be able to do your quilting in the hoop you will be framing with later. Or you can enlarge the project by basting strips of fabric along each side. These extensions will fit into the quilt frame and hold the work in place.

ALERT!

Don't be confused into thinking lap quilting means quilting with no hoop at all. It is possible to quilt this way, but without stretching the quilt out flat in a hoop, your stitches will be too tight and your finished quilt will be puckery.

Ruffle

If it seems appropriate to your picture, you may want to put a ruffle around your wall hanging. A length of commercial ruffle a couple of inches longer than the circumference of the hoop/frame will be sufficient. Ruffle is available in many colors, sizes, and styles. Again, it is best to have your fabric with you when you shop for the trim. Be sure the ruffle is stiff enough that it will stand out around the hoop.

Other Supplies

The other supplies that you'll need for this project are:

- Quilt batting
- Backing fabric
- Quilting thread
- Basting thread
- Needles and pins
- A thimble
- Liquid or hot glue

FACT

Colored quilting thread is going to show up more than white or cream-colored thread, even on dark colors. Many quilters shy away from it for fear it will call too much attention to any less-than-perfect stitches. If it looks like fun to you, don't be afraid to experiment with it.

Assembling Your Quilt

Since you may need to wash your hanging after you've stitched it and before you frame it, it would be wise to wash both the cover and the backing fabrics before you begin. Iron them both smooth, and you will be ready to assemble your quilt.

Cut

Cut the printed fabric in a square 2" or 3" larger than the hoop frame you have chosen. Your cutting doesn't need to be exact, since you will trim it into a circle later. This is now the cover of your miniature quilt.

Place your cover right side up on the quilt batting and smooth both layers out with your hands. Cut the batting slightly larger than the cover. Place both of these layers on the wrong side of the backing fabric and cut around it as well, making it the same size as the batting. If these layers were cut exactly the same size as the cover, they would have to be placed exactly on top of one another to ensure that there is batting and backing behind all the edges of the cover. This rule becomes more important when cutting a full-sized quilt than with this little project, of course.

Baste

Pin baste the layers together, checking the back to be sure it is as smooth as the front. A pin every 2" or 3" will be enough.

With a contrasting thread, baste the layers together. Knot the thread and begin in the center with a running stitch. To do a running stitch, weave the needle in and out of the fabric several times before you pull it all the way through. These stitches can be 1/2" long or longer and don't have to be pretty. You'll be removing them as you quilt. Stitch to one corner and cut the thread. Repeat for the other corners, always beginning in the center.

As you baste, be sure the backing remains as smooth as the cover. Check it constantly for wrinkles or puckers. If you discover one, remove what basting stitches you need to, smooth the fabric, and baste again. Remove the pins as they become unnecessary.

If your hanging is more than 6" or 7" across, you could run stitches from near the center to the sides and to the top and bottom as well. The purpose of basting is to hold the layers securely so nothing shifts when you quilt.

The Quilting Stitch in Theory

The ideal quilting stitches are straight, even stitches through the layers of the quilt that look the same on the back as the front. Expert quilters take as many as ten or twelve stitches per inch. Beginners should be happy with eight.

To make the stitches equal on the front and on the back, the needle must run through the layers of the quilt at as close to a right angle as possible. The temptation is to take one stitch at a time, pulling the needle through the layers, then taking another stitch from the underside back to the top. The problem with this is that your stitches will be crooked.

In order to keep your stitches in a straight line, you will need to take a form of running stitch, only much tinier than you did when you were basting. Because the needle is straight, the stitches taken together will be straight as well. However, a usual running stitch is going to put the needle through the layers at an angle closer to twenty degrees than ninety.

The trick, then, is to bend the quilt so the needle can enter the layers at a right angle, both from above and from below even during a running stitch. One finger of your off hand pushes up from underneath and the thumb of the sewing hand pushes the fabric downward. The needle, once it is started, is guided and held entirely by the pressure of the thimbled middle finger of the sewing hand.

The Quilting Stitch in Practice

For this project, you will begin by quilting along the outline of your picture. Follow these steps and practice making stitches that are as tiny and even as possible. A few lines of stitching inside the picture can be very effective. However, don't try to outline every detail. Think in terms of foreground and background and outline a few key areas.

Bury the Knot

Thread an 18" length of quilting thread onto a between needle. Tie a simple knot in the thread close to one end. Along the stitching line and about 1" away from where you want to begin stitching, insert the needle through the top layer of the fabric only and out at the point where you will begin stitching.

Pull the needle through and gently tug the knot through the cover so it will be hidden in the batting. Sometimes scratching it with your thumbnail will encourage it through the cloth. If you are having trouble, you might use the tip of the needle to lift the fabric near the knot and pull it over the knot as you tug on the thread.

Be sure to enter the thread on the line where you will be stitching. This prevents the shadow of the knot or any tail behind the knot from showing as it might if you bury the knot outside the stitching line. This is especially important if you are using colored thread.

Downward Stitch

With the index finger of your off hand under your work at the point where you will begin stitching, balance the frame against your body. Insert the tip of the needle about $1/16''$ from the exit point of the thread. Use your index finger to stop the needle as soon as it emerges from the quilt.

FIGURE 4-1

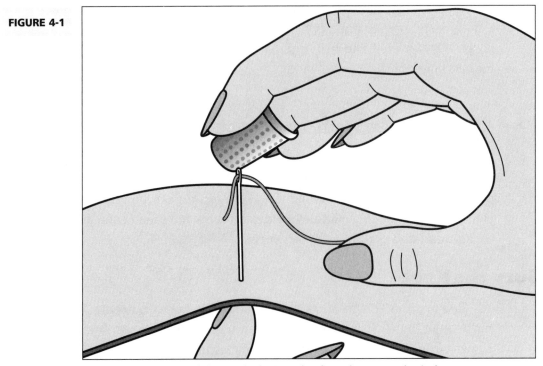

▲ A cutaway view of the quilt during the first downward stitch.

Upward Stitch

Gently place your thimble-protected middle finger on the eye end of the needle, and rock the needle to the side until it is nearly lying on the surface of the quilt. Push up with your finger under the quilt. At the same time, push down on the top of the quilt with your thumb, just ahead of the needle. This makes it possible for the needle to get into a position nearly perpendicular to the part of the quilt it is going to enter.

The index finger under the quilt pushes the needle through the layers and the thumb stops it as it emerges. The thumb is the key to tiny stitches on top and the index finger is the key to tiny stitches on the bottom.

FIGURE 4-2

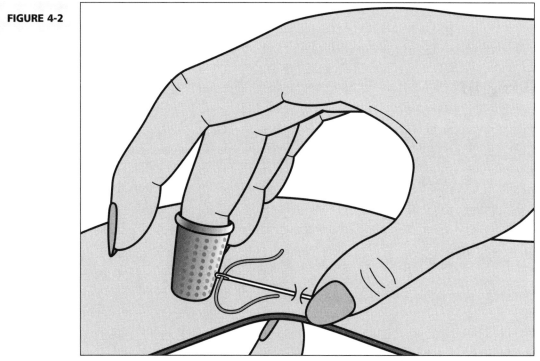

▲ A cutaway view of the quilt during the first upward stitch.

When the tip of the needle comes through the fabric and is stopped by the thumb, relax your thumb and rock the needle upward again, forcing the tip back through the layers. Your hand should look like **FIGURE 4-1** again except there will be a stitch on the needle.

Does it have to be the index finger working under the quilt?
No. Some quilters find the middle finger more convenient to use. The trick is to figure out which finger lets you relax your hand the most. Since your middle finger is longer, it might be the one.

Running Stitch

At first you might want to push the needle on through the cloth after only one or two stitches. Practice making tiny stitches initially, then see how many stitches you can get on a needle before you have to pull it through. There is a limit to how many stitches will work before you need to use pliers to get the needle through all the layers, but four or five stitches on the needle will help ensure your stitching is straight.

Tying Off

When the thread is getting short enough to cause difficulty, it is time to tie it off and begin with another length of thread. While the thread is still on the needle, tie a knot in the thread about $1/4$" to $1/2$" from the surface of the quilt. If you poke the end of the needle in the loop as you tighten the knot, you can guide the knot to end where you want it to.

Run the needle into the top layer of fabric at the point it had emerged and out again about 1" away. Be sure you do this along a stitching line. Pull until the knot has gone through the fabric and is in the batting layer. Tug the thread a little and clip it near the cloth. The knot and tail will be buried inside the quilt.

Echo Stitching

Once you have gone all the way around the picture on your quilt, try echo stitching to get in some more practice. Echo stitches are rows of stitches running parallel to a design, mimicking its curves and angles. Think of the ripples on the surface of a pond.

To judge where to run the row of echo stitches, use a ruler and hard lead pencil to mark a few spots $1/4$" from the finished row. A dot every 1" or so should be enough to guide you around the picture again. Continue the echo rows until you have filled the entire area that will be visible when the picture is centered in the hoop.

When a row of basting stitches is in the way of your quilting stitches, cut it and pull out a stitch or two. Leave the rest of the row of basting to hold the unquilted layers. If you stitch over a basting stitch, it will be difficult to remove when the quilting's done.

Finishing the Miniquilt

Now it's time to remove the quilt from the hoop and examine your handiwork. Don't dwell too much on the imperfect stitches. Find a few really good ones and congratulate yourself. Just a few more details, and you can hang it on the wall.

Finishing Touches

First, be sure to remove any remaining basting stitches. Erase any pencil marks that are visible. If your work seems smudged by your pencil marks or prolonged handling, you may want to wash it.

Your quilt will seem surprisingly puckered after being quilted and washed. Be certain all the pencil marks are gone and then iron it. Ironing a finished quilt isn't usually recommended because it flattens the batting. However, this project will look better on your wall if it is ironed. Stretch it out as you go so you don't iron puckers or creases in the unquilted areas.

Framing the Quilt

Center your miniature quilt over the inside hoop of the embroidery hoop frame. Loosen the outside hoop and center the adjustable screw at the top of the picture. You will be hanging the finished quilt from this screw.

Push the outside hoop down over the inside hoop, adjusting the quilt to see that it stays centered. Tighten the screw a little at a time, pulling the ends of the quilt tight as you go.

When the quilt is centered and before the screw is completely tight, ease the outside hoop off a fraction. Run a few drops of glue between the exposed inner hoop and the quilt and along the line between the back of the outside hoop and the quilt. Slide the hoop back in place and tighten thoroughly, making any necessary last-minute adjustments. Allow the glue to dry. Next, trim off the excess fabric flush with the back of the hoop frame.

ALERT!

You should not be getting cramps in your hands. If you are, see if changing the position of your hoop will help. Be sure you are using a between needle. Too long a needle will strain your thumb.

Adding the Ruffle

Trim the raw edge at one end of the ruffle. Press and stitch under a narrow hem. Use the ruffle to measure around the hoop frame to find where to put the second hem. Starting with the hemmed edge at the center top, lay it out carefully around the hoop. You will be gluing the base of the ruffle against the raw edge of the quilt and the back of the hoop. Ideally, the gathering stitches of the ruffle should just be hidden behind the hoop frame.

Find the point where the ends of the ruffle will meet, allow for the hem, and trim and hem the second end. Glue the ruffle in place. If you are using liquid glue, you might need to push an occasional pin through the ruffle into the edge of the quilt to hold the ruffle in place until the glue dries. Inserting the pins at a sharp angle is going to be most effective. Let the glue dry; then hang your first quilt on the wall to enjoy.

FIGURE 4-3

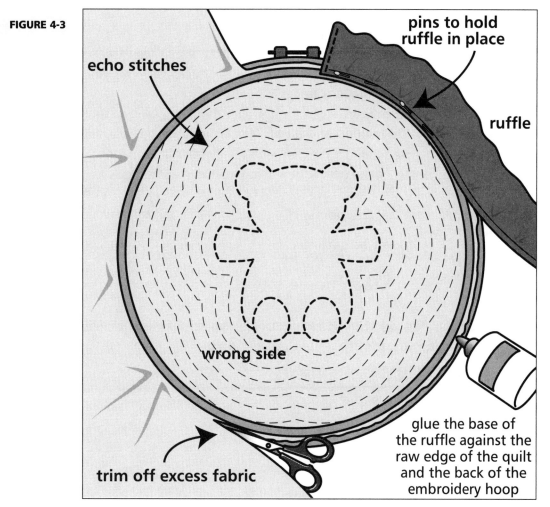

pins to hold
ruffle in place

echo stitches

ruffle

wrong side

glue the base of
the ruffle against the
raw edge of the quilt
and the back of the
embroidery hoop

trim off excess fabric

▲ The back view of the miniquilt during the finishing steps.

Battling Sore Fingers

Your fingers are bound to be tender the first few times you quilt. Besides the pressure of the needle, there are going to be a few pricks and scratches. Quilters have battled these for generations and have found a few solutions.

The thumb and the index finger that guides and pulls the needle are especially vulnerable to soreness. Quit before a blister actually forms.

Wrap the sore fingers in paper tape or adhesive bandages when you quilt until they heal enough to toughen up a bit. Finger cots sold in pharmacies are an alternative, or you can make your own from rubber gloves or the end of tube balloons. The rubber actually helps your grip when you're pulling the needle.

Soaking your hands in warm water after a quilting session can ease the soreness. This is a great reason to leave the dinner dishes until you've had some quilting time. You don't want to quilt immediately after doing the dishes, since overhydrated fingers are going to get sore faster.

Keep some small adhesive bandages in your sewing box to cover the inevitable scratches and pokes. The new spray bandages are worth a try as well. Treat any cut with antiseptic so it will heal faster and get you back to quilting sooner. As you form calluses, the number of punctures and cuts will be greatly reduced.

ALERT!

One of the worst things about poking your finger is the tiny drop of blood you sometimes get on your quilt. Treat it immediately with a wet cotton swab. Some quilters swear their own saliva somehow "neutralizes" their own blood and takes it out the best.

Try Other Projects

If you enjoyed this project and want to do more, consider different fabric prints for display in different rooms of your home. Holiday and seasonal prints would make good temporary decoration. You might even find hoops intended for display of needlework small enough to hang on a Christmas tree. A lot of fabric stores stock Christmas prints all year round.

If you can find a print made to look like patchwork, consider this project: Quilt an outline around each of the printed "patches" and leave the raw edges outside the frame instead of adding a ruffle.

Is your favorite eight-year-old interested in quilting? Set him or her up with a hoop and a picture print. Don't expect a child to do the quilting stitch, however. In and out without too many finger pokes is enough to expect.

Chapter 5

Log Cabin Potholder

This quick and easy project is designed to be sewn entirely with a sewing machine. The Log Cabin pattern is one of the old standards and lends itself to piecing and quilting at the same time because it is pieced from the center outward with no seams to match.

Supplies Needed

The traditional Log Cabin block has a center square of a solid dark color. The logs are added in a "circular" pattern around this center square. Half the block, divided on the diagonal, is generally of light-colored fabrics and the other half dark. Usually the same fabric is used for the horizontal and vertical stripes that are the same distance from the center and on the same color tone half of the block.

FIGURE 5-1

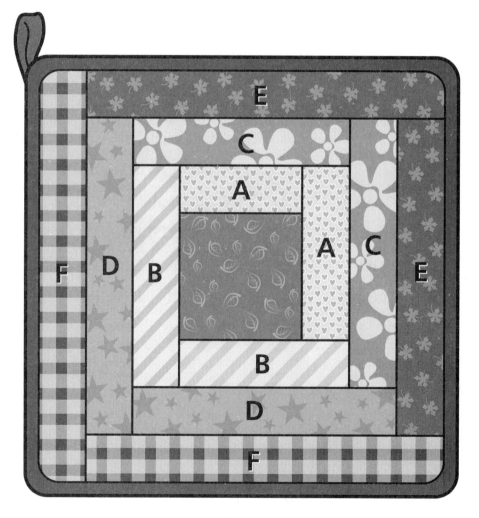

▲ Log Cabin potholder.

You will need:

- 9" by 9" square of batting or heavy flannel
- 9" by 9" square of backing fabric
- Approximately 1 yard of extra-wide, double-fold bias tape
- Fabric scraps for the cover

Choosing Cover Fabrics

Collect together the fabrics you want to use for the cover. The largest scrap will need to be at least $8^1/2$" by 3" or 16" by $1^1/2$", so keep this in mind as you collect the scraps.

FACT

You can make your potholder look like a slice of watermelon. Make colors A, C, and E white and the center square dark pink or red. Make B pink, D light green, and F dark green. Add some embroidered seeds if you want.

Arrange the scraps from the darkest to the lightest. Decide if you are going to use seven or thirteen different colors—that is, if you want to match the horizontal and vertical logs on half of each round or make them all different. These instructions assume you are using seven different fabrics. Simply pair up your colors if you decide on thirteen.

Pick the darkest color for the center. The rest will be logs. Referring back to **FIGURE 5-1**, decide on the arrangement of the other colors.

Cut by Measure

Since all the pieces are either squares or rectangles, you will be cutting them by measure, so there is no need to make templates. Be sure to iron the fabric first so your measurements will be accurate.

The Size of the Pieces

You will need a $2^1/2$" square of the darkest fabric for the center. All the rest of the cover will be cut from strips $1^1/2$" wide.

You will need strips in the following lengths:

- Color A: $2^1/2$", and $3^1/2$"
- Color B: $3^1/2$", and $4^1/2$"
- Color C: $4^1/2$", and $5^1/2$"
- Color D: $5^1/2$", and $6^1/2$"
- Color E: $6^1/2$", and $7^1/2$"
- Color F: $7^1/2$", and $8^1/2$"

Rotary Cutting

If you have acrylic rulers and a rotary cutter, you can make short work of cutting. Line the ruler along one long side of the fabric on the grain and cut away any uneven edge by running the cutter along the ruler. Line up this new cut with the appropriate mark under the ruler and cut a strip of that width. In the same way, cut the strip to the required length.

Ruler and Scissors Cutting

To cut the pieces with a ruler and scissors, you will need to start with a straight edge of fabric cut on the grain. If the edge isn't already straight, pull a thread and cut along the line as you did when you straightened the fabric as described in Chapter 3. Measure the appropriate distance from this straight edge and pull another thread. Measure and cut the strip to the proper length.

Quilt as You Piece

You will be piecing, assembling, and quilting your potholder all at the same time. The only tricky part is getting that first piece centered on the batting and backing.

Centering the First Piece

Begin by laying your batting on the wrong side of the backing piece. Pin them together at each corner. Use a ruler and a pencil to gently draw crossing lines on the batting from corner to corner. Be as accurate as possible since this will determine the center of your potholder. Put a large knot on the end of a piece of basting thread. Run the thread from the center back through to the center of the batting. Find the center of the square piece. You may be able to do this by pressing a crease in the center with your fingers as you fold it in each direction. Run the basting thread through the center of the square piece.

FIGURE 5-2

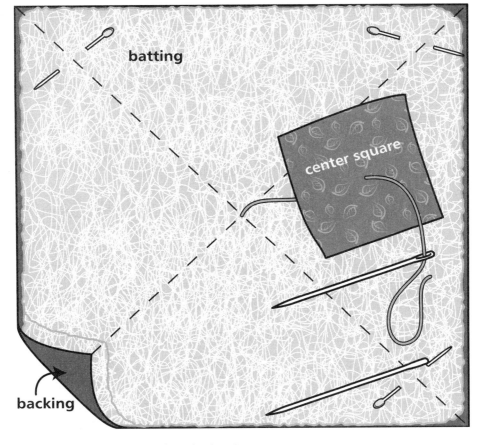

▲ Center the square piece on the batting.

Besides being centered, this first piece must be squared with the outside edges of the backing and batting for all the other pieces to fit. Line up the corners of your center square with the lines drawn on the batting. If your lines are accurate and your square is true, this will center the piece exactly. Measure each side if you want to be sure. Use the basting thread to tack the piece in place, stitching no closer to the edge than $1/4$". Check the back to see that it is still smooth and has not shifted.

The standard way to knot a thread is to wrap the end around the tip of your moistened index finger twice and slide it off. With practice you can do this even while wearing a thimble. This works for regular thread when you're piecing and basting, but quilting thread needs a simple end-through-the-loop-type knot.

Piecing the First Log

With right sides together, line up one long edge of the smaller Color A strip with one side of the center piece. Machine stitch $1/4$" from the edge. Your thread is going to show more on the back than on the front. Keep this in mind when you pick your thread color. Avoid too great a contrast with the cover fabric, however, or it will show. Consider the stitches on the backing to be decorative and pick a color that complements the backing rather than disappearing. To make the stitching on the back of the potholder look more like regular quilting, stop and start the stitches $1/4$" from the corners.

ALERT!

Tempting as it may be, never try to save time by skipping the ironing. Your finished project will look sloppy. Before you stitch across any seam, it should be pressed. The only exception is small hand-stitched cotton pieces that can be finger pressed instead.

FIGURE 5-3

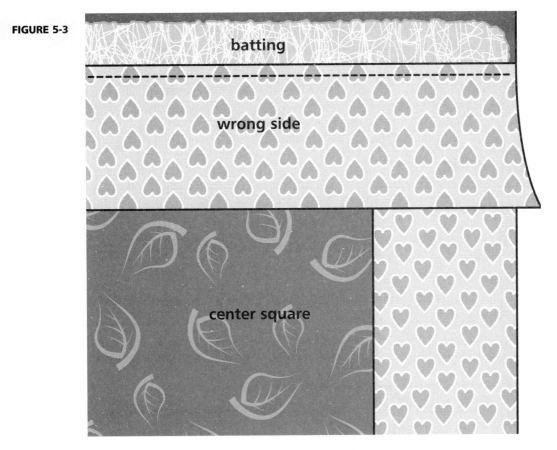

batting

wrong side

center square

▲ Sew the logs to the center, right sides together. Open and press.

Backstitching a couple of stitches at the end of the seams will eliminate any danger of the seams' coming loose. However, there won't be any pressure on the seams, so it isn't necessary.

If the strip isn't already cut to the proper length, use the edge of the square under it as a guide and trim it. Open the piece and iron it flat against the batting. The fabric will cling to the batting, and you probably won't need to pin it in place.

You can save time by having the strips arranged in order on the end of your ironing board. When you press one piece down, you can pick up the next piece to sew.

Continue Piecing

With right sides together, line up one long edge of the larger Color A strip with one side of the center piece and the short edge of the first strip. The strips are added in a circular pattern. Stitch and iron the same as for the first strip. Continue around the center using the smaller, then the larger, strips of Colors B, C, D, E, and F.

Trim to Fit

You will notice that there is a lot of batting and backing surrounding the last rows of logs in your Log Cabin block. If you centered the first piece exactly, there will be about 3/4" all around. Allowing this excess is important in case your centering is less than perfect. How did you do?

If the strips you trimmed away are straight but not all the same size, you lined your center piece up well but miss-measured the center of the backing. Once the excess is trimmed away, no one will be able to tell the difference.

FACT

Log Cabin quilts are generally made without separating panels between the blocks. Depending on how the blocks are turned when they are arranged together, the dark and light halves of the blocks next to one another create a design on the cover of the quilt, forming such patterns as Zig Zag, Pinwheels, Straight Furrows (diagonal stripes), Barn Raising (diamond shapes), and many others.

If the excess batting and backing are the shape of long triangles, your problem arose when you squared up that first piece. The backing won't be straight with the grain, but it won't matter with this project.

If one or more of the logs extends over the edge of the batting, you probably let the center piece slip out of place when you basted it, or you attempted to center it by vision alone. Trim all the sides equally. A slightly smaller potholder will still be fine.

Commercial Binding

There are many ways to bind the outside edge of a quilt. One is to use commercial binding such as bias tape. You will be practicing this method on your potholder.

Preparing the Binding

Commercial bias tape claims to be preshrunk and colorfast. If you are using a very dark tape, you may want to color test it to be sure. However, washing it in a machine will turn it into a tangled mess. Soaking it in hot water will minimize the damage, but you'll still lose the creased folds that are going to make it easy to work with. One solution is to cut a couple inches of binding and soak it in very hot water. A teacup that is white on the inside works well for checking colorfastness.

You could measure your piece before and after to check for shrinkage, but an unnoticeable amount in your 2" piece could still show up in a full-sized quilt. You'll have to trust the manufacturer and take your chances. This is one reason a lot of quilters make their own binding. Another is to get an exact match to one of the quilting fabrics.

Trim the starting edge of the binding in a straight line and open out the folds.

Stitching to the Back

Clip a small triangle off three of the corners of your potholder to aid in rounding the ends. The larger the triangle cut away, the more rounded the curves and the easier it'll be to sew on the binding. Whatever size triangle you choose, be sure you cut them all the same. Leave one corner square. This is the corner where you will work a loop with the binding so you can hang your potholder.

With the backing side facing you, begin at the squared corner. Hold the bias tape, right side down on the potholder, lining up the cut edge of the bias tape with the corner and the side edge just over the raw edge of the potholder. Using thread that closely matches the bias tape, stitch along the first fold. Be careful not to stretch the bias tape as you sew.

FIGURE 5-4

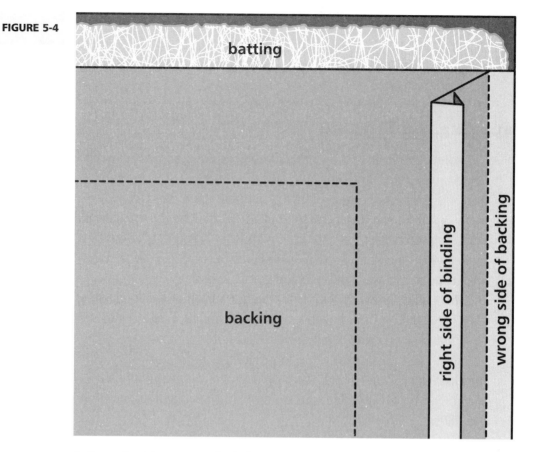

batting

backing

right side of binding

wrong side of backing

▲ Open the bias tape and stitch it to the back of the potholder.

Ease the binding around the trimmed corners, gathering it a little, and stop just before you stitch over the binding where you started. Cut the binding about 3" beyond the edge of the potholder.

QUESTION?

Why not stitch the binding on in one step?
You can try, but it's hard to keep from missing the binding on the bottom. Also, it becomes very difficult to ease the binding around the corner when you are worrying about what's under as well as what's on top of your potholder.

Stitching to the Front

Turn the potholder over and pull the binding around to the front. If you stitched right on the fold of the binding, you shouldn't need to press it to get it to fold. If it's a tight fit to pull the binding over the front stitches, trim the potholder just a fraction before starting to sew.

The idea of the next step is to get the binding to cover the row of stitches that the last step left on the front. These new stitches done from the front should look as even as possible along the binding. They should go through the binding on the back as well so they do not show against the backing.

Because the easiest way to sew is clockwise and you've turned your potholder over, you will be starting at the same place you quit before, leaving the few inches of bias tape that will cover the top corner of the potholder and form the loop to finish later. Stitch close to the edge of the tape all around to the end, gathering as needed at the corners.

Now, encase the unfinished corner that has the stitched-down binding within the fold of the loose bias tape. Overlapping the stitches for about 1/2", stitch through all the layers, over the corner, off the potholder, and along the excess inches of the binding, sewing the binding shut.

Making the Loop

Turn the excess binding into a loop of whatever size you want. Trim and stitch securely to the back of the potholder. A zigzag stitch will prevent the necessity of turning the edge under. Be sure that the stitches will be on the binding where they are unlikely to show and not on the face of the potholder. Zigzag across the edge, backstitch, and cross it forward again to be sure it holds.

FACT

How to Make an American Quilt by Whitney Otto (New York: Ballantine Books, Inc., 1991) is a novel about the lives of the members of a quilting club. "Quilting Patterns" scattered through the book use quilting as a metaphor for the women's lives.

Same Technique, Different Product

The Log Cabin pattern is a favorite because there are no seams to match within the block. Traditionally, the blocks are pieced as you pieced this potholder, only without sewing the pieces directly to the batting and backing. You can piece the block, of course, and hand quilt it to the batting and backing afterward. Normally, the quilting outlines each log $1/4"$ inside the seams.

If you enjoyed quilting as you pieced, you can use the same technique to make a variety of things. Remember, you can make the center square and the "logs" any size you wish. Consider a seasonal print in the center with coordinating colors around it for the center of the table. If you make the upper and lower logs narrower than the sides, you could make matching placemats.

Or start with a child's picture print and coordinate wide strips around it for a quilt-as-you-piece baby quilt. Just be certain you've squared that middle piece. The larger your project, the more potential for overhanging pieces.

Instead of making something bigger, you could make miniature versions of the potholders (with probably two rows of "logs" around the center instead of three). Use Christmas fabric and combine them with the tiny hoops mentioned in Chapter 4 for a true quilting fanatic's Christmas tree.

An alternative to the Log Cabin design is to stitch strips to both sides of the center square, then to the top and bottom. The process is repeated again on the sides and so on. This creates borders or frames for the center fabric. If the center square is tiny, the same size as the width of the strips, it's called Courthouse Steps and is usually done in two colors, one for the horizontal strips and one for vertical. Ⓔ

Chapter 6

Nine-Patch Baby Quilt

Making a Nine-Patch baby quilt is a great weekend project. It is sewn entirely on the machine and is tied, which is much faster than hand quilting. Baby quilts are great to have on hand to use as gifts or for donations to fund-raising bazaars.

Fabric Requirements

Nine-Patch refers to a pattern of nine squares, generally of only two colors, which alternate in three rows of three. The nine-square blocks are framed with panels of a coordinating fabric to keep the blocks from blending into one huge checkerboard. This 36" by 52" quilt calls for six blocks made of nine 4" (finished size) patches, separated and framed by 4" panels.

FIGURE 6-1

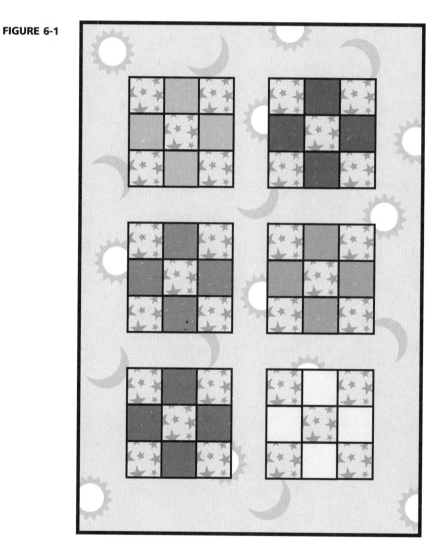

◀ The layout of a Nine-Patch baby quilt.

Choosing Fabrics

Since this is for a baby, use soft fabrics. One hundred percent cotton is recommended, either in broadcloth weight or flannel. Beware of any finishes on the fabric that might cause irritation to a baby's sensitive skin.

FACT

Just because this is called a baby quilt, don't let that limit your thinking. The same size quilt would make an excellent lap robe or throw. Consider colors that match a favorite chair in the den or your living room décor.

Soft colors are traditional for anything for babies, and you will find a lot to choose from along these lines. However, tiny babies can see only bright colors and sharp contrasts except at a very limited range, so don't discount them as possibilities.

Amounts of Fabrics

The yardages that follow assume the fabric you are buying is about 42" wide. If the width of the fabric is significantly different, adjust the yardages accordingly. And remember, it's better to have too much than too little. You can start your stash of scraps for future projects.

You will need:

- 1 yard of a primary print for panel and border pieces
- 2/3 yard of a secondary print
- 1/6 yard each of six solid-color fabrics that coordinate with the prints
- 1 2/3 yards for backing
- Piece of batting at least 38" by 54"
- 10 yards of yarn or crochet cotton for ties
- A sharp tapestry needle or large embroidery needle

With a little applied geometry, you'll discover that you should be able to cut the thirty secondary-color patches from exactly 1/2 yard of fabric. Unfortunately, it's unlikely the clerk in the fabric store is going to measure and cut the fabric exactly straight. Usually the clerk will try to be generous, but until you've washed the fabric and pulled a thread to even out the ends, you don't know how much will be wasted if the fabric's off grain.

If you are using the primary print fabric for the backing, 2½ yards should be sufficient for the panels, borders, and the backing. One yard of the secondary fabric should be enough if you want to use it for the backing as well as the thirty patches. Cut the backing piece first and cut the smaller blocks or panels from what is left.

ALERT!

Neither of the print fabrics should have a one-way design. The panels and borders will be especially difficult to cut out while accommodating a one-way print. If you aren't careful, part of the quilt will look sideways or upside down no matter how you turn it.

Cut and Arrange the Pieces

Since all the pieces are squares or rectangles, you will cut them by measure as described in Chapter 5. Pull a thread to even up the edge of your fabric and be sure it is straight. The patches on the finished quilt will be 4" by 4". Allowing ¼" all around for the seams, each patch will need to be cut 4½" square. Measure 4½" from the cut edge of your fabric and pull another thread or cut with a rotary cutter. If you are using a rotary cutter, you can fold the fabric and cut through as many as four layers at once if you are careful about keeping the edges lined up. Remember to cut away the selvage before you cut your strip into 4½" squares.

The Patches

You will need thirty squares of the primary color and four of each of the six solid colors. But here is the fun of the Nine-Patch. If you discover you are short on the print fabric, use it for four patches per block instead of five and cut one more of each of the solid-color fabrics. Or, if you have a lot of scraps of juvenile prints, use a different print for the patches in each block. You could pick a different solid color to go with each print or choose one that goes well with them all.

It's also not unusual to have the center patch different from the other patches in the block. If all of your blocks are going to be of a different print and different solid color, one fabric repeated in the center of each block will make them look more of a piece. Perhaps it could match the border and panel fabric.

Panels and Borders

You will need to cut the border and panel pieces $4^1/2"$ wide. You will need nine pieces $12^1/2"$ long to fit vertically between and on either side of the blocks, and four pieces $36^1/2"$ long to run horizontally above, between, and below the rows of blocks.

Cut the fabric into seven strips $4^1/2"$ wide. Four of these strips will be used for the horizontal panels and borders. The other three will become the vertical panels and borders. Trim away the selvages, but there's no need to cut the strips to the exact length. You can save time by doing that as you sew.

Backing and Batting

The finished cover will be slightly less than 36" by 52". Your backing and batting will both need to be cut a couple of inches larger than this. Be sure you have straightened the backing fabric as described in Chapter 3. Pull a thread to cut the edge with the grain; fold the cut edge in half, selvage to selvage. Pull on the diagonal until the selvages hang evenly.

Machine Piece the Blocks

The directions for this quilt are for machine piecing. It's quicker, more accurate, and sturdier. Hand piecing will be addressed in a later chapter with a project that cannot be machine pieced accurately. However, if you do not have a machine, you can, of course, stitch the pieces by hand.

If your machine wants to eat your fabric when you begin, make a "thread bunny." This is simply a folded scrap you put under the back of your presser foot next to, not on top of, your fabric that is about to be stitched. It raises the back of the presser foot enough that it isn't pushing the edge of your fabric into the machine.

Three Patches Equal a Row

Begin with two patches that will be next to each other in a block. With right sides together, line up the edges and stitch 1/4" from the raw edge. Being sure to keep track of which patch should be in the middle of the row, stitch a third patch to the first two. Set this row aside and repeat the process with each row of patches. You should have eighteen rows.

If all your blocks are the same, you can sew 4½" strips of fabric together in the order the blocks should be arranged in the top and bottom rows. Cut the connected strips into 4½" units. Do the same with strips arranged for the middle row. This can save considerable time if you are making a full-sized quilt.

Press the seam allowances toward the darker fabric. This ensures that the allowance will not show through the front of the cover.

Matching Seams

Group the pressed three-square units together by block again. With right sides together, line up the edges and seams. To be sure the seams match, pin the strips together exactly on the seam line. The seam allowances should be pressed to stagger rather than overlap, minimizing the bulk. You will not be sewing through more than four layers of cloth when you stitch the strips together. This also makes it easier to line up the seams. Run a pin in and back out along the stitching line of the unit you've placed on top. Check the bottom unit. Does the part of the pin that is visible line up exactly with the stitching? If not, make the necessary adjustments.

When both seams are matched, check the fabric between the pins. Is it lying flat naturally? You need to be able to stitch without gathering or stretching one patch to fit the other. If you can't, you need to redo a seam. Use another unit to help you determine which seam is the culprit. It's easier to make a piece smaller than larger, but don't automatically solve the problem that way. Your finished block might end up a different size than the rest of the blocks and your problems will have increased considerably.

Don't be reluctant to rip out a seam and redo it. It may feel like a lot of work for what may be an ⅛" mistake. But consider how you'll feel about the finished project. If that little mistake keeps other components of your quilt from fitting right, your little mistake will look like a big one.

Three Rows Equal a Block

When the seams line up, stitch the units together ¼" from the edge and repeat the process with the third row of patches. Set the new block aside and make the other five blocks the same way.

Press the seams. The direction isn't going to make a great deal of difference because whichever way you choose, you will be pressing darker allowances toward lighter fabric about half the time. An alternative would be to press the seams open, but this is a little more time consuming. If you have a great deal of contrast between the hue of the fabrics in your quilt, it might be worth the extra effort. Otherwise, consistency is probably more important than what direction you choose.

Unless your blocks are all the same, you'll need to decide their placement on the finished quilt. Lay them out on a large surface such as the floor. You can spread your panel/border strips between them to get a better idea of what your quilt will look like. Trade the blocks around until you are satisfied.

Once you've made your decision, stack your blocks in order, bottom row blocks, middle, then top row. Left and right won't make any difference at this point unless you have used one-way fabric. In which case, you'll need to keep careful track of what you are doing.

You may notice that, in spite of your best efforts, a few of the seams don't match exactly. This may be because the fabrics slid a little as your presser foot went over a pin. Don't worry about a slight misalignment. In this particular pattern, it will be covered by the ties.

Set the Quilt

At the sewing machine, with the stack of blocks nearby, spread three of the panel strips across your lap. With right sides together, sew a panel strip to one side of the first block. You won't need to pin since there are no seams to match. Simply line up the edges and sew. When you come to the end of the block, cut the thread and trim the strip, using the block as a guide.

Repeat the process with the other end of the block. Sew the second block in the stack to the panel you've just trimmed, and then sew a third panel to the other end of it. You now have a completed row of your quilt.

Set this aside to press and repeat the process with the rest of the blocks. Iron the seams toward the panels and lay them out to re-create your chosen layout.

Return to the sewing machine and spread the remaining four panel strips across your lap. Sew the strips and the rows of blocks together, trimming the excess from the panel strips at the end of each row. Press the seams toward the panels and your quilt cover is finished.

Easy Assembly Method

This method of assembling a quilt works well with small projects. The idea is to sew the cover and the back together with the right sides of the fabrics facing each other, a little like a pillowcase, then turn it right-side out. This saves the need for any form of binding or hemming of the edges of the quilt.

Backing and Batting

Spread the batting out on the floor or other large surface. Smooth out any wrinkles. Spread the backing piece over it, right-side up and pin them together in a few places. Baste the pieces together loosely and remove the pins. You won't need a great many basting stitches in order to hold these together for the next step.

ALERT!

Don't try to get by with pin basting alone. The pins, if they are on the backing side, will catch when you try to turn the quilt. If they are on the batting side, there is a chance you'll leave one *inside* the quilt!

Assemble

Spread the cover, right-side down, on top of the backing. Carefully smooth out any wrinkles. Place a pin every few inches around the outside edge. The edges of the backing and batting should extend beyond the edge of the cover.

Stitch a 1/4" seam around the outside edge of the cover, leaving only 10" to 12" open on one side of the quilt. Backstitching is recommended at the beginning and end because there will be considerable stress on these stitches when you turn the quilt right-side out.

You will need to stitch the backing to the batting at the opening. Move the cover out of your way and stitch along what would have been the stitching line, coming as close as possible to where the cover is stitched down without catching the cover in these stitches.

Some Sewing Hints

You will want to sew with the batting down and the underside of the cover facing you. Besides the fact that your cover is your guide for your stitches, you do not want to try to sew with the batting on top. It will catch on the presser foot and tear.

When you stitch the corners, take a stitch or two on the diagonal instead of making a sharp turn. This allows you to trim off more of the excess fabric and actually makes a sharper corner on the finished quilt.

Trim and Turn

Trim the backing to about $1/16$" outside the cover's edge. The finished edge will lie smoother after it's turned if the two fabrics in the seam allowance are of different widths. Trim the batting close to the stitching and clip the four corners almost to the diagonal stitches.

Turn the quilt right-side out through the opening you left. Use the blunt end of your seam ripper's handle or the eraser end of a pencil to poke the corners out. Never use a sharp object for this as you can easily rip open the seam or poke a hole in the fabric.

Press around the edge of the quilt, being careful to open the seam out as much as possible. Rolling the seam between your fingers helps to open it out. Turn the edges under in the opening and press them flat. Remove the basting stitches from the backing.

The Blind Stitch

You need to close up the opening you left to turn the quilt, but you want it to look as much like the machine stitches as possible. If done correctly, the blind stitch is nearly invisible.

FIGURE 6-2

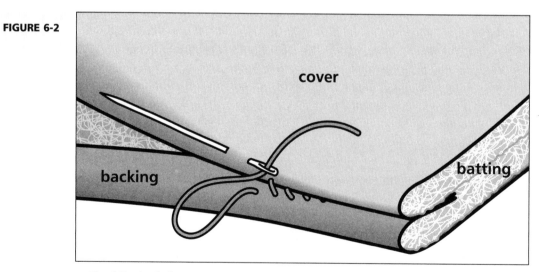

▲ The blind stitch.

Refer to **FIGURE 6-2** and follow these steps.

1. Knot an appropriate length of the same thread you used to stitch around the quilt.
2. Bury the knot in the seam allowance, bringing the needle out at the end of the machine stitching.
3. Holding the layers between the thumb and forefinger of your off hand, take a tiny stitch exactly on the crease of the cover.
4. Insert the needle in the backing even with where the needle left the cover and take another tiny stitch.
5. Repeat with another tiny stitch in the cover beginning exactly across from the end of the last stitch.

The trick is to do all your forward movement with the thread inside the folds of cloth and not in the space between the layers. Following this technique will make your hand stitching almost indistinguishable from the machine stitching.

If you want the stitches to be especially secure, you can do a backstitch. It's done the same way except you'll take your forward stitch at about twice the length as the machine stitches, then take a tiny stitch in the opposite direction in the other layer of fabric. Again, try to be sure the thread enters one piece of fabric straight across from where it left the other piece so the stitches are hidden in the fabrics' fold lines.

Tie the Quilt

The only thing left to do is secure the layers together. This quilt is going to be tied at the corners of every patch. This puts ties evenly spaced over the entire surface of the quilt at close-enough intervals to hold the batting in place.

Baste

Spread the quilt out on a flat surface again and smooth it out. Begin in the middle and pin the layers together every 6" to 8". Flip the quilt over to be sure the backing is as smooth as the front. Move pins if necessary.

Since this is a relatively small project, pin basting will be sufficient while you tie. However, if you are reluctant to get a few scratches from the pins as you work, baste the layers together, beginning in the center and working outward the same way you basted the miniquilt in Chapter 4. Knot your contrasting thread and work a running stitch from the center to each corner, then from the center to each side. You may find it easier to use large safety pins instead.

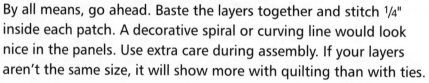

What if I want to hand quilt instead of tie?
By all means, go ahead. Baste the layers together and stitch ¼" inside each patch. A decorative spiral or curving line would look nice in the panels. Use extra care during assembly. If your layers aren't the same size, it will show more with quilting than with ties.

QUESTION?

Yarn for Tying

Cotton or acrylic yarn is recommended for tying. Some quilters use wool because it shrinks and frizzes into tight little knots when the quilt is washed, and there is no danger of the ties coming out. There's also no danger of anyone lying on the quilt, because those knots are as hard as buttons. Acrylic and cotton ties will last well enough and, if done correctly, will not come out anyway.

The color you choose for the ties will depend on whether you want the ties to decorate the surface of your quilt or blend to near invisibility. There's no rule that says the ties must all be the same color, either. Consider how your yarn or yarns look with all the different fabrics before you make your decision.

The Tie Stitch

There is no need to cut a length of yarn from the skein. Simply thread the loose end of it onto your sharp tapestry needle or embroidery needle. The smallest needle available that will still allow the yarn to go through the eye will be easiest to draw through the layers of your quilt.

Beginning near the center of your quilt, insert the needle about $1/8''$ diagonally from the corner of a patch and out again $1/8''$ on the other side. Draw about 4" of yarn through the quilt. Take a second stitch back through the same holes. Tie the yarn in a double knot and trim to about $3/4''$ or whatever length you desire.

FIGURE 6-3

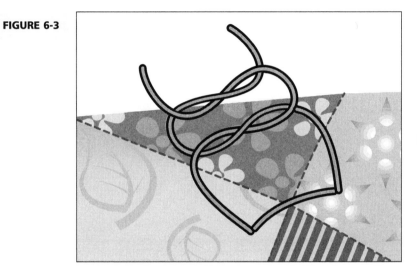

◀ Double stitch and double knot to tie.

With the thumb and forefinger of your off hand, untwist the yarn slightly. Stick the needle in the yarn just above the knot and run it outward to fray the yarn. This will decrease the chances of the knots coming untied.

Rethread the needle and repeat across the surface of the quilt, working outward from the center. Sometimes it's easier to catch any skipped sites by checking the back of the quilt. The little loops of yarn should be evenly spaced over the entire surface.

Sometimes ties are tied in bows instead of frayed. This can be very pretty but is not recommended for a baby quilt as tiny fingers can catch in the loops. It might work well on the living room throw, however. Ⓔ

Chapter 7

Puff Lap Robe

Puffed quilts, also called biscuit quilts, are made by pleating a square of fabric onto a slightly smaller square and adding some stuffing between the layers. In this pattern, the size of each finished square is 1 3/4" across. It takes 832 squares to make a 45 1/2" by 56" lap robe.

What You'll Need

This is a great pattern for using up some of those smaller scraps. Distribute the various colors completely at random across the cover of the quilt, or, if you prefer, choose larger amounts of coordinating colors and establish a pattern with the pieces.

Lap Robe

For the lining, or smaller squares, you will need approximately 3 yards of fabric, depending on the width. You can use up less desirable fabric for the lining pieces since they will not show as long as they are a lighter color than the cover or backing fabrics.

The backing requires a piece at least 46½" by 57". You will need a small bag of cotton or polyester stuffing. Ten to 20 yards of sport-weight yarn, crochet cotton, or embroidery floss will be sufficient for the ties.

For the binding, you will need 5⅔ yards of commercial binding or bias tape or about ⅓ yard of fabric to make your own binding.

FACT

If you are intimidated by the number of squares you will need, consider making them over a period of time, putting together a few from scraps at the end of other sewing projects and collecting them in a basket. You might be surprised at how quickly they accumulate.

Other Sizes

This and most other quilt patterns can be converted to any size quilt you desire. The following measurements allow approximately 15" for overhang on the sides and bottom and for a tuck under the pillows, except for the crib size and the lap robe.

Bed	Mattress	Quilt	Puffs
Lap robe	N/A	45½" × 56"	832
Crib	27½" × 52"	28" × 52"	480

continued on following page

Bed	Mattress	Quilt	Puffs
Twin	39" × 78"	69" × 108"	2,480
Double	54" × 78"	84" × 108"	2,976
Queen	60" × 78"	90" × 108"	3,224
King	72" × 84"	102" × 114"	3,770

ALERT!

A pieced cover will be slightly smaller than the sum of its parts. This is primarily because the thickness of the fabric keeps it from lying perfectly flat at the seams. The more pieces that make up a quilt cover, the more it will vary from the mathematically calculated size.

Cut, Pleat, and Stuff

Cut the pieces by measure as described in Chapter 5. Cut the fabric into strips, then squares, either by pulling a thread or using a rotary cutter. You will need 832 cover pieces 3" square and the same number of lining pieces $2^1/4$" square.

With wrong sides together, pin a cover piece to a lining piece at the corners. On three sides, pleat the excess fabric and pin. If you pleat left to right, you'll be stitching with the pleats instead of against them. (See **FIGURE 7-1**.)

Insert a small amount of stuffing through the unpleated side. In order to use as close to the same amount of stuffing as possible in each puff, set aside a piece to use as a guide. Don't overstuff the puffs or they will become very difficult to sew and will be less attractive. Use just enough to give them some lift but still allow them to settle against each other a little when they are finished.

An alternative to the stuffing is to cut 1" squares of batting. Your puffs will not stand out as much as they would with the stuffing, but it will be easier to get them all the same.

Pleat the fourth side and pin it in place. Your puffs will look like little insects with steel legs. Stitch all around each square close to the edge, and you'll see why they are sometimes called biscuits, though at this point they look more like ravioli.

FIGURE 7-1

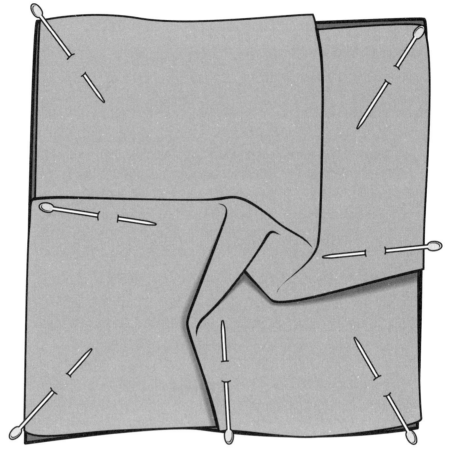

▲ Pleat the cover to fit the lining.

Chain Piece Shortcut

When you are sewing many pieces together, especially if they are to be pieced at random, you can save some time by stitching them together in a "chain."

Getting Started

Begin by having all your pieces handy to the sewing machine. These are already stuffed, with the pleats stitched to the lining. If you want the pieces arranged in a particular pattern, lay them out so that you can keep straight which two pieces need to be stitched together. Normally when you are chain piecing, you can stack your pieces, but the stuffing in these pieces prevents that.

Put the first two pieces right sides together, lining up the edge to be stitched. Stitch the $1/4''$ seam as you normally would, except stop stitching just as you reach the edge. Leave the pieces under the presser foot.

Prepare the next two pieces, right sides together, and ready them in front of the presser foot. Take two or three stitches off the first pair and feed the second pair under the presser foot. This saves the time it normally takes to raise the foot, cut the thread, and start the next pair. When you are dealing with 832 squares, the total time saved becomes significant.

Separate and Chain Again

When you have finished, cut the pieces apart with a snip of the scissors and pair them up again. Stitch all the pairs together into rows of four, the fours into rows of eight, and so on until you have twenty-six rows of thirty-two squares.

QUESTION?

But don't you have to backstitch?
Backstitching is generally a good idea. You don't want the stitches coming out later. However, the few stitches that were made beyond the pieces will knot, providing a little protection. The crossing seams do as well. It becomes a matter of weighing the time saved against the possible risk.

Finish the Cover

Press the seams open. One of those clever little mini-irons comes in handy for this since the stuffing interferes with the full-sized iron. If you don't have one, a sleeve board or a tightly rolled towel placed under the seam can help you get the puffs out of the way and the iron onto the seam.

Match the seams as you did in Chapter 6. Place two rows together, right sides facing, and pin at each seam. Stitch the rows together. Don't be terribly concerned about a slight mismatch of seams, as the puffy nature of the quilt will help to hide the seam junctions. A tiny bit of gathering isn't going to show either, since the pieces already have pleats. Iron these seams open as well.

Assemble and Tie

Though its appearance is different, the puffed quilt is assembled much like the miniquilt in Chapter 4. Because of the puffs, but also because of its size, it can be a bit trickier.

Backing and Batting

Cut your backing piece slightly larger than the cover. It may be necessary to piece it. In this particular quilt, having the seam across the middle isn't going to show on the front of the quilt. Press any seams in the backing open.

Lay out the backing, right-side down. Because there is already stuffing as well as two layers of fabric in the cover, you can skip the batting if you wish. However, the batting will make your lap robe heavier, stiffer, and warmer.

Spread the batting, if you are using it, on top. Spread the cover, right-side up, on top of that. Pin baste them together as you did the baby quilt in Chapter 6 after it had been turned. Begin at the center, making sure all the layers are kept smooth. Check the back and make any necessary adjustment with the pins.

Tie

Because of all the layers you will be tying, regular four-ply knitting yarn is going to be too heavy. The lighter sport-weight yarn, crochet cotton, or embroidery floss will let you use a smaller needle, which will go through the layers easier.

You will tie a double knot the same way you did with the baby quilt in Chapter 6. Since these squares are much smaller than the patches in the baby quilt, you don't need to tie at the junction of every seam. Every three to five squares will be enough.

What color yarn or thread you use to tie will depend on what effect you are after. You might experiment with having the frayed thread or bow on the backing side of the lap robe.

If you are having difficulty running your needle through the quilt to tie, you might try pulling the needle with pliers. Experienced quilters often keep a small pair in their sewing box.

Stitch around the outside of your quilt through all the layers at about $1/4$" from the edge of the cover. Trim away the excess backing and batting.

Make the Binding

Next, you will need to bind the edge of your quilt. Binding strips, either commercial or homemade, that are cut on the bias are easier to use on projects with curved corners, like the potholder in Chapter 5, because they stretch a little. The puffs in this quilt, however, don't leave much room for clipping corners. Mitered corners are going to look better, and they are easily made with binding you make yourself with fabric strips cut on the grain of the fabric.

Cut the Binding

Begin by preparing your binding fabric. Cut away the uneven edges and straighten the fabric by pulling on the required biases. Cut away the selvages.

Fold the fabric in half, right sides together, lining up the edges where the selvages were. Now move one layer of fabric down 2". The edges should overlap for 10", with one layer of fabric extending beyond for 2" on either side.

FIGURE 7-2

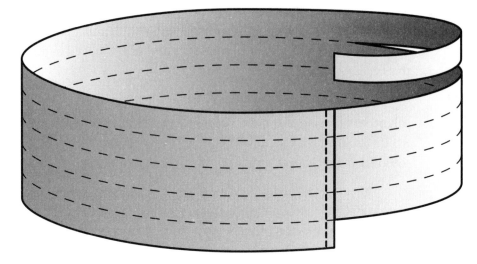

▲ Cut a continuous strip of binding as indicated by the dashed lines.

Stitch $1/4$" from the selvage edge along these 10", creating a large loop of fabric. Press the seam open.

Beginning just above the overlap, cut a strip 2" from the lengthwise edge. Continue cutting through the seam and around in a spiral until you have one continuous strip 2" wide.

Don't be alarmed if your fabric is less than 12" long when you've cut away the uneven edge. Five lengths of even 42" fabric will go all the way around your lap robe.

Press the Binding

You will need to press the edges of your binding toward the center of the wrong side. This will make your binding look like commercial single-fold binding tape. A pin guide on your ironing board will make this chore a lot easier. To establish the folds, press the edges of your binding until they almost meet in the middle for about 3".

Take a long pin and just catch it under about $1/8$" on the cover of your ironing board. Do this near the center of your board with the point of the pin toward you. Push the pin through until about 1" extends beyond the anchor. Slide the folded binding under the pin as close to the anchor as possible without wrinkling the binding. This is easiest if you can push down on the ironing board cover on either side of the pin and down on the head of the pin at the same time.

Adjust the pin so that it is anchored on the other side of the binding as well. Try to get the pin to enter the ironing board cover as close to the near edge of the binding as possible without actually catching the binding. The binding should slide under the pin the long way but should not shift back and forth under the pin.

As you slide the binding through the pin guide, the edges will turn up and you can press them flat. This will not be one smooth movement, but rather pull and press and an occasional readjustment. Still, it is much easier and more accurate than folding each edge and trying to keep your fingers out from under the iron. When you are finished, you can press the binding in half to give you the center fold as a guideline if you wish.

Binding the Quilt

Because you are mitering the corners, you aren't going to get to hide one row of stitching inside the binding as you did with the potholder. It's too difficult to manipulate the binding into a position to do that. You will still stitch the binding to the backing side first, though, because whichever side you stitch first will have two rows of stitching and look less tidy as the second side.

Sewing on the Binding

Open out the center fold of your binding. You have a 1"-wide strip with the ends folded under and a crease down the middle. With the backing side of the quilt facing you, line up the center crease of the binding to just a fraction beyond the outside edge of the quilt. This slight extension beyond the edge allows for the thickness of the quilt. The turned-under raw edges of the binding strip should be facing down.

Beginning anywhere along a side, sew the binding to the quilt, stitching close to the fold of the binding. Your stitching will be slightly more than $1/4$" from the raw edge of your quilt and probably inside the stitching that is already on the quilt.

Mitering the Corners

When you approach a corner, continue stitching straight to the edge of the quilt and backstitch a couple of stitches. Remove the quilt from the sewing machine and cut the thread.

Fold the binding back against itself along the edge of the quilt. With a pin, hold the top layer of binding against the bottom layer just over $1/4$" from the quilt edge. Fold the binding ninety degrees so it lines up with the next side of the quilt and finger press the diagonal crease in the binding.

FIGURE 7-3

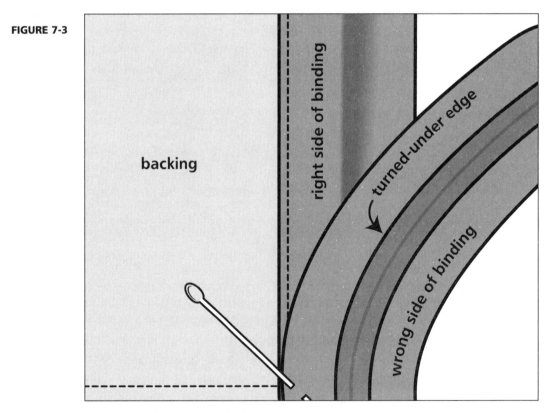

▲ Fold the binding and pin $1/4$" from the edge.

FIGURE 7-4

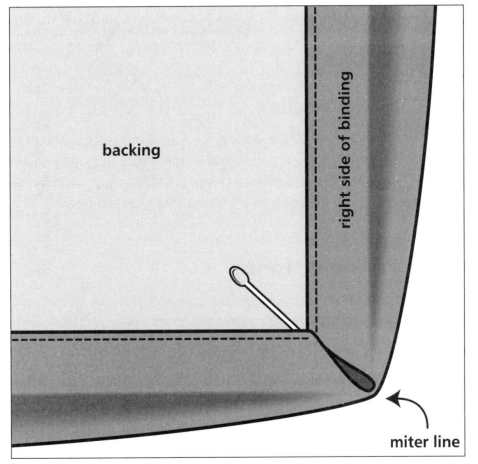

▲ Crease the miter line and stitch along the next side.

Finishing

When you've stitched almost all the way around the quilt, determine how much binding you will need, allowing about 1/2" to lap over where you started. Cut away the excess. With your fingers, press the raw edge of the binding under about 1/4". Continue stitching the binding in place, taking a few stitches beyond the folded edge.

Turn the quilt over. Fold the binding to the front. Stitch the binding in place as you did the other side. When you come to a corner, stop stitching when you are the same distance from both edges, at the point where you need to turn the corner. Backstitch a couple of stitches.

Hold the binding down as if you had stitched to the edge of the quilt, and fold the binding for the mitered corner. The binding will fold easily into position because it is already being pulled around the corner. Press the crease firmly with your fingers. Stitch forward again, onto the fold, and turn the corner.

This quilt can make a great group project. Many hands will make short work of the pleating and stuffing. Any child old enough to handle pins can be trusted to stuff. A little adjustment just before sewing can take care of any inaccuracies caused by small fingers.

Consider Variations

The puff quilt is a fun and rewarding project. If you've enjoyed your time spent on this endeavor, you may want to try out your creative style on a few more.

Shiny fabrics are particularly effective on the puff quilt because of the play of light on the curving surfaces. If your lap robe is not going to get particularly hard use, you might consider making it out of silk. Plan for a deeper seam allowance to make up for the extra fraying you'll have to deal with in using these fabrics.

Different-Sized Puffs

You can make the puffs any size you want, and the ratio between the cover and the lining doesn't have to be the same as described here. Using smaller lining pieces or larger cover pieces will make the puffs stand up higher. Less difference between the two layers will give the quilt a more subtle texture. In this last case, the square of batting will probably work better than the ball of stuffing. Remember, the overall size of the quilt will be determined by the size of the lining pieces.

Chapter 8

Christmas Tree Wall Hanging

Quilts have always been used to commemorate special occasions and events. Today's popular quilted wall hangings can do the same. This Christmas tree wall hanging comes together quickly and lets you practice several aspects of pieced quilting while you are decorating for the holiday season.

Reading a Pattern

Most patterns for pieced quilt blocks are simply a picture of the block shown on a grid. This is often called a block pattern. Knowing how to read and use a block pattern makes it possible to reproduce any pattern you see and to create your own.

FIGURE 8-1

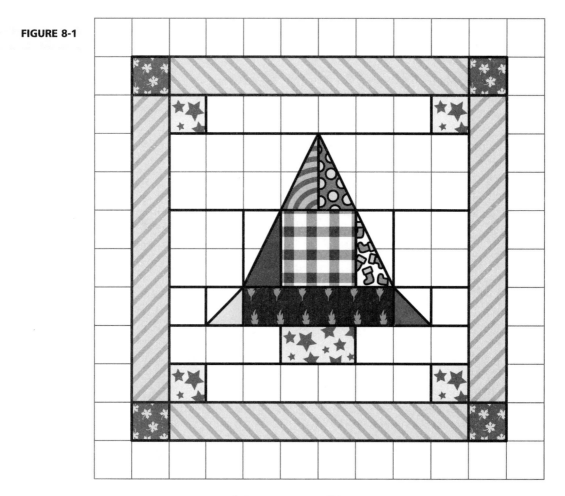

▲ Christmas tree wall hanging pattern.

Size

The size represented by the squares on the grid will be determined by the size you want the finished block to be. For example, if the squares in the grid in **FIGURE 8-1** each represent 2", the finished hanging will be approximately 20" by 20". Let them represent more if you want a larger hanging.

FACT

Before women could vote, they sometimes expressed their political views in their quilts with symbols or by naming their quilts after political movements. Consider these quilt names: Fifty-Four Forty or Fight, Free Trade, Tippecanoe and Tyler Too, Whig Rose and Democrat Rose, Union Quilt, Yankee Pride, Underground Railroad, and The Little Giant, named for Stephen A. Douglas.

Determining Supplies

The pattern shows you what fabrics you will need to make the cover. In this case, red, white, and green fabrics are used plus a red-and-green Christmas print on the border. You can use one fabric of each color or make your tree of several different green scraps. If you are buying new fabric, $\frac{1}{8}$ yard of each of the colors will be sufficient to make a 20"-by-20" hanging.

The batting and backing will need to be slightly larger than the cover.

This pattern has already split the tree and the background into pieces that will be easy to stitch into rows. If the pattern simply showed the outline of the tree on the background, you would need to determine the rows to know how to cut the pieces.

It would be possible to divide the pattern vertically instead of horizontally. The tree could be pieced together first and the white background could be two large triangles. Most patterns are going to leave that decision up to you.

Cutting the Pieces

Remember to add $1/4$" all around each piece for the seam. The pieces, such as the red squares in the corners, will be the size of the square plus $1/2$". For a 20"-by-20" hanging, these pieces will be cut $2^1/2$" square. The green square in the middle of the tree will be $4^1/2$" square. The length of the border strips are eight times the size of the corner squares plus $1/2$" or $16^1/2$" by $2^1/2$", and so on.

Cut the triangles as if they filled the whole square. Do this for both halves of the triangle. In other words, cut a rectangle of white and a rectangle of green for the pair of triangles that occupies one rectangle on the pattern.

It is possible to cut out the triangles by calculating the diagonal seam allowance. Easier yet, draw the finished triangle, add the seam allowances, and use the template to cut the pieces. The difficulty comes in trying to keep the fabric from stretching out of shape when you take a narrow seam on the bias.

Pairing and Piecing

The wall hanging is pieced similar to the Nine-Patch in Chapter 6. However, the pieces are of several different sizes and the triangles must be made first.

Turning Squares into Triangles

The half squares at the lower corners of the tree are easy to turn into triangles. Place a white square on top of a green square and stitch them together across the diagonal. For accuracy, use a pencil and ruler to mark this line before you stitch.

Trim one-half of the square away $1/4$" from the stitches. Open out the square and press the seam allowance toward the green triangle. Repeat for the second corner. You don't have to worry about directions or even which half you trim away because you can simply turn the square to make the triangle fit into either position.

ALERT!

If you have chosen a one-way fabric, such as a print that must be turned right-side up, you will need to take extra care in cutting, stitching, and trimming. It will not work to turn it to fit the tree the way you can other fabrics.

Turning Long Rectangles into Triangles

The two-square-by-one-square triangles are a bit more complicated. Place the white rectangle on top of the green but instead of matching them up, turn the white piece until the upper left corner is on top of the green piece's upper right corner. The lower right corner of the white piece should be paired with the lower left of the green piece.

FIGURE 8-2

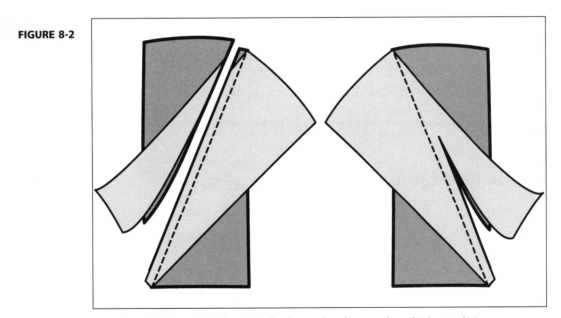

▲ Left and right triangles: Stitch along the diagonal and trim to ¼" seam allowances.

Mark and stitch from corner to corner and trim away one side the same way you did the squares. Again, it won't matter which half you trim away because you can rotate the piece. However, which diagonal you stitch will make a difference. You will need to make two triangles as described and an additional two triangles with the upper right corner of the white matched with the upper left of the green. Press the seams toward the green triangles.

Piecing the Rows

Put the pieces together into rows following the diagram, leaving the outer borders for last. Press the seam allowances toward the green or red pieces and stitch the rows together, matching seams where applicable. Sew two of the borders to the top and bottom of the block. Press these seams toward the top of the hanging. Sew the green corner pieces to the remaining borders and sew these to the sides of the hanging. Press the allowances outward.

QUESTION?

How do I decide which direction to press seam allowances in?
There are two basic rules: press toward the darker fabric or press in the direction that minimizes bulk. Sometimes there is no clear choice; you follow one to break the other. In those cases, do whichever seems easier.

Mark the Quilting Lines

Before you assemble the layers of your wall hanging, you need to mark the quilting lines. The tree and the border pieces can be outlined or echo stitched as you did the miniquilt in Chapter 4. A round of quilting stitches close to the tree and concentric rounds outside that, each approximately 1/4" from the last, won't have to be marked.

If you want to mark scallops for boughs of the tree, make a circle on cardboard using a protractor, if you have one. Otherwise, anything perfectly round can be used as a pattern. The circumference of the circle shouldn't be larger than the length of the bottom of the tree.

Fold the circle twice and cut it into wedge-shaped fourths. Use the curve of the wedge as a guide to draw even scallops on the surface of the tree.

Another suggestion is to embroider ornaments on the tree before you assemble the hanging. Or stitch on sequins or buttons of appropriate sizes. Or maybe you'd rather wait until it is assembled and, instead of quilting, tie your hanging with little red bows on the tree and white, silver, or light blue "snowflakes" over the background.

Assemble and Quilt

Assemble the wall hanging the same way you did the baby quilt in Chapter 6. Layer in this order: batting, backing right-side up, and cover right-side down. Stitch $1/4$" inside the cover's edge. The hole left for turning the hanging can be as small as 6" or 8", depending on the size of the hanging. Turn, press, blind stitch the opening, and baste the wall hanging from the center outward the same as you did the baby quilt.

If you have enlarged the pattern to anything more than 36", you should consider assembling the more traditional way as described in Chapter 4. Layer the backing wrong-side up, the batting, and the cover right-side up. Baste together and plan to bind the edge. The larger the quilt, the more difficult it is going to be to get the backing exactly right before you turn, unless you baste the layers together from the center outward. A tied quilt, like that in Chapter 6, can be turned to bind with little worry because any errors in size will be less detectable between the ties than between rows of quilting.

Quilt the marked lines and whatever areas you've decided to stitch, the same as you did in Chapter 4. Begin near the center and work outward.

How to Hang

It's not a wall hanging until you can hang it on the wall. There are decorative hangers made especially for small quilts. Some are designed to look like old-fashioned hangers and come in a range of sizes. There are also special brackets designed to hold dowels and rods made like curtain rods with clips for the quilt instead of hooks. There are also many more inexpensive options.

Loop Method

Make four small loops out of ribbon and stitch them to the back of the quilt far enough below the upper edge that they will not show. Cut a dowel 1' shorter than the width of the quilt and cut a small notch at the center. Slip the dowel through the loops and balance the notch on a nail in the wall. This works best with a lightweight hanging under 2' long.

If your hanging is slightly larger, use more little loops and hang it on two nails instead of one. Use a carpenter's level to be sure the nails are aligned so the quilt won't hang crookedly.

Quilts can make some powerful statements. The AIDS Memorial Quilt, made by thousands of quilters in memory of loved ones lost to AIDS, covers several acres when all the sections are laid out. The quilt was begun in 1985 and, unfortunately, is still growing.

Casing Method

If your quilt is much more than 20" wide, the loops aren't going to be enough. To ensure that your quilt doesn't sag in the middle, make a casing or sleeve for the dowel. Cut a strip of cloth about 2" shorter than the width of your hanging and about 2" wide. Press the raw edges under all the way around and stitch them down. Hand stitch the casing to the back of the quilt, leaving the ends open to insert the dowel through. Be sure you stitch to the backing only and not through to the front of the quilt. The dowel should extend beyond the casing far enough to rest on two nails but not far enough to be seen beyond the edges of the hanging.

If you are binding your wall hanging instead of turning it, stitch the casing on just before the binding. The top edge would not need to be hemmed but can be covered by the binding.

Tab-Top Method

A more elaborate method is to use a decorative curtain rod that extends beyond the sides of the quilt. The quilt hangs from this rod on tabs sewn to the quilt. The tabs are generally made from fabric used elsewhere in the quilt such as the background or binding fabric.

To make these tabs, cut a strip the desired width of the tabs, times two, plus 1/2". If you want 2" tabs, cut the strip of fabric 4 1/2" wide. The strip will need to be the desired height of the tabs, times two, plus 1", times the number of tabs you want. The more tabs you have, the less likely the hanging will sag or bunch together. Often the space between each tab is equal to the width of the tabs. If you want tabs 2" wide and 3" high evenly spaced on a 20" hanging with 2" spaces in between, you will need five tabs. Cut your strip 35" long.

Fold the strip in half the long way, right sides together, and sew a 1/4" seam along the edge. Turn the strip right-side out by fastening a safety pin to the corner of the seam allowance, then running the pin through the "tube."

Press the strip flat with the seam centered on one side rather than on the folds. Cut the strip into the appropriate lengths. Fold the tabs in half with the seam sides together, and sew them at even intervals to the back of the quilt. Turn the raw edges under for a more professional look.

FACT

Several religious and charity organizations sent donated quilts and blankets to New York City and Washington, D.C., after the September 11 attacks. Some of these organizations also sent blankets and quilts to children in Afghanistan.

These can be stitched to the quilt before it's assembled. Space the folded tabs across the top of the cover. The raw edges should be in line and the tabs lying with the looped ends toward the center of the quilt. Stitch them in place, then assemble the quilt. When the quilt is turned, the raw edges of the tabs will be inside the seam allowance of the cover and backing.

Run the curtain rod through the tabs and hang the quilt from the appropriate end pieces or from two hooks hidden as much as possible by the tabs.

Care of Wall Hangings

If your hanging is to be on the wall for an extended period of time, there should be space between it and the wall. Oil in paint and untreated wood can stain the cloth. The quilt needs to "breathe" so molds and mildew won't be able to grow on it. Commercial hangers are usually designed to do this.

If your hanging becomes dusty, shake it out or air fluff it in your dryer. Vacuuming is also a possibility. If your hanging is in your kitchen where grease will be in the air, you might want to spray it with fabric protector. If you have chosen all washable fabrics, you can wash your quilt as you would a baby quilt.

Making Your Own Patterns

Now that you know how to follow a pattern illustrated only by a picture on a grid, you can create your own patterns. Consider illustrating an occupation or another hobby. Draw the desired shape on graph paper. Move all the lines and curves to the nearest graph lines or diagonals.

If your drawing seems too complicated to piece after you've reduced it to triangles and squares, don't despair. Save it until you've learned to use templates.

Simple shapes are going to be easiest to translate into patterns. Try drawing tulips, birdhouses, and cats. Different fabrics or embroidered details will make your creation unique. Have fun putting your new knowledge into practice.

FACT

Quilted wall hangings may seem like a new idea, but tapestries were hung on the walls of medieval castles. Pioneers hung their quilts on log cabin walls for the same reason: to cut down on drafts. Modern quilters have just borrowed the idea and modified it to their decorating tastes.

Signing Your Work

Any work of art deserves to carry the artist's signature. Your quilted wall hangings, especially ones that express your special interests or milestones, should be signed. Many quilters include their maiden name to help future genealogists. Some quilters put their name and whatever other information they want on a piece of cloth and stitch it to the quilt, while others sign directly on the quilt.

Front or Back

Most quilters put their names on the backs of their quilts. The information is on the quilt forever, but doesn't detract from the appearance of the quilt.

Generally, if a quilter puts her name on the front, she will try to make it less conspicuous. Some will use quilting thread to sew their names in tiny stitches taken only through the cover of the quilt. A few will even work their names into the stitching pattern.

Ink or Thread

You can sign your quilt with ink or a permanent marker or sign it in pencil and stitch over the lines. Cursive letters are easier than printed letters because they are joined. A single strand of embroidery thread works best for the stitching. Use a simple backstitch, sometimes called a stem stitch. On the face of your fabric, the thread takes a small stitch from left to right. The needle is working from right to left and comes back to the front in the middle of the stitch.

FIGURE 8-3

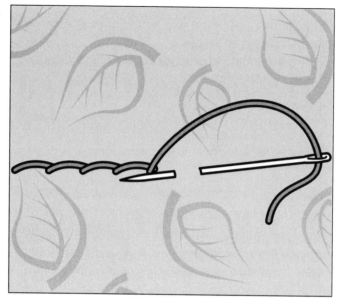

◀ The outline stitch is ideal for signatures.

Refer to **FIGURE 8-3** and follow these steps.

1. Bring the needle up from the back at the beginning of the line.
2. Insert the needle about ¼" along the line and back out halfway between this point and the starting point.
3. Insert the needle about ¼" from this point and back out at the end of the last stitch.
4. Always let the stitch fall on the same side of the loose thread.

If you decide to sign in ink, iron over it to set it. Covering the signature with a cloth dipped in vinegar and water and then wrung out and ironing over that is even better—you don't want the ink to run when the quilt is washed. If you are signing a piece of cloth to appliqué to the quilt, backing it with iron-on interfacing or butcher paper first makes it easier to sign. Remove the paper before you sew it to the quilt.

Nearly all quilters put their names on their quilts. Most also include the date—at least the year. Some record the date the quilt was begun as well as the date it was finished. Many include the quilt's name and sometimes more information about the pattern. Ⓔ

Chapter 9
Rising Star Pillow

There are many versions of the eight-pointed star pattern. The Rising Star features a star within a star. If you put triangles in a pinwheel design in the center of the block in place of the inner star, it becomes a Martha Washington.

Read the Pattern

If each square in the block pattern represents 2", the finished block will be approximately 16" by 16", a good size for a pillow. You can reduce or enlarge the size to suit your needs by changing the dimensions of each square or by adding a border. For purposes of giving specific instructions, assume each square equals 2" and adjust your measurements accordingly.

FIGURE 9-1

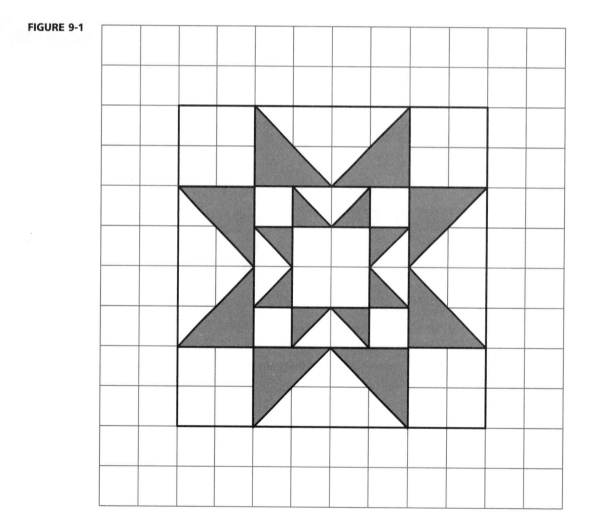

▲ Rising Star pattern.

Planning Your Project

The Rising Star is often done in just two colors, but there's no rule that says you can't use more. The star points ought to be darker than the fabric around them or the star image disappears. Consider making the star points of a solid fabric and the rest of a coordinating print. Or perhaps you'd like to make the inner star red and the outer star blue with a white background for a patriotic block.

You will need a piece of backing and a piece of batting slightly larger than the block. To make the block into a pillow, you will also need another piece of fabric the same size as the block for the back and you'll need stuffing. If you wish to add a ruffle, you'll need about $1^3/_4$ yards of commercial ruffle or approximately $^1/_4$ yard of fabric to make your own.

If you wish, you can make two rising star blocks and put them together for a two-sided pillow. Consider opposite placement of colors on the two blocks.

Piecing from a Block Pattern

Unlike the Christmas tree pattern in Chapter 8, the Rising Star pattern doesn't lend itself to being divided entirely into rows. Remember the Log Cabin in Chapter 5 and start at the center. What group of pieces can be sewn together to make a unit equal in length to the center square? What should be sewn together so that a partial row will fit this new unit? Group the pieces so that you are sewing together units or rows of equal length, even if they are not complete rows in the pattern.

FACT

The names of quilts can indicate their age. *Old Maid* isn't a term we use much anymore, and how many of us have seen a *Mill Wheel?* Yet these were common terms when the quilt patterns were named. What will today's quilt names tell the next generation about us?

Plan to put the triangles together first, then sew the star points into pairs. You will sew pairs of small star points to two sides of the center square and the small corner squares on either side of each of the remaining small star points. Sew the three rows together to form the inner star. Then you'll piece the larger outside star to the small star in the same manner.

Triangle Shortcut

You will notice that there are eight small star points made up of dark and light triangle pairs. There are eight larger pairs. You can cut squares and turn them into triangles, as you did the corners of the tree in Chapter 8, by sewing across the diagonal to form pairs of triangles, but, since all the triangle pairs are made out of the same two fabrics, there is an easier way. Sew the fabrics together on the diagonal, several at a time; then cut them out.

FIGURE 9-2

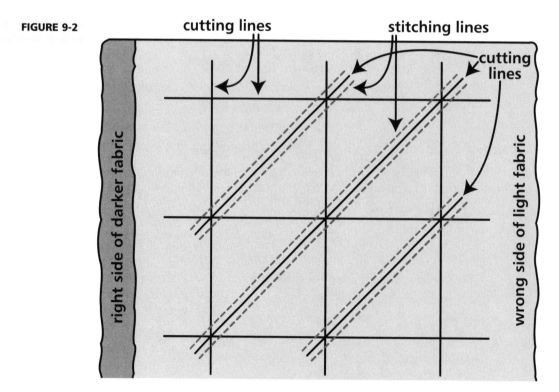

▲ Triangle shortcut.

Determine the Size

The first step is to determine exactly where to do this diagonal stitching. The outside triangle pairs are going to open out into 4^1/$_2$" squares. Allowing for the seam allowances on the diagonal, the triangles, if you were to cut them out individually, would need to be slightly more than an additional ^{1}/$_4$" on the two short sides. Since you will be cutting two triangles out of each marked square, you'll need to allow for two diagonal seam allowances.

If you can figure out exactly how large these triangles need to be, your old geometry teacher would be proud of you. The size of the finished square (in this case 4" by 4") plus ^{7}/$_8$" is probably very close. If your ruler doesn't divide into eighths or you're afraid you won't be able to mark that accurately, use 5" and plan on trimming the finished triangle pairs later.

Mark the Fabric

Begin by drawing a grid on the wrong side of the lighter fabric. An acrylic ruler works the best, but any straightedge will do.

Mark 5" intervals as close to straight with the grain as possible. Be sure your horizontal rows are at right angles to the vertical. You will only need four squares to make the eight triangle pairs. Mark a diagonal line across each square in your grid. These lines will be your cutting lines.

A ballpoint pen or fine permanent marker is all right for marking a *cutting* line. As a safety precaution, trim away any ink on the seam allowance after stitching the piece so it doesn't bleed when the quilt is washed. Be careful not to get ink on your fingers or tools, where it can smear onto your fabric.

Stitch and Cut

Pin the marked fabric on top of the star point fabric, right sides together. Stitch ^{1}/$_4$" along *each* side of the diagonal lines. Next, cut along all the lines you drew. Open out the triangles and press the seams toward the darker triangles. There will be a few stitches across the corners of some of the triangles. Remove them carefully with a seam ripper or scissors.

Trim the new squares down to 4½" by 4½". Be sure the diagonal seam remains centered on the square. You will want to trim away the little ears of excess seam allowance fabric left at the ends of each of the seams.

Repeat the process with a 3" grid for the inner star points. This shortcut is especially helpful when making a full-sized quilt, which can have hundreds of identical triangle pairs.

Another quilting shortcut is to complete a particular step on all the blocks for a quilt before moving on to the next step, rather than completing the blocks one at a time. To be sure you're doing the step correctly before you repeat it forty-two times, complete one whole block first.

The Quilting Design

Cut the square pieces called for in the pattern and piece the cover as you did the pattern in Chapter 8. Begin at the center and follow the order described earlier. Be sure to press seams before you cross them with another and match seams where appropriate. With that done, it's time to mark the quilting design. The center square and the corners provide a perfect opportunity for something special.

Choosing a Design

Generally, geometric pieced quilts are quilted in rounded, curving designs, and elaborate appliquéd quilts in straight, geometric designs. There are instances, however, when the quilting design mimics the pieced or appliquéd designs, as in the case of echo stitching. With that in mind, the center block of your Rising Star block might be quilted with the outline of an even smaller star in the center. The same design would be somewhat less effective in the four outside corners. They could echo the two perpendicular lines until they disappear off the edge.

Quilters use all kinds of things as quilting patterns. Plates for large circles, fluted gelatin molds for scalloped-edged circles, even cookie cutters are called into service to get just the right design. Modern quilters can use computer programs to make their own designs and print them off, ready to transfer. Remember making snowflakes from folded paper back in grade school? Try it again for an interesting quilting design.

Perhaps the easiest thing to use is a commercial stencil. If your stencil isn't the right size, see if you can't add or leave out a loop or two. If you don't have a stencil and want a curving design, one is provided in **FIGURE 9-3**. All you need to do is enlarge it and transfer it to your block.

FIGURE 9-3

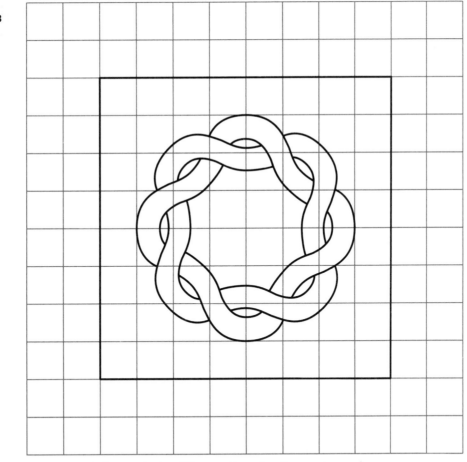

▲ Suggested quilting pattern for the center and corners.

ALERT!

Because of the sharp contrast between the star point fabric and the background fabric, it is important to press the seam allowances toward the dark fabric as much as possible. Even a loose thread can show through the cover.

Enlarging a Design

There are several ways to enlarge a design. Enlarging photocopiers are readily available to a lot of people. A more traditional way is to resize the design using a grid.

In order to enlarge a printed design like the one pictured in **FIGURE 9-3**, you need to reproduce it in the correct size. Follow these easy steps.

1. Draw a square the same size as the center square of the block.
2. Divide the square into eight squares by eight squares, the number in the diagram.
3. Mark the points in the large grid where the lines of the drawing cross the grid lines in the small grid.
4. Fill in the curves between these points to complete the design.

QUESTION?

How do you know what a quilting design will look like on the quilt?
Draw the quilting design on wax paper or some other transparent material and pin it to the quilt. This will give you an idea of how it fits with the shapes around it.

Transfer the Design

One quick way to transfer your design onto the block is to use dressmakers' tracing paper as if it were carbon paper and draw around the design. If you are using the same design on the four corners as well as the center, you might want to make a second copy of your design before you start, as one copy might not hold up to five tracings.

The trickiest part of transferring this way is to get your design centered, since you can't see the square under the tracing paper. Use your fingers to find the seams and center the picture accordingly.

Another method is to trace the design onto plastic template material. Make holes in the plastic at key points in the design with a nail. Heating the nail tip on a candle flame will make it pierce the plastic more easily. Use the holes to mark dots on the fabric with a pencil, then fill in the lines between the dots.

A third idea is the light box method. Position a piece of glass on a stable surface that allows for a light underneath. Tape the design on the glass and position the quilt over the design. Unless the fabric is very dark, you'll be able to see the design through the cloth, and you can trace it with a pencil.

Ready to Assemble?

Cut the backing and batting and layer them with the cover. Be sure that the seam allowances in your star are all lying in the direction you ironed them. Baste the layers together as you did the miniquilt in Chapter 4, beginning in the center and working outward. Be sure all the layers are smooth before you begin to quilt.

Besides quilting around your design in the center and corners, quilt the star points. Stitches on the lighter fabric along the edges of the triangles will show less and therefore won't need to be as perfect as stitches on the darker fabric. They will also be easier to do because most of the seam allowances are ironed toward the darker fabric.

FACT

There are people who enjoy piecing a quilt cover but don't like the quilting (or are afraid to try it). They hire professional quilters who charge by the spool of thread or square inch. Look for their ads in local papers or quilting magazines. Many use special quilting machines rather than stitching by hand.

Make a Ruffle

If you have decided to put a ruffle on your pillow, trim and straighten the ¼ yard of fabric, split the fabric into two long strips, and sew the ends together to make a loop. Don't forget to cut away the selvage.

Press the seams open and fold the ruffle in half, wrong sides together. Machine stitch ¼" from the raw edge all around the loop.

With pins, mark the two points halfway between the seams; then mark the points halfway between the seams and the first set of pins. The loop is now divided into eight equal parts.

Match the pins or seams to the corners and the centers of each side of the pillow top. The raw edge of the ruffle should align with the raw edge of the cover side of the pillow top, and the folded end of the ruffle should be pointed toward the center of the pillow top.

Use a pin to pull up the stitches at close intervals on the ruffle, gathering the ruffle until it fits the pillow top. Rounding off the corners with the ruffle is going to be easier than trying to make a sharp turn. Allow a little extra ruffle at the corners as you gather, but otherwise distribute the gathers as evenly as possible around the top. Stitch the ruffle onto the pillow top, stitching directly over the gathered stitches.

Or Pipe It Instead

Perhaps instead of making a ruffle for the edge, you would like to pipe it. Piping is merely a cord covered with fabric. It gives a pillow a tailored, professional look.

Materials

You will need wide bias tape of the appropriate color, or you can cut a binding strip the way you did in Chapter 7. This should be about 1½" wide and 2" longer than the distance around your pillow top.

You will also need the same length of cording. Cording is sold in the fabric section of most department stores and comes in several thicknesses. Choose one of the medium-sized cords to show up well on your pillow. If the cord's diameter is more than about ¼", you will need to cut your binding wider.

Ready-made piping is available, though the color choices are usually limited. Neutral-colored piping will still give your pillow a more finished look than none at all. Don't discount black as a dramatic possibility.

Making the Piping

Press open the folds in the commercial bias tape. At the sewing machine, fold the bias tape or binding strip in half, wrong sides together, over the cord. Stitch as close to the cord as your machine will allow without catching the cord under the needle. A zipper foot is useful here if you have one, because it will allow the needle to get closer to the cord. Trim the binding to ¼" from this row of stitches.

FIGURE 9-4

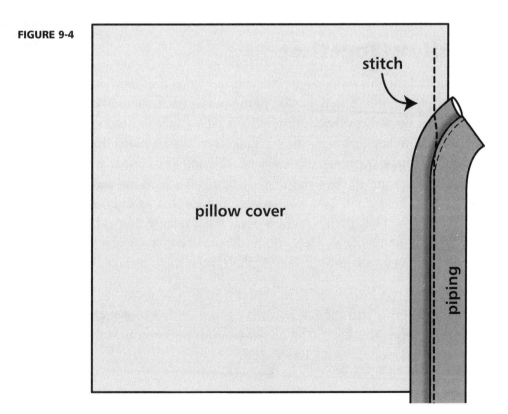

▲ Curve the end of the piping into the seam allowance.

Assemble Your Pillow

You will sew your piping to the pillow top much as you did the ruffle, except you don't need to gather it. Also, you will be hiding the ends in the seam allowance.

To do this, begin about 1" from the end of your piping. Pin it in place in the center of one side of the pillow top. Curve the piping into the seam allowance until the outside tip is along the raw edge of the pillow top.

Stitch over the piping along the $1/4$" seam allowance. Sew the piping in place easing a little at the corners.

When you come to the last couple of inches of piping, curve it off to the side, the same way you did the beginning, overlapping the ends so both begin to curve outward at the same point. This will show less than any turning or matching you could try to do.

Put the Pillow Together

Sew the back of the pillow to the top the same way as the baby quilt was assembled in Chapter 6. The right side of the pillow back should be facing the front of the quilted cover with the ruffle or piping tucked between.

If you sew the back on with the backing side of your pillow top facing you, you have your previous rows of stitching to use as a guide. Stitch directly over the stitches you made when you sewed the ruffle or piping in place. This is the best way to keep the gathers looking as sharp as possible. Begin a few inches from a corner, backstitch, then stitch all the way around the pillow to within about 4" of your first stitches. Backstitch again before you remove the pillow from the sewing machine.

ESSENTIAL

Pack the stuffing into the pillow with a blunt-ended tool such as a wooden spoon. This keeps the pillow from developing that limp understuffed look once it's been used.

Trim the batting close to the stitching and clip the excess fabric off at the corners. Turn the pillow right-side out. You won't need to poke the corners out because pulling on the ruffle or piping will accomplish that. Press the seams flat. Stuff, blind stitch the opening closed the way you did the opening in the baby quilt in Chapter 6, and your pillow is finished!

Going Further

The Rising Star pattern, like most geometric quilt designs, is made from squares and right triangles. Even some seemingly complicated diamond shapes can be made by placing two triangles of the same color back to back. Try out a few designs of your own on graph paper. Feel free to use your imagination both with your design and with the name you decide to give it.

Pillows

Any of the other quilting projects described in the previous chapters can be turned into pillow tops. Enlarge the Log Cabin design from Chapter 5 to fit a pillow. Reduce the Nine-Patch from Chapter 6 to a square one-fourth the size of your desired pillow top and make two. Alternate them with plain quilted blocks.

Is your basket of puffs from Chapter 7 growing too slowly? Turn thirty-six or forty-nine puffs into a pillow top. Skip the batting step; it will only make your pillow top harder to work with and won't show anyway.

If you have some throw pillows you've grown tired of, you can renovate them with quilted pillow shams or cases. Make your quilted top slightly larger than the pillow it's intended to cover. When you sew the front to the back, you will need to leave one whole side open to insert the pillow. Sew the opening closed after you've inserted the pillow if you wish, or finish the seam allowance on the open end with seam binding and leave it open for easier laundering. A couple of snaps or ties will keep that end from gaping open. You can also make the back in two overlapping sections.

Perhaps your favorite five-year-old has a loose tooth. Let him pick out the fabrics and piece a small tooth fairy pillow. Put a pocket in the center for the tooth and add ties to hang it from his bed or doorknob.

Full-sized Quilt

Or was it the Rising Star block that you enjoyed? Alternating star blocks with plain blocks or separating the stars with panels as you did the Nine-Patch blocks in Chapter 6 would make a very attractive full-sized quilt. If you put the star blocks directly beside one another, you create even larger plain squares where the corners meet, leaving perfect opportunities for more creative quilting. With the triangle shortcut and chain piecing, any of these quilts will go together more quickly than you might think. And there is no end to the possibilities.

Chapter 10

Old-Fashioned Block Patterns

All block patterns are read much the same way. Some cannot be reduced to squares and triangles the way the Rising Star pattern can. Because of the shape of the pieces or the way these pieces must go together, these patterns require the use of templates.

Robbing Peter to Pay Paul

The idea of a Robbing Peter to Pay Paul quilt is to take two different-colored squares and appear to take a piece out of each and trade them. **FIGURES 10-1** and **10-2** show two different Robbing Peter to Pay Paul designs: the Love Ring, also known as Nonesuch, and the Steeple Chase. The bottom right corner pieces reveal what the individual squares look like. These squares have names as well: Drunkard's Path and Bows and Arrows. In a true Robbing Peter to Pay Paul quilt, there are exactly the same number of each of the two types of squares.

FIGURE 10-1

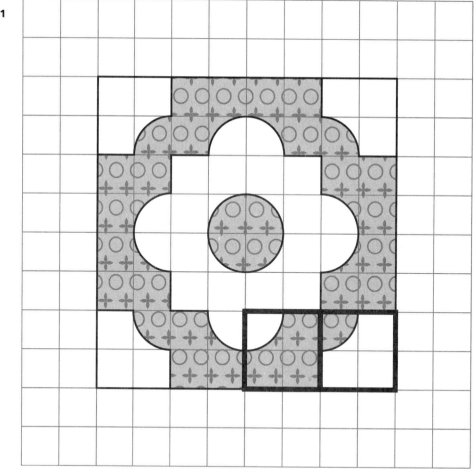

▲ Love Ring, or Nonesuch. The blocks are Drunkard's Path.

FIGURE 10-2

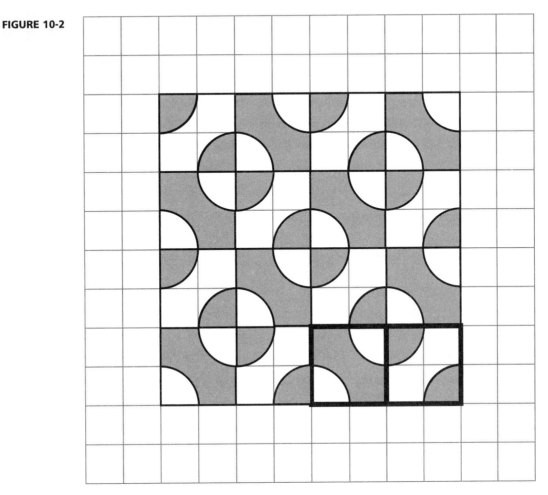

▲ Steeple Chase. The blocks are Bows and Arrows.

Rearrange and Rotate

Many of these arrangements go by one or more names as well as the name of the particular Robbing Peter to Pay Paul square. For example, **FIGURE 10-1** is a Robbing Peter to Pay Paul quilt made with a Drunkard's Path shape arranged in a Fool's Puzzle design.

If the pieces illustrated in **FIGURE 10-1** were laid out to alternate dark and light, with the quarter circle always in the same corner, the resulting diagonal stripe design would become the Vine of Friendship. If the direction of the quarter circle is changed to create a series of *X* stripes, it is called Drunkard's Path or Rocky Road to California. Further variations of these two become Fool's Puzzle and Old Maid's Puzzle.

FACT

These patterns are traditionally done in solid red and white or blue and white and were popular in the late nineteenth and early twentieth centuries. This corresponded to the Arts and Crafts period of decorating, which encouraged simplicity after the more elaborate Victorian period.

Put the pieces together so the quarter circles form complete circles made of crossed light and dark quarters while the square pieces form larger single-tone squares and you have a Mill Wheel. The overall effect is almost a checkerboard, with the circles at the corners of each square looking as if they've been rotated one quarter turn.

Make Your Own Pattern

The Robbing Peter to Pay Paul patterns don't have to be quarter circles in squares. Figuratively clipping the corners off or taking "orange slice" slivers off each side can qualify as well. Play around with different designs and create your own pattern.

Make a Template

Since the pieces in most Robbing Peter to Pay Paul quilts are not easy squares or rectangles, you cannot cut them out by measure. You could use paper patterns as you would in clothing construction, but templates are much more accurate for these smaller pieces.

Drawing the Pattern

Begin by drawing your pattern. This is easily done with a ruler and a protractor. Draw a 4" square and use the protractor to define the quarter circle of a little more than 2" radius to make the Drunkard's Path.

For Bows and Arrows, take out two quarter circles.

If you don't have a protractor, come at it from the other direction. Find something to use to make a perfect circle approximately 4" in diameter. Draw the circle, cut it out, and fold it twice to separate it into fourths. One-fourth of this divided circle is the quarter circle of the pattern. Measure and complete the square outside the quarter circle. For Bows and Arrows, fold the finished pattern in half on the diagonal to trace the first quarter circle for the second.

Transferring the Pattern to the Template Material

If you are using transparent template material, you can simply trace the pattern through the plastic. If you are using cardboard, glue the drawing to the cardboard and cut it out. Make three or four if you are making a full-sized quilt, as cardboard will wear down with use. Be sure that they are all the same size.

Other template materials favored by quilters include cereal boxes, plastic lids, and the cardboard from the backs of legal pads. Some quilters use very fine sandpaper because it won't shift out of place on the fabric.

Butcher Paper

The plastic side of butcher paper will stick to fabric when ironed lightly. You can draw your pattern on the paper side and cut it out. Iron the plastic side to the wrong side of your fabric and cut $^1/_4$" outside the edge of the paper. The butcher paper can be left on the fabric until the cover is pieced, serving as a stitching line without marking the fabric. When you're ready, you can peel it off. Warming it with an iron will loosen any stubborn pieces. However, you will need to cut a pattern piece of butcher paper for each piece of the quilt. This method is more practical for a quilt that uses many different sizes of pieces rather than a great many of one size.

ALERT!

With this pattern it won't matter, but with some you will need to invert your pattern onto the butcher paper or press it onto the *right* side of your fabric. It is less effective as a stitching guide on the right side.

Using the Template

You will need to cut an equal number of squares and quarter circles from your two colors of fabric. Eight of each will make a 16" by 16" pillow top. (Refer to the table in Chapter 7 to determine the number of 4" squares you will need to make the different-size quilts.)

Draw around the templates on the wrong side of your fabrics. This line is the stitching line. Cut around the piece approximately 1/4" outside these lines.

The reason for this is accuracy. It is very difficult to stitch an outward curve to an inward curve and stay exactly 1/4" from the raw edges of both pieces. The pencil line gives you a guide and makes it possible for you to be certain you are stitching exactly where you need to stitch. If you are inaccurate in piecing the quarter circles to the squares, your quilt cover will not lie flat.

Besides the usual hard lead pencils and quilting pencils, quilters use mechanical pencils with the finer leads, colored pencils, and silver architect's pencils. For darker fabrics, some swear by tailor's chalk and even slivers of soap.

Stitching Curves

Not all quilters agree on marking the stitching line as opposed to the cutting line. Some will add the seam allowance to their templates no matter what. A good rule for beginners is to mark the stitching line for hand piecing and the cutting line for machine piecing. Because it is so important that you follow the stitching lines on both pieces, it is recommended that you piece the curves by hand.

Clip the Curves

To make the inward curve on the square flex enough to fit the outward curve of the quarter circle, you need to clip the seam allowance. Make tiny cuts about every 3/4" into the seam allowance to within a thread or two of the stitching line. Be careful not to cut across the line.

Pin the Pieces

Pair up a square with the opposite quarter circle. Put right sides together. Insert a pin in the quarter circle stitching line where the curve meets the straight line of the side. Manipulate the square piece until the pin comes out in the corresponding corner of the stitching line on the square. This will ensure your corners meet exactly.

Anchor the pin along the straight seam lines of both pieces. Repeat the process with the other side. This will not look like the pieces should fit, but it's important that the corners match.

Let the clips on the inward curve open out until the curves fit together. Place several pins along the curved seam, matching up the stitching lines by inserting the pin on the line of one piece and exiting on the line of the other.

FIGURE 10-3

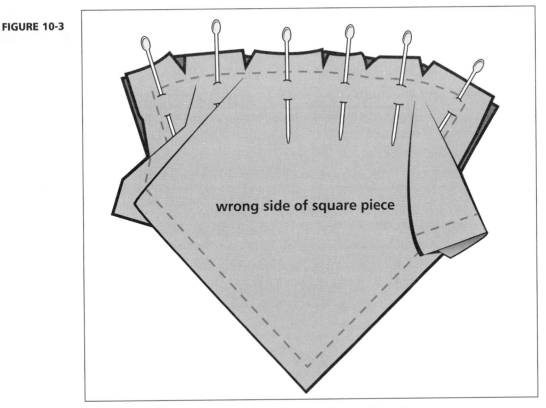

▲ Clip the seam allowance and pin along the stitching line.

FACT

In the 1920s and '30s, many magazines and newspapers expanded their readership by including easily copied quilt patterns such as the ones described in this book. Today there are many magazines, stores, Web sites, and even festivals devoted entirely to quilting.

Hand Stitch

Stitch along the seam line with tiny running stitches. The running stitch is described in Chapter 4 for use as a basting stitch and simply means the needle goes in and out of the fabric several times before it is pulled all the way through. In this case, the stitches need to be about the size of sewing machine stitches. It's a good idea to check the back piece to be sure the needle is exactly on the stitching line of both pieces before pulling the needle through.

Although your marked stitching line ends at the intersection with the straight side's line, extend your stitches to the raw edges of the pieces. This goes for the beginning as well as the end of the piecing stitches.

Securing the ends of your row of stitching is more important when hand piecing than machine stitching because the larger single-thread stitches pull out more easily than machine stitches. Take several overlapping stitches at the beginning and end of each row or turn and stitch back over your stitches for 1" or so. Knots are acceptable, too.

QUESTION?

Why did the two-tone quilts fall out of favor?
The Great Depression drove quilters back to their scrap bags. The Double Wedding Ring and Grandmother's Flower Garden became favorite quilts because they called for small amounts of lots of fabrics, while the two-toned quilts required buying new fabric in order to have enough.

Press all the seam allowances toward the square piece. This eliminates the necessity of clipping *V*s out of the quarter circle's seam allowance in order to make it lie flat. If the quarter circle is darker than the square fabric, trim the darker allowance shorter than the lighter to reduce the chances of it showing through to the front of the quilt.

Choosing an Arrangement

The best way to decide on an arrangement for your quilt is to lay your two-toned squares out and move them around. If you are making a full-sized quilt, the bed itself might be the best place to do this. You can use one-fourth of your squares and either repeat the design you choose or mirror it in the other three-quarters of the quilt.

Another idea is to work out designs on graph paper first. You might refer back to the beginning of this chapter and try some of the layouts mentioned. It's surprising how much difference rotating a few pieces can make in the appearance of even a pillow top. Imagine the possibilities if you were making a full-sized quilt.

FACT

If you like a design but not the name, rename it. You won't be the first to do so. In fact, naming your quilt is part of the fun. Often quilts are named because of an overall impression that might depend on the colors as well as, or instead of, the pattern of the quilt. Autumn's Tints and Calico Puzzle are examples. Sometimes quilts are named for the quilter or the recipient, such as Flo's Fan and Loretta's Rose.

Piece, Assemble, and Quilt

When you've settled on an arrangement, stack the pieces by rows and move them close to the sewing machine. Chain-piece the squares as you did the puff squares in Chapter 7, running one pair under the needle of the sewing machine right after another.

Since the squares need to go in a particular order, sew the top blocks from the first two rows together, then feed the second pair through after it, and so on down the first and second rows. Leaving the chain intact to keep the blocks in order, chain-piece the third vertical row to your first set and so on until all the blocks are in rows. Cut the connecting threads and press the seams open or toward the darker squares. Sew the rows together, matching the seams as you did the Nine-Patch rows in Chapter 6. Press the seams.

Generally with Robbing Peter to Pay Paul quilts, there are no blank places needing elaborate quilting, so there is nothing to mark. Once the cover is set and pressed, the quilt is ready to assemble. Assemble it the way you did the miniquilt in Chapter 4, basting the layers together.

If you want to machine quilt you can "stitch in the ditch," or stitch directly in the seam line. This serves the technical purpose of quilting, yet the stitches don't show. Begin near the middle and work outward. For best results, use the walking foot attachment on your machine and stitch slowly.

There are two recommended ways to quilt a Robbing Peter to Pay Paul quilt. Outline either the individual squares or stitch only along seams that separate different colors. The former accents the original pattern shape, while the latter accents the overall arrangement. Whichever you choose to do, quilt close to the seam line or $1/4"$ on both sides of the seams.

Bind a Quilt

Once you've quilted your project, all that's left to do is finish the raw edges. If you've made a full-sized quilt, you can bind the edges the way you did the potholder in Chapter 5 with commercial bias tape, rounding the corners, or you can miter the corners using your own binding the way you did the puff quilt in Chapter 7. Your choice will be determined by whether you want to square up the corners of your quilt like the squares in the pattern, or round them off gently, highlighting the quarter circles.

Child's Mix-and-Match Pillow

If you've chosen to make a pillow, you can add a ruffle or piping first, then put the pillow together using the method described in the previous chapter. If you enjoyed making the Robbing Peter to Pay Paul pillow, you might try a variation.

Consider making a child's pillow using four large Drunkard's Path blocks instead of sixteen smaller ones. Choose a juvenile print and a coordinating solid to make a true Robbing Peter to Pay Paul pillow. Or use four different prints for the four squares and one solid for the quarter circles. Set the quarter circles in the center and position the four prints in the corners. This will need to be planned before you cut the fabric if your fabrics are one-way prints.

If the child is old enough, let him or her choose the fabric scraps to make the pillow. The quarter circles can be made from prints, too, if those are what he or she likes.

A child six or older might be interested in doing some of the piecing if you'll pin it first. If you decide to let him or her do it, don't be too particular about the outcome. You may have to skip the quilting phase and simply make the pillow with a pieced top to save time if the child is impatient to have the pillow.

FACT

After Charles Lindbergh's record-setting solo flight from New York to Paris in May 1927, pieced designs featuring airplanes became popular. Some feature an appliquéd propeller. There is also a pattern called Airport, which resembles Swing in the Center, a reference to square dancing.

Schoolhouse Quilt

Another old block pattern is the Schoolhouse. It was popular in the early 1900s and was usually done in red and white. Modern quilters are more likely to use different calicos for each schoolhouse on their quilt or even make the house and roof of different fabrics.

FIGURE 10-4

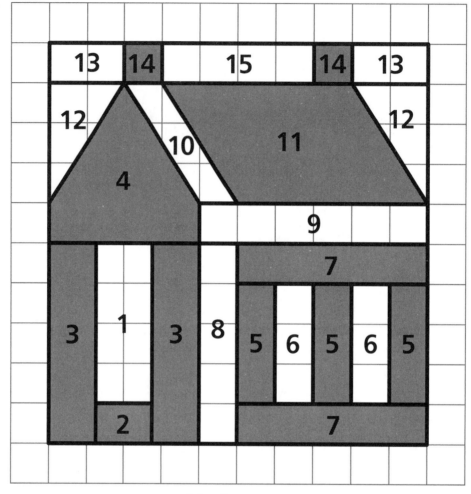

▲ Schoolhouse pattern.

The Pattern

Enlarge the pattern, letting each grid square equal 1". This will make a 10"-by-10" block. Plan on panels at least 3" wide between the blocks. Refer to the chart in Chapter 7 to determine how many blocks you will need. Making adjustments in the width of the panels is going to be easier than trying to change the size of the blocks.

Because all the stitching lines are straight, you can piece this on the machine. The only tricky parts are the peak of the roof and the corner where pieces Nine and Ten join piece Four.

Cut by Template

Pieces Four, Ten, Eleven, and Twelve will be easiest to cut if you make templates. Enlarge at least that portion of the pattern on graph paper. Cut those four pieces out. The two Twelve pieces should be exact opposites of each other, and you need only turn one into a template. Glue or trace these pieces onto cardboard or other template material. Add $1/4$" all around each piece. The easiest way to do this is with an acrylic ruler. Cut out the templates.

Cut the roof-level pieces using the templates. Remember to cut two of piece Twelve, one with the template face-up and the other with it face-down, unless your fabric is the same on both sides.

ALERT!

You can't reduce this pattern to only squares and rectangles and cut it all by measure, piecing it the same way you did the Christmas tree pattern in Chapter 8. The problem is piece Ten. The grain-straight width on the pattern is 1". The width that you would need to use to cut it by measure is difficult to determine.

Cut by Measure

Cut all the other pieces by measure. Note that pieces One and Two are $1^1/2$" wide when finished and need to be cut at 2". The number Three pieces are $1^1/4$" wide and need to be cut at $1^3/4$". The number Seven pieces are the same length but are cut at $1^1/2$". Don't get the Three and Seven pieces mixed up after they are cut.

If you are making a full-sized quilt, using the same fabric for all the schoolhouses, you can leave most of the pieces in long strips to be trimmed later. Pieces One and Two and the template pieces are the only ones that need to be cut to the exact length.

You can join the number Five and Six strips together and slice the $3^1/2$" units off to save some piecing time. The same can be done with the

Thirteen, Fourteen, and Fifteen pieces. Just remember to cut your strips by the horizontal width, rather than the narrow width. In other words, for the number Fifteen pieces, cut a strip $4^1/2$" wide. Determine its length by taking $1^1/2$" times the number of schoolhouses in your quilt (plus a little extra for good measure).

Piecing the Schoolhouse

In this pattern, all seam allowances should be pressed toward the darker schoolhouse fabric before it is crossed by a new piece of fabric. It is important that the pieces go together in a logical order to minimize the difficulty of stitching the points of the roof.

Begin by sewing pieces One and Two together. Add the number Three pieces to each side. If you have cut Three as a long strip, sew it to one side, trim it to the proper length, then sew it to the other side and trim. Sew piece Four to the top and set the section aside.

ALERT!

Be sure the edges of the fabric meet at the stitching line rather than at the cutting line when you place them together to stitch.

Arrange the Five and Six pieces as shown in **FIGURE 10-4**. Sew the pieces together or sew, press, and slice the strips into $3^1/2$" units if you are making several schoolhouses from the same fabric. Add the number Seven pieces to the top and bottom of the window section. Sew on piece Eight and then Nine. Set this section aside.

Sew the chimney row together either as individual pieces or as strips that are sliced to $1^1/2$". Sew the number Ten and Eleven pieces together.

Sew the Sections Together

Mark the intersection of the stitching lines on the peak of piece Four and also at the side corners. Mark the same spot on both corners of piece Ten and the corner of piece Nine where these pieces meet Four. Also mark the corner of the stitching line at the non-right-angle corners of the number Twelve pieces.

Match the dots on the front and the side sections. Begin stitching on the dot, taking two stitches forward and backstitching over them again. Then sew the seam to the bottom of the house.

Match the dots on Ten and Four and stitch these sections together the same way, beginning and ending the stitching at the dots. Move the seam allowance from the earlier stitching out of the way so you don't catch it in the stitching. Do the same with the lower part of the roof and piece Nine. This horizontal seam can extend to the ends of the pieces.

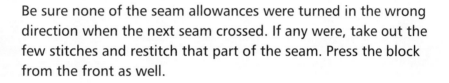

Be sure none of the seam allowances were turned in the wrong direction when the next seam crossed. If any were, take out the few stitches and restitch that part of the seam. Press the block from the front as well.

Sew one of the number Twelve pieces to the left side of piece Four. Match the dots again and begin stitching at the point where the earlier stitching stopped. At the lower end, the edges of the fabric should cross at the stitching line.

Clip *V*s in the seam allowance at the two corners of piece Four where the rows of stitching meet. Press all the seams toward the darker pieces. The point at the top of Four will have the seam allowances of Ten and Twelve extending above it. Press these open or let them overlap.

Next, sew the other number Twelve piece to the right-hand side of the roof. The edges of the fabric should cross at the stitching line at both ends of this seam. The stitching should cross the seam between pieces Nine and Eleven 1/2" from the outside edge. This will make it possible to sew a panel on the side and have the corner of the roof come to a perfect point. Last, sew the chimney row to the top of the roof. Press all the seams again.

Finishing

Sew your blocks together with the panels as you did the baby quilt in Chapter 6. Mark the quilt pattern on the fabric. A diagonal hatchwork that stops at the blocks and continues beyond them is very effective. You will want to quilt around the blocks as well—outlining the colored sections by stitching on the white is recommended. Your stitches won't show on the white and you will be stitching over a minimum of seam allowances.

Assemble the layers and quilt your marked lines. Bind the quilt with the fabric you used for the background, backing, or schoolhouses as described in Chapter 7, or with commercial bias tape as described in Chapter 5.

If you are making a pillow, consider a narrow border of background fabric and a wider border of an apple print. A ruffle or piping made to match the schoolhouse would be very effective. This would make a great gift for a teacher.

Miniquilt

Log Cabin Potholders

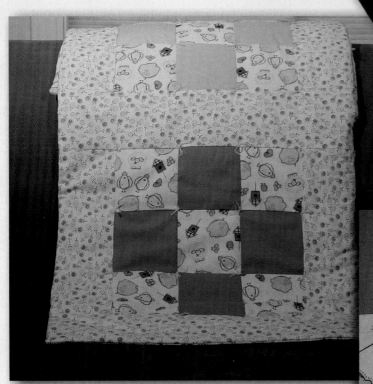

Nine-Patch Baby Quilt

Christmas Tree Wall Hanging

Rising Star Pillow

Robbing Peter to Pay Paul Pillow

Take-Along Quilt

Cathedral Window Quilt

Crazy Quilt Vest

One-Patch Quilt

Stained Glass
Wall Hanging

Sunbonnet Sue
Baby Quilt

Tea Time
Placemat

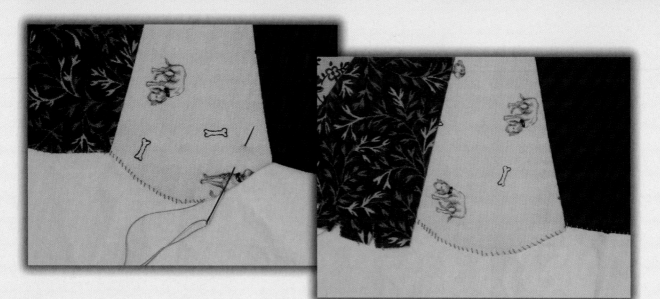

Dresden Plate Quilt

Chapter 11

Take-Along Quilt

A full-sized quilt, even for a twin bed, is not very portable. If you find yourself with potential sewing time away from home and a quilt frame, you can assemble your blocks, quilt them, then sew them together afterward. This quilt is also a good alternative if you don't have a large quilt frame and want to do your quilting with a hand-held hoop.

Design Your Quilt

Before you can decide on the design of your quilt, you need to understand the basic idea of the take-along quilt. The blocks are pieced, marked, assembled, and quilted, much like the pillow tops in Chapters 9 and 10, then sewn together using one of two methods.

The Easy Method

In the easy method, the quilted blocks are sewn together and the seam allowances are hidden by a narrow piece of fabric called a finishing strip. Any quilt that is pieced in blocks will work for this type of take-along quilt. However, the quilting pattern must be complete within each block and not flow from one block to the next. The Log Cabin block from Chapter 5 lends itself well to this easy method.

The Traditional Method

The other, more traditional method of piecing the quilted blocks together involves sewing the three layers—cover, batting, and backing—together separately. This method requires the quilting stitches to stop at least 1" from the edge of the blocks to make it possible to get to each layer when you sew them together. Additional quilting stitches can be added after the quilt is complete, but that partially defeats the purpose of quilting the blocks before they are set.

A solution might be to frame each of the blocks with 1" strips of a single fabric, which, when sewn together, will give the appearance of $1^1/2$" panels. It won't seem strange to have the quilting stitches stop at the panels. In the easy method, there will be a deeply indented seam down the center of these panels, which will look very much like quilting stitches from a distance.

Working with Restrictions

With these restrictions in mind (a pattern worked in blocks and self-contained quilting designs on each block), decide on a pattern for your quilt. Pieced blocks that alternate with plain quilted ones can be very effective. Use the chart in Chapter 7 to determine the size and number of blocks you will need. Allow extra backing fabric for 1" strips to cover all the seams between the blocks if you are going to use the easy-assembly method.

FACT

While the restrictions imposed by this type of quilt construction might seem complicated at this stage, once you get started you'll discover it's easier than tackling a regular full-sized quilt. If you are marking smaller portions, you can start quilting before you finish piecing, and, fabric permitting, you can change your mind about the size of your quilt clear up to the time you bind it.

Cut and Assemble

Once you have settled on a design and picked out your fabric, you are ready to begin. Cut the pieces by measure or with templates, whichever is appropriate for your pattern. Cut out the entire quilt top to be sure you have enough fabric. Remember to allow for the seams.

Consider whether the triangle-piecing shortcut or chain piecing will save you time. Piece one complete block to be sure you're using the right techniques. Then piece the blocks, completing the first step on all the blocks, then the second, and so on. Mark your quilting design, and assemble the blocks as if you were making a pillow top.

Quilting on the Go

Now you have a stack of blocks to quilt. These make easy pick-up work or projects to travel with you to doctors' appointments, on vacation, or even to break time at work. With a little planning ahead, quilting away from home can be a rewarding experience. It's wonderful to accomplish something during what would otherwise be wasted time, especially if it's also a fun activity. You may even make new quilting friends when they see your supplies and handiwork.

Packing to Go

Along with your blocks you'll need a few sewing supplies. Keep them together in a box or bag that won't let them spill if you happen to drop it. Sealable plastic food containers work well and come in a wide range of sizes. A rubber band around a shoebox will work, too. Clear plastic bags are often the best choice for the work itself. They keep the work clean and allow you to see what's inside while taking up the least amount of space.

Thirty-five-millimeter film containers hold needles and pins perfectly and take up less room than a pincushion. A magnet can serve as a pincushion while you're working and is handy to help with cleanup if your pins spill. The kind with the sticky back can be attached to the lid of your sewing box.

If your scissors are too large for your box and you drop them in the bag with your block, put a cork on the end so they can't damage your fabric. Also, include an emery board to smooth out rough fingernails that snag on your thread. A few small adhesive bandages for needle pokes are a good idea, especially if you are sewing in a moving car. They are also handy if you discover a weather (or climate or altitude) change has loosened up your thimble.

If you travel with your quilting a lot, you should consider getting duplicates of items like scissors and thimbles. This will mean your sewing's always ready to go with you and you aren't forever shifting the items back and forth between your travel box and your work basket at home. You'll decrease the chances of finding yourself away from home and unable to use some sewing time because of one or two missing items. Be sure to take extra needles, too, as they are easily lost.

E ALERT!

It is no longer be possible to take your sewing scissors on an airplane, except, possibly, round pointed ones like baby-fingernail scissors. Pack your sewing in your checked baggage and use your flying time to plan your next project instead of sewing. It can be a little crowded on airplanes to try to sew anyway.

Working Away from Home

Respect those who will come after you and bring something to collect your trash. A paper cup is the easiest thing to drop your clipped threads into while you sew, but it must be dumped before you can pack it back into your box. A paper bag is better in some respects because you can roll it closed when you're ready to leave.

If you will be quilting in a hotel room, pack a seventy-five- or one-hundred-watt bulb in case the lighting is inadequate in the hotel. For long stays, buy the bulb when you arrive; but for short car trips that involve an overnight, take one along in your sewing box if there's room. Save the original cardboard sleeve so the bulb doesn't roll around, and remember not to put anything too heavy on top. Be mindful of any wattage restriction posted on the light, however; you don't want your bulb to start a fire.

ESSENTIAL

As tempting as it may sound, don't forgo chances to sightsee in favor of staying behind to quilt. Who knows what inspiration might turn up on a trip to a new place. And there will be other opportunities to quilt.

Sewing the Blocks Together—Easy Method

This method of putting your blocks together is relatively quick and virtually foolproof. The seams between the blocks are deeper than quilting stitches and give the quilt top a slightly pillowed effect, but it's not extremely noticeable. The difference is more in the feel of the quilt than in the appearance. The ridge created by the seam allowances and the strip that covers them is visible only from the back, but it can be felt through the quilt.

Trim the Blocks

Once your blocks are quilted, measure them against each other to find the smallest block. Trim the rest to match it. It is important that your blocks be all the same size before you sew them together or the seams won't match. Stretching or puckering the fabric to make the blocks fit will not do justice to the blocks you quilted so carefully. The most accurate way to trim your blocks is with an acrylic ruler and a rotary cutter.

Finishing Strip

Cut strips of backing fabric 1" wide. You will need several that measure the same as the width of your quilt. The number will be the number of rows of blocks minus one. You will also need shorter strips to sew between the blocks within each row. These can be cut to the proper length as you sew.

Pair up two adjoining blocks, right sides together. Fold the strip in half, wrong sides together, and align the raw edge with the edges of the blocks.

FIGURE 11-1

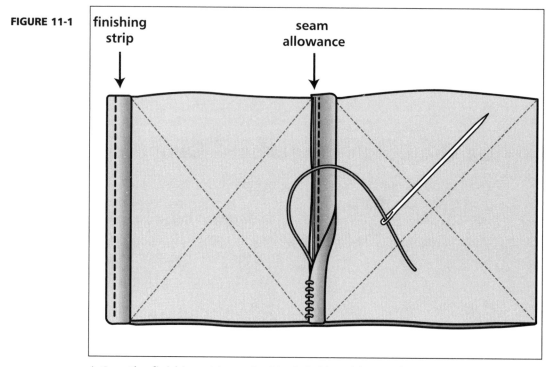

▲ Sew the finishing strip to the block (left). Fold over the seam and blind stitch to hide the raw edges (right).

Sew them all together with a $1/4''$ seam. Open out the finished blocks and trim the batting close to the seam. If you run the cover side of the seam over the edge of your sewing table, the allowance will open up and you can get at the batting easily. Remember, there are two layers of batting to trim.

Fold the finishing strip over the seam allowance and blind stitch it into place, covering the raw edges.

You will notice that the strip is not exactly centered between the two blocks. The machine stitching line is the center and the strip is offset slightly. To keep the back of your quilt looking neat, put all the finishing strips on the same side of the blocks within a given row. The rows will go together easier if you alternate the strips' placement from one row to the next.

In other words, if you sew the strip to the left block while sewing together the top row, sew the strip to the right block on the second row. This prevents the necessity of sewing through two strips on top of each other when you sew the rows together. It isn't the strip itself that creates the problem, but rather the six seam allowances and the edge of two layers of batting under it.

Put the rows together with the long finishing strips, matching the seams. Place the strips so they all fold in the same direction. That way, they will be the same distance apart on the back of the quilt.

FACT

You can create an interesting hatchwork on the back of your quilt by choosing a color fabric from the front of the quilt to use as the finishing strips instead of matching the backing. Alternating sides may change the effect you are after. Weigh the difficulty of stitching through two of the seam allowances against the somewhat unbalanced look of the offset strips.

Sewing the Blocks Together— Traditional Method

The traditional method of sewing the blocks together is actually not a great deal more difficult than the method already discussed. Both involve a step on the sewing machine and the same amount of hand sewing. The only additional step is trimming the batting pieces and sewing them together separate from either the cover or the backing. When it's done, the quilt will be nearly indistinguishable from one that is set and quilted in the traditional way.

Join the Covers

Trim the blocks down to the same size as described for the easy method. Arrange the blocks in order. Because your quilting stitches ended at least 1" from the edge of the blocks, you can fold the batting and backing out of the way and stitch only the covers of two blocks together. Be careful not to tear the batting. Iron the seam allowance open or toward the darker block.

Join the Batting

Cut a piece of heavy cardboard just under $1^{1}/2$" wide. This is used to protect the quilt cover when you trim the batting. Ideally, the cardboard should be as long as the length of the blocks, but this isn't necessary. Simply move it along the seam as you cut.

Lay the joined pieces on a flat surface, cover-side down, and place the cardboard against the finished seam. Overlap the batting on top of the cardboard. Fold the backing out of the way and pin it. Be sure the blocks are lying flat.

With the cardboard to protect the cover, cut through both layers of batting. When the scraps are discarded, the two pieces of batting will fit together perfectly even if your cut wasn't absolutely straight. Whipstitch the batting together—that is, simply bring your needle down through one layer and up through the other. Use large, loose stitches that hold the two pieces of batting next to each other without pulling.

Join the Backing

Fold the edge of the backing on one block under $1/4$" and hand stitch it to the backing of the other. Use the blind stitch as you did

FIGURE 11-2

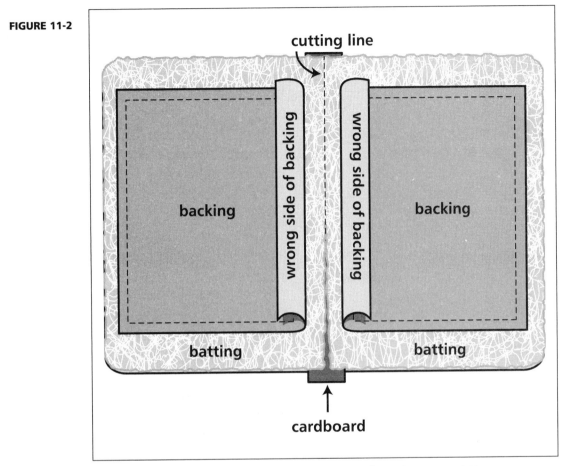

cutting line

wrong side of backing

wrong side of backing

backing

backing

batting

batting

cardboard

▲ Cut through both layers of batting, using cardboard to protect the cover.

when sewing up the end of the baby quilt in Chapter 6, except here you are sewing a folded edge to a flat piece of cloth instead of two folded edges. Be sure to enter one layer of fabric exactly even with where you left the other so your stitches will look almost like machine stitching.

Repeat the process with each of the blocks. The rows are put together in the same manner. Be sure to move the cardboard along the row as you cut the batting to keep from damaging the cover. When this is done, your quilt will be the same as any other in which the quilting is finished.

Binding the Quilt

Chapters 5 and 7 discussed a couple of possibilities for binding your quilt. Either of these will be fine. With this method of construction, you can also make separate border pieces and borrow from the turning method you used with the baby quilt in Chapter 6.

ALERT!

This method of finishing the edges of your quilt is faster in some respects than the usual methods of cutting, folding, and sewing on binding strips, but it can be a bit tricky and isn't recommended unless you are an experienced sewer.

Border Pieces

When your blocks are all sewn together, measure for your border pieces. Your side borders will need to be the length of the finished blocks plus 1/2" for seams and 1" for possible shrinkage caused by the quilting stitches and whatever width fits your bed. Cut border pieces, batting, and backing the same way you did the blocks. The top and bottom borders will be the width of all the blocks plus the width of the two side borders and seam allowances.

Mark the quilting stitches on the covers of the borders. Stop the pattern 1 1/2" from the edges on the side borders to allow for possible altering. It will be possible to add more stitching when the quilt is done if you wish.

Instead of putting the layers together as you do the blocks, put the cover face-down on the backing and batting and stitch them together as you did the baby quilt in Chapter 6, except stitch only the outside edge on the side borders.

Stitch the ends and the outside length of the top and bottom pieces. If you are using the traditional method, begin and end your stitches 1/4" from the inside edge. Trim the batting, turn, and baste in preparation for quilting. Quilt these pieces as you did the blocks. Sew the side borders onto the quilt the same way you sewed the rows together. If you are using the easy method, sew the top and bottom borders on the same way as well, except the raw edges of the ends of the finishing strips will need to be turned under before they are sewn in place.

With the traditional method, the top and bottom will be a bit tricky. At the ends, the batting may need to be cut away from the seams a bit in order to trim it. The backing will not be easy to fold out of the way. Remove a few stitches if necessary and replace them with blind stitches when you sew the backing pieces together.

Alternate Border Ideas

A simpler, though possibly more time consuming, alternative that will look nearly the same is to assemble and quilt the borders as you did the blocks and attach them to the rest of the quilt using whichever method you used to connect the blocks themselves. Trim $1/4$" off the batting. Press the seam allowance of the backing under, tuck the seam allowance of the cover over the batting, and blind stitch the two together. You will have to remove some stitches at the seams in the borders, but it can be done.

Some quilts have borders on the sides and bottom only. The part of the quilt that covers the pillows remains the same as the body of the quilt. If you decide to do this, you can finish the top edge of each of your top-row blocks with the turning method before you quilt them.

Remember to turn under the ends of the finishing strip on the top if you assemble with the easy method. The problems faced in the last step of the traditional method will be multiplied by the number of blocks in the row. But they are not insurmountable if this is the quilt you want to make.

QUESTION?

What if you don't know which blocks will be on top?
Finish the sides and the bottom in the way described, except don't stitch and turn the top edges of the side borders. Bind the top row of blocks and borders with seam binding after the rest is done.

Raw Edge Quilting

A technique similar to the easy method of sewing your blocks together is raw edge quilting. With this method, the raw edges are left to fray, creating their own kind of rustic charm. This isn't going to work with every quilt or with every fabric, but under the right conditions, it can be very effective.

Flannel Baby Quilt

Cut flannel squares in a variety of sizes that fit together like a puzzle. As with a lot of seemingly random arrangements, this will take some planning. Cut two squares of each size, one for the cover and one for the backing. The backing, as well as the cover, should be a variety of colors.

Assemble the individual blocks as you did the blocks for the take-along quilt. Batting is optional. Two layers of flannel will probably be thick enough for a baby quilt. Without batting, you can easily machine quilt the pieces together by crossing them with stitches on the diagonal. Remember, this is intended to look rustic, so nothing fancy.

Sew the blocks together and, if you used batting, trim it close to the seam. Sew around the outside edge and let it fray, too, or bind the edge as you desire.

Fraying the Edges

Next, wash the quilt a few times in a washer with a lint filter. If your washer doesn't have a cleanable lint filter, use a commercial washer to wash the quilt the first few times. The lengthwise threads at each seam will pull out and the short threads will tangle, stopping the fraying before it reaches the seam. Since it is flannel, these tangles will be soft.

ALERT!

Don't be confused between the lint filter in your washer and your dryer. All dryers have lint filters but these threads will come off in the washer. If your new quilt requires a service call to fix the washer, your future quilting activities may be met with less-than-wholehearted support by the rest of your household.

Chapter 12

Trip Around the World Quilt

The many different Trip Around the World quilts are part of the Amish contribution to quilt patterns. They are made entirely of 2"-by-2" squares arranged in a pattern that works outward from the center. Let's take a look at the center of one such arrangement.

Variations of the Pattern

The Amish made their Trip Around the World quilts out of solid fabrics. More often today, some, if not all, of the rounds are of prints. The only hard-and-fast rule seems to be that all the pieces in any given round will be of the same fabric.

FIGURE 12-1

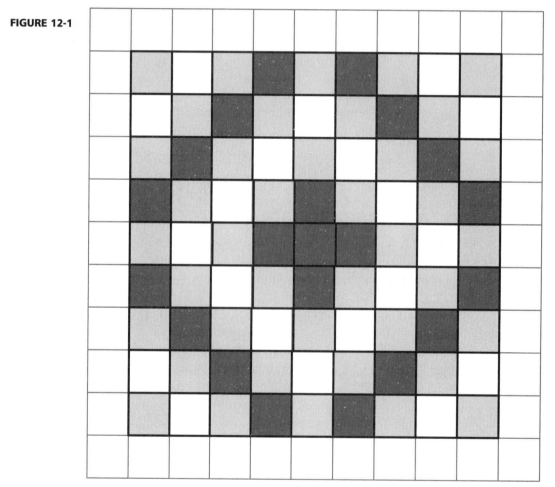

▲ Center of a Trip Around the World design.

The Standard Pattern

Generally in a Trip Around the World quilt, the rounds alternate light, medium, dark, and medium, then light again. In other words, the center might be dark and light red with a white ring. Next would be a ring of light green, then dark green followed by another light green. This would be followed by a white round, then light, dark, and light rounds of perhaps yellow and so forth. The color pattern is eventually repeated.

The center is usually a cross, though the very center square might be the same fabric as the first round outside the cross, giving the center the look of a Nine-Patch. The rings of colors are actually concentric diamonds, and the corners are squared up with a continuation of the pattern. The finished quilt is normally just as long as it is wide.

It is possible to manipulate the center on a square-centered quilt to make it a rectangle. A straight row down the center or a row that alternates two colors would do this. However, it doesn't work as well as the row of diamonds does when the pieces are on point.

Sunlight and Shadow

A variation of the pattern is the Sunlight and Shadow quilt. In this quilt three or four rounds of each color spread out from the center, graduating from light to dark. The dark round of one color is followed by the lightest color of the next and so on. Often these lighter rounds are made up of prints, so the light background will make them appear lighter while the color actually matches the solid in the dark row. Sometimes the colors go through the spectrum from red in the center to violet at the outside edge. Though this gradual change in color seems to be the primary distinction between Trip Around the World and Sunlight and Shadow, the names are sometimes used interchangeably.

Block Repeats

A variation on the pattern is to make blocks like the one illustrated in **FIGURE 12-1**. These blocks can each be of a different hue as long as the lights and darks are more or less equivalent from one block to the next.

Between each block is a row that completes the diamonds begun in the blocks. These might be black, gray, and white and would separate all the colored blocks. This creates an illusion of more blocks with four different colors in the diamonds or of a black-and-white grid separating the colored diamonds. (This design can also be done using only three colors for an all-over tilelike repeat.)

FACT

Other quilts that are made up of squares about this size include the Crossword Puzzle, which uses lots of white and usually three or four other colors, and Golden Glow, a sunburst-type design generally done in shades of yellow.

On Point

Another way to lay out this pattern is to put the pieces on point. The rounds of colors are now squares and all the rounds are completed, meaning the outside round will be all one color. The finished quilt is square with a zigzag edge.

When the quilt is done on point, it is easier to get it proportioned the way our modern beds are. You can begin with any number of center pieces placed vertically point to point. The next round circles all of these. Each subsequent round is a rectangle.

Planning Your Quilt

Since the Trip Around the World quilts are usually made of 2"-by-2" squares, it will take a lot of them to make a quilt. A 28½"-by-39" baby quilt will need 19 by 26 squares, or 494 squares in all, with eight pieces running down the center.

Use the chart in Chapter 7 to determine the number of squares you will need. The finished squares will measure 1½" by 1½", so divide the dimensions of the quilt you want by 1.5. The number of squares needed for the width will tell you the number of rounds you will need. The number of squares needed for the length minus the number for the width plus one will tell you the number of squares you will have to use in the center to get the shape you want.

Next, determine what colors you want to use for each round. You can figure the total number of squares you will need for each color as well.

E ALERT!

If you cut more squares than you need for your quilt, save them. The Watercolor quilt discussed in the next chapter and the Cathedral Window quilt in the chapter after that both use the same size squares.

Cutting the Squares

The task of cutting so many small pieces may seem daunting. There are, however, a few shortcuts that speed up the process.

From New Fabric

All but the innermost circles are going to take a great many squares and will probably require buying new fabric. The handiest tools for cutting these squares is an acrylic ruler and rotary cutter. In the absence of these, you'll need a sharp pair of scissors and a short ruler.

Preshrink the fabric you'll be cutting. Pull a thread, trim, and straighten the fabric. If you use a rotary cutter, fold the fabric twice: selvage to selvage and then center fold to selvage. The newly cut edge should line up on all the layers.

Put the acrylic ruler on top and line up the cut edge with the 2" mark. Slice clear across through all four layers. Figure about twenty squares per width of fabric and slice as many 2" strips as you will need.

With the rotary cutter, you can now trim off the selvages and center crease. Cutting through four layers at once, slice your strips into 2" squares.

If you don't have a rotary cutter, the most accurate way to cut the strip is to pull another thread 2" from the cut edge. If you are careful, you can cut through two layers at once. A piece of cardboard 2" wide can be a helpful guide to cut the strips into squares.

Cutting from Scraps

You will probably be cutting squares from scraps of fabric, too. Whenever reasonable, cut the squares straight with the grain. An acrylic ruler can be used. A template works well, also. If you are pressed to have enough of a particular fabric, you can sacrifice the straight-of-the-grain without causing yourself any problems unless the fabric is striped or checked.

The acrylic ruler, rotary cutter, and protective mat are well worth the investment if you are going to do much quilting. The savings in time, as well as the increased accuracy, will make the whole experience more fun. Try to fit them into your quilting budget if possible. You can get a starter kit for around $40, less if you are near a well-stocked discount store.

Piecing the Quilt

This quilt can be pieced by hand or by machine. When this quilt was popular in the 1930s, it was probably hand pieced beginning in the center. This meant that quilters did not need to cut all the squares out at once, but rather cut each new color as needed or whenever it was convenient to do so. If you enjoy hand piecing, you might want to do it this way.

Begin and end the stitching ¼" from the edge of each square to avoid the necessity of pressing the seam allowances all the time. Once the quilt top is together, the allowances can be pressed in whatever direction you want.

If you are machine piecing, either lay the pieces out or plan the design on paper carefully enough that you will collect the correct pieces for each row. If you have chosen to set your pieces on point, the rows will begin at a corner. The first will be one piece, the next three, then five, and so on. It might be best to press the seam allowances on each row as it's done and sew it to the previous row before piecing the next. The stitching at the edges should end ¼" from the fabric edge to make it easier to turn the seam allowances under to finish.

Chain Piecing

Chain piecing, running one pair of pieces under the needle right after another, is not recommended if your pieces are on point. If your pieces are laid square, you can do it. Stack the vertical rows or columns and take two to the sewing machine. Piece them in pairs, leaving the chains intact so the pieces stay in order. Chain the third column to the pairs and so on. When all the horizontal rows are pieces, they will be held with "chains" to each other. There is no need to cut the joining "chains" unless they are long or annoy you.

Sewing the Rows Together

Alternate the direction you press the seams on the rows. This will make it easier to match the seams when you put the rows together. (See Chapter 6 for tips on matching seams and correcting errors.) Alternate the direction of your stitching when you sew the rows together to keep the quilt from stretching out of shape.

ALERT!

Press the seams; do not iron them. A rubbing motion with the iron can make such little squares stretch on the bias. A pressing and lifting motion will keep them in good shape.

Quilting and Finishing

Assemble the quilt in the usual manner. Quilting on a pattern like this is usually done by stitching-in-the-ditch, which means stitching right on the seam line. This can be done on the machine or by hand. End the stitches 1/2" from the edge to allow for turning the edges under.

Many quilters feel that quilting stitches done in a straight line, especially on the bias of the quilt, are more likely to break if the quilt is stretched. For this reason, they will quilt in a zigzag pattern across the quilt, eventually getting around every block. This is less necessary if you are machine quilting. And, of course, a broken thread is more easily mended on the machine.

Trim the batting and backing to match the edge of the cover. If you set your pieces square, you will be cutting in a straight line. Turn the quilt cover-side up and, holding the batting and cover out of the way, press the edge of the backing under $1/4$". Turn the quilt over and trim the batting $1/4$" to match the folded edge of the backing. Fold the cover over the batting and press it as well. Blind stitch the edge closed the way you did the opening in the baby quilt in Chapter 6.

If you set the pieces on point, you will trim the backing and batting to match the zigzag edge. Clip the inside angles of the backing not quite $1/4$" and press the seam allowance under. At the outside points, fold one side down and the other side over it. Trim the batting an additional $1/4$" to match the backing.

On the cover, the inside angles should fold under easily if you stopped stitching at the seam line. At the outside points, fold under and over the same way you did the backing. To minimize bulk at the points, try to fold each one in the opposite direction as the corresponding point of the backing. Blind stitch all the way around the quilt. An alternative to the blind stitch would be to machine stitch very close to the edge. If you have machine quilted, this would fit in well.

ESSENTIAL

If you set your pieces on point, you may be tempted to clip the seam allowances of the outside points to keep them from feeling too thick. This is not recommended, but if you do so, be sure not to clip them too close since the points will be vulnerable to fraying.

Other Ideas

A quilt made up entirely of small squares can lead to many possibilities. Get the graph paper out and do some brainstorming. A few suggestions to stimulate your imagination are offered here.

Granny Squares

You can make a quilt inspired by crocheted granny squares. Begin with a bright center on point and surround it with only four rounds of colored squares, then one of black. Make as many of these blocks as you'll need for the size of quilt you want. Each block can use the same fabrics or each can be different, using up scraps the way granny square afghans often do. You could bind this quilt with black to match the outside round rather than turning it under, if you would like.

QUESTION?

What is a postage stamp quilt?

A postage stamp quilt is one made from pieces that are less than 1" square plus the seam allowance. Usually every tiny square is made from a different fabric. A sewing machine would eat pieces that small, so they have to be pieced by hand.

Counted Cross-Stitch

Victorian ladies used counted cross-stitch patterns to design quilt covers. Small squares of fabric were substituted for each cross in the pattern. There are a multitude of cross-stitch patterns available. Consider how much larger your fabric squares will be than the size of cross-stitch canvas when you choose your pattern. You will have more opportunity for subtle shading with cloth squares, however.

Consider a teddy bear or other child design for the center of a baby quilt. Or choose a holiday pattern and make a wall hanging. You can make your own pattern by transferring a picture onto graph paper, then moving lines to the nearest square. You can plan on splitting a few squares into two rectangles or triangles to better shape the picture, if you need to.

The large areas on the cross-stitch pattern that call for the same color thread can be made either of several individual 2"-by-2" pieces or of one large piece. Remember to subtract all but the outside seam allowances if you decide to cut larger pieces. Also consider how each of these pieces will stitch to the ones around it. You can avoid situations where you need to sew a piece into a corner like the roof in the Schoolhouse pattern in Chapter 10 by simply squaring off the large piece and using individual pieces for any protrusions from it.

Carry the idea of a picture on a quilt one step further with the Watercolor quilt in the next chapter. Ⓔ

Chapter 13

Watercolor Quilt

Watercolor quilts are so named because the colors in the pieces blend into one another like a wash of watercolor. They are generally made from 2"-by-2" squares cut from many different fabrics arranged to give merely the impression of something. They often convey movement as the colors flow from dark to light. Watercolor quilts are almost always intended as wall hangings.

Watercolor Fabric

What you envision for your quilt will influence which of your fabric scraps you choose to use. Likewise, the fabrics you have available will inspire you further and change your original concept.

Using Print Fabrics

Print fabrics that do not contain an entire repeat of the motif within the 2" square are good choices for Watercolor quilts. Very busy prints with lots of different colors are great, as are fabrics with prints that are large enough that only undefined colors and shapes are left when cut into the small squares. You may be able to cut several squares from these fabrics that look nothing alike.

Fabrics made to look like sky, ocean, or watercolors may not be the best choices because from a distance they look like solids, and solid colors do not blend well with the squares around them. Tiny repeating prints will also look like solids from a distance. Prints with too great a contrast between the value (lightness and darkness) of the print and the background may stand out too much in your quilt. Too little contrast and they will also appear to be solids.

Variety Is Best

As you go through your fabrics, or the remnant bins at your fabric store, choose a wide variety of colors, values, and scales of motif. Include some questionable prints as well, if you like them. It's hard to know at this stage how a fabric might fit into your future quilt.

ESSENTIAL

Don't be too limited by the rules. Use tiny prints, stripes, and even solids if you want. Just be aware that the line from one square to the next is going to be more defined by the use of these types of fabrics.

Cottons are best, but you can use any fabric. You are dealing with such small pieces that a mix of fiber content isn't going to make much difference and a shiny piece might be just what you want. Since this is intended for the wall, you aren't going to be washing it a great deal. However, avoid fabrics that easily fray. Otherwise there won't be anything left by the time you're ready to sew.

At this point, don't worry about border fabrics or backing. You wouldn't pick out a frame before you've painted the picture. You can decide what goes best with your Watercolor quilt once it is together.

Designing Your Watercolor Quilt

Don't try to be too exact in designing a plan for your Watercolor quilt. You won't actually create a pattern but rather a rough guide for choosing and arranging your squares.

On Paper

Decide on the size you want for your quilt. The finished squares will each be $1^{1}/_{2}$" by $1^{1}/_{2}$". From this, determine the number of squares you will have vertically and horizontally.

On graph paper, outline the appropriate number of squares. Make several of these outlines. Lightly draw the shape you envision within each of these outlines. If you have no idea yet, draw a heart in your space, just to get the idea. Your heart can be centered, offset, symmetrical, or one-sided.

With the side of your pencil, shade the interior of your shape from light to dark. Try several different schemes: dark on one side of the heart to light on the other, dark at the center to light at the line of the shape, and vice versa.

Now shade the area outside your shape to create a contrast with the shape. In other words, on the darkest side of the shape, make the background very light and make the background darkest where the edge of the shape is the lightest.

Perhaps none of these fit your vision. Outline and shade landscapes, mountains, clouds, whatever strikes your fancy. You might try looking through some photographs or remembering a setting to get you going.

Don't try to draw an exact picture, only outlines that give the impression of what you see or feel.

FACT

Many Watercolor quilts are inspired by the Impressionist artists because they are more interested in the impression presented by the play of light on an object than in what the object really looks like. Try studying some paintings for inspiration for your quilt.

Back to the Fabrics

Once you have settled on a general plan, go back to your fabrics. What do your fabrics suggest for your project? What types of fabrics are you lacking? Remember, in Watercolor quilts, the value, or the relative darkness and lightness, matters more than hue, or color family. As you collect more fabrics and refine your plan, you can begin cutting out your squares.

Cutting the Squares

A small 18"-by-18" wall hanging will take 144 squares to complete. You will need to collect more than that to give yourself some choices when you arrange them for your quilt. Cut the pieces the way you did for the Trip Around the World quilt in the last chapter. If you cut a 2" square of transparent template vinyl and frame the edges with $1/4$" of masking tape, you'll have a window that will show you exactly what the square will look like finished. This can be very helpful when deciding exactly where in a motif you want to cut your square.

Arranging the Squares

Cut a collection of squares, sorting them into dark, medium, and light groups. When you can't wait any longer, start laying them out for your quilt.

Where to Arrange Them

The easiest way to see what you are doing is to hang a large piece of heavy white flannel on the wall. Your squares will stick to it the same way cloth pictures stuck to the flannel board back in grade school. If your quilt pieces are on the wall, you'll be able to view them in a way that more closely resembles the way they will eventually be displayed.

The best way to hang the flannel to the wall is to stick it there with thumbtacks. If this isn't possible, turn one end under to form a pocket and buy a piece of quarter-round or other trim from the lumberyard that is long enough to use to hang it. Try to make it as stable as possible. You don't want it to ripple like curtains or your pieces will fall off.

If your flannel is pinned to the wall, you can mark off a grid with string and more pins. It isn't necessary to make a 2" grid; 6" by 6" or 10" by 10" will be enough to keep your pieces aligned. You can also mark your grid lines on the flannel with a pen.

If you don't have a wall you can use, spread a white sheet across a guest bed or on the floor. Find a place where your pieces will not be disturbed during the process of arranging. If you have an old sheet you can donate permanently to the cause, draw your grid lines directly onto it.

How to Arrange Them

Find the lines of sharpest contrast between light and dark on your plan; then locate the corresponding squares on your grid. Arrange your darkest and lightest pieces in the appropriate places and work from there. As you go, you'll discover a need for more of certain types of squares and have to go back to the cutting table.

You might need pieces that are half dark and half light, perhaps divided on the diagonal. This is where the vinyl template comes in handy. Working like a viewfinder, it allows you to see exactly what you'll get before you cut. You may discover you need to cut some pieces at odd angles instead of with the grain.

In most quilts you try to separate similar colors, but in Watercolor quilts that might not be the best choice. Experiment with creating little pockets of color, say a spot of red in the center of your darkest shade.

Don't discount the wrong side of fabric squares. Perhaps the more subdued print is exactly what you'll need somewhere. Turn pieces, trade pieces, and discard pieces until you create the effect you are after.

ALERT!

You can split pieces if you need to in order to get the right effect. First try to find pieces that can be cut on the edge of motifs to accomplish the same thing. Extra seams, especially diagonal ones, will add more bulk to an already seam-heavy quilt.

And Rearrange

When you think you have your quilt arranged, leave it for a day or so. Come back and look at it again from a distance. Stand on a chair to look down on it if it's spread on the floor or bed. Squint your eyes or take off your glasses.

What you are looking for is any piece that stands out, any piece that interrupts the flow you are after. You may need to eliminate some pieces and cut new ones. Something you rejected earlier may seem to fit now in a new place.

Give yourself as much time as you need. Hurrying this phase could produce a wall hanging with some flaw that will torture you every time you look at it (even if no one else seems to notice). Cutting and stitching this many squares is too much work to go through and still end up with something you aren't pleased with.

Medium shades of gray or tan thread will blend with all the colors without looking too light on the dark colors or too dark on the light.

Piece the Cover

Now you need to get all those squares together, not only in the exact order but turned the correct way as well. Move your sewing machine near your layout if at all possible. Even so, you won't want to be taking the pieces one by one to the sewing machine. Here are a few suggestions.

Stacking the Rows

On a piece of paper about 4" square, write the word *top* near the top. Pin the square from the lower left-hand corner of the quilt (bottom square of the first column) to the paper. It should be right-side up with the top of the square just under the word *top*. Stack the rest of the squares from that column, or vertical row, on top of the first square. When you get to the last square in the column, the square from the upper left-hand corner of the quilt, put a pin in it near the top to mark the top of the row. Leave the rest of the rows and columns on the flannel or sheet.

Sew the pieces together, beginning with the marked top piece and the one directly below it in the pile. The *top* on the paper and the pin on the top piece will help you keep your squares in order and turned correctly. Keep the pin in place on the top piece in case you are called away before you finish sewing the column.

When you have sewn the last piece in the column, press the seam allowances and pin the row to its place on your flannel or sheet. Don't be shocked by how much shorter this is than the pieces waiting to be sewn together. Repeat the process one column at a time. Alternate the direction you press the seams, up on odd columns and down on even, the same way you did the Trip Around the World quilt. When you sew the rows together, alternate the direction of your stitching, top to bottom then bottom to top, to keep the quilt from stretching out of shape.

If you are feeling confident, stack up two columns, each on its own paper, and chain piece the pairs together as you did the pieces of the Trip Around the World quilt in the last chapter. Be extra careful that you don't turn any of your pieces as you go.

Blocks

An alternative to sewing the quilt together in rows is to sew it in blocks of nine or sixteen. Lay these blocks out near your sewing machine and stitch them together as you did the Nine-Patch in Chapter 6. Sew the pieces together into rows, press the seam allowances so they will stagger, and sew the rows together, matching the seams. Repeat with another group of pieces. When the whole quilt has been stitched into blocks, sew the blocks together in rows, then stitch the rows together.

Mark the pieces however you need to in order to help keep them straight. You will still need to alternate directions as you sew the rows together within the block and when you sew the blocks together.

Fusible Interfacing

You can buy fusible interfacing—that is, interfacing with one side that will stick to fabric when it is ironed to it—that is marked with either a 1" or a 2" grid. You can also mark regular fusible interfacing in the same manner.

Iron your pieces to the interfacing within the grid marks, right-side up, in the exact order you have arranged them. Fold the interfacing along a marked horizontal line between the rows of fabric pieces. The fabric pieces will be right sides together and the interfacing will be on the outside. Sew $1/4$" inside the line as a seam. Repeat this with all the horizontal lines.

Clip the interfacing at the corner of each square just past the stitching. This will allow you to turn the seam allowances, which are under the fold of interfacing, in opposite directions. Sew the vertical seams, checking that the seam allowances turn in opposite directions as you go.

The interfacing will stiffen and stabilize the quilt, but it is still a good idea to alternate directions as you sew. If the interfacing isn't large enough for your hanging, you may need to work it in two or four parts, sewing the parts together after they're stitched or as the first row of stitching.

Finishing Touches

Once your cover is together, press the seams until they lie flat and then press the cover from the right side as well. Hang it on your flannel or pin it to curtains, anything to get it on the wall where you can see it. You have a few more choices to make.

Borders

Most Watercolor quilts benefit from a border. A wall hanging is like a picture and it needs a frame. Perhaps two rows of border will be most effective, like matting a picture as well as framing it.

ALERT!

Embroidery and even appliqué can enhance the appearance of your watercolor quilt. Don't dismiss the possibility of some small but significant addition that might serve as a focal point, or the value of outlining for depth.

Sometimes quilters add more squares to part of the border, making the picture seem to spill over onto the frame. If you choose to do this, pick the area carefully so it is a natural outgrowth of your work. Cut your borders and add them to the cover. You might want to back your border pieces with fusible interfacing to make them the same weight as the rest of your hanging.

Quilting Design

Now hang the quilt on the wall again. What quilting lines are suggested by the shadings on the quilt? Simple freehand waves and curls are going to be more effective than traditional quilting patterns. Practice drawing lines on your shaded graph paper. Consider what inspired you in the first place. What shapes or symbols enhance that particular image?

Decide if your quilting should extend into the borders or if the quilting in the borders should be different. When you've decided, mark the lines with your choice of marking tools.

Assemble and Quilt

Layer the cover with the batting and the backing in the usual way. Baste it together and quilt. Don't forget to sign your quilt somewhere, perhaps the lower right-hand corner on the front where an artist would sign a painting.

Bind and Hang

Bind the quilt using any of the methods already discussed. Matching the outside border with the binding will keep from adding another color around the quilt.

Since your Watercolor quilt is probably larger than the wall hanging in Chapter 8, you will need to hand stitch a sleeve to the back of the quilt. Cut a strip of backing fabric about $2^{1}/_{2}$" wide and a few inches shorter than the width of the quilt. Turn all four sides under and stitch them. Hand sew the top and bottom of the sleeve to the back of the quilt just under the edge of the binding. Put a dowel through the sleeve and balance it on nails. Make sure your nails will allow your quilt to hang level, and enjoy your work of art.

ESSENTIAL

For heavy quilts use a straight piece of lath instead of a dowel. It has the advantage of being flat and you can drill holes in each end so you don't have to rely on balance to keep your quilt on the wall. It will need to be longer than the sleeve but shorter than the quilt's width.

Watercolor Bed Quilt

Consider using the Watercolor idea or a counted cross-stitch pattern to make a center block for a bed quilt. Surround it with a neutral-color fabric to cover the surface of the bed and decorate the overhang with pieced blocks using the primary colors of the Watercolor. A checked effect with three rows of 5" squares of five or six different fabrics might pick up the idea of the Watercolor without trying to match it.

A shortcut to creating a series of repeating blocks is to sew strips of fabric together in the order of the repeat. These strips will be the width of your desired blocks but as long as your fabric will allow. Once the strips are all together, cut them to the proper length through all the fabrics, creating sets of sequential blocks. Sew the sets together to make the repeating series.

Chapter 14

The Cathedral Window Quilt

The Cathedral Window quilt is the origami of quilt making. A 7" square is reduced to 3" by a series of folds. These squares are sewn together, becoming a background for 2" squares, generally made from a multitude of different fabrics, which are sewn on using flaps of folded fabric as frames.

Background Fabric

The primary expense of a Cathedral Window quilt is the background fabric. This fabric takes the place of backing and batting. By the time you've finished folding, there will be four layers of background fabric over most of the quilt.

Types of Fabrics

The background fabric is traditionally muslin, which is soft and easy to fold and sew. It often comes in widths of 100" or even 108", which makes it relatively inexpensive.

Any solid-color fabric will work as long as it is fairly lightweight. Instead of cutting a multitude of colorful scraps for the inside squares, you can choose one or more print fabrics that coordinate with your solid color. Consider a very dark background fabric with one light-background, large-motif print for the inner squares.

If you want to emphasize the comparison to a cathedral window, consider a subtle gray like the stones and concrete of a cathedral or a dark rich gray or even black like the lead between pieces of glass. Rich jewel colors would work best with these backgrounds.

QUESTION?

What kind of fabric can be used for the colored squares?
Anything washable. Here is your chance to use dotted-swiss, seersucker, checks, stripes, and most of the other fabrics quilters usually avoid. Use knits if you want, depending on the look you are after. Extremely loose weaves or fabrics too stiff or heavy to sew easily are the only cautions.

Determining the Amount

To determine how much background fabric you'll need, refer to the chart in Chapter 7 for the size of your quilt. From those dimensions, calculate how many 3" squares you will need. If, for example, you are making a twin-bed quilt and you want it to be approximately 69" by 108", you'll need 23 by 36 squares, or a total of 828.

These squares will need to be cut as 7" squares. Take the width of your fabric and divide it by seven. Drop any fraction from your answer. If your fabric is 108" wide, you can cut fifteen squares across the width of the fabric.

Divide your total number of squares by the number of squares per row to find the number of rows you'll need to cut (828 divided by 15 equals 56). Round up any fraction and take that number times 7" to find the number of inches you'll need (56 times 7 equals 392, or approximately 11 yards).

It isn't necessary to make your Cathedral Window quilt in these dimensions. Smaller squares would be difficult to handle, but larger ones can be very attractive and have the added attraction of sewing together faster.

Since the colored squares will cover both the horizontal and vertical seams between the background squares, you can determine the number you'll need by multiplying the number of horizontal background squares minus one, by the number of vertical squares. Add that to the number you get when you multiply the number of vertical squares minus one by the number of horizontal squares. For the quilt described here, you would need 35 times 23 plus 22 times 36—1,597—colored squares.

For all practical purposes, that means only that you need to cut a few from all of your scrap fabrics and add to your cache as you acquire more fabric for other projects. Start with the squares you cut but didn't use in your Trip Around the World quilt from Chapter 12 or your Watercolor quilt from Chapter 13.

Tearing the Squares

The easiest way to cut hundreds of 7" squares from muslin isn't to cut them at all but to tear them. Muslin will tear easily along a thread line, and this will be more accurate than trying to cut across fabric that might be more than 100" wide.

Extreme widths of fabric are difficult to straighten, which isn't necessary if you are tearing your pieces. The individual pieces can be straightened once they are separated.

Tearing isn't usually recommended because it stretches the edges of the fabric and frays them more than cutting does. One-half-inch seam allowances have been used in this pattern to compensate for these problems.

The edge of the fabric where the store clerk cut it will need to be trimmed. If this is difficult to tear because it's so close to the edge, pull a thread the usual way and trim it. Measure down 7" from this edge. Clip through the selvage, tear the fabric all the way to the other selvage, and clip it as well. The strip can be torn into 7" squares in the same way. Remember to trim or tear away the selvages.

If you've chosen a muslin fabric that your store normally stocks, you don't need to tear all your pieces at once. Three or four rows will be enough to get you started. If you've made a mistake in figuring or measuring, you can go back later and still be able to match your fabric. If you have chosen some other fabric, cut or tear all the pieces as soon as possible to be sure you have enough while there's still a chance of getting more.

First Fold

To make the first fold with your background piece, you will need to have a 1/2" seam allowance pressed up on all sides. Since the pieces have frayed a little from being torn, the most accurate way to do this is to make a pressing guide.

Pressing Guide

Cut a piece of cardboard or other heat-resistant material 6" by 6". Center it on the wrong side of the background square. This will help you determine if your square needs to be straightened. Tug at the appropriate corners until the seam allowances visible around your guide are equal and even.

Hold the cardboard in place and press the seam allowances over the cardboard. Don't try to miter the corners; just press two sides over the other two. Do about a dozen of these to get started.

There is no right or wrong side to muslin until you've pressed up the seam allowances. You don't have to worry about keeping your torn blocks right side up as you go. Other fabrics need to be checked closely in case one side has a different shine than the other.

First Seams

Fold one background piece in half, wrong sides together. The pressed seam allowances will be on the inside. Beginning at a corner, blind stitch to a point halfway between the corner and the fold. Stitch the other side of the piece in the same manner.

FIGURE 14-1

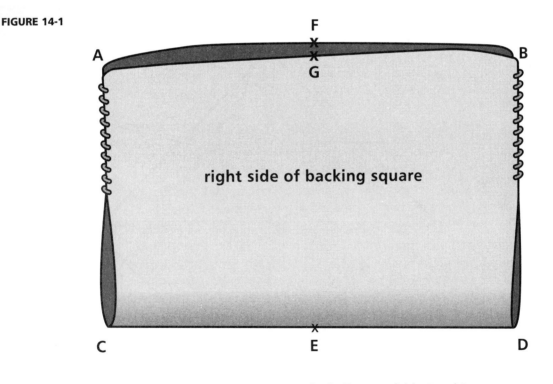

right side of backing square

▲ Stitch from corners A and B halfway to folds C and D.

You can find the halfway point by folding the seam line in half. It might be easiest to fold and find the center first and start the stitching there.

The half of the seam nearest the fold is left unstitched to allow for some adjustment and give when you fold again in the last step. There are bound to be minor inaccuracies in pressing, folding, or stitching, but also there is some inevitable stretching of the fabric since much of the folding is going to be on the bias.

Second Fold

This second fold is really a completion of the first one. Open the piece as though you were opening a bag or pocket and close it the other way, matching the two seams. Blind stitch from halfway between the fold and the completed seams to the corresponding point on the other side.

FIGURE 14-2

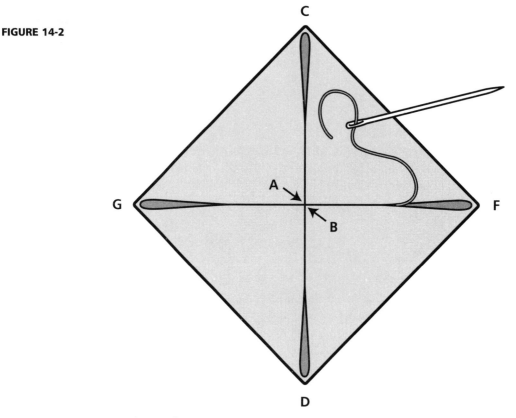

▲ Match seams at A and B and stitch halfway to folds G and F.

If you don't like doing the blind stitch, you can put these pieces right sides together and make small running stitches along the creases. Once the first two steps are complete, turn the square right-side out through one of the open corners. You can even try stitching these short seams on the machine.

Flatten the piece out so the junction of the seams is in the center of the square. Essentially, what you have done is taken your 6"-by-6" square and folded the corners into the center. This new square will measure 6" across the diagonals and be about $4^1/4$" on a side.

Make sure the seam allowances are open and lying flat inside. At the corners, tuck the allowances in or pull them out until the new square is lying as flat as possible. The corners should be sharp but the flaps of fabric where the seams were left unstitched shouldn't overlap.

Third Fold

As in the first two steps, you will be folding the corners to the center again. It's easier this time because you don't have any raw edges to hide as allowances and you need only to catch the corners in at the center.

FACT

Stained glass windows and quilts have more in common than their bright colors. They were both originally created to fulfill a particular function and have evolved into works of art without losing any of their functionality. The arches on cathedral windows, like the three layers of a quilt, were intended to add strength even as they increase the windows' beauty.

With the crossing folds of your square facing you, bury the knot under the junction of the seams. Run your thread through to the center of the plain side of the square. Catch this layer securely to the seam junction with two or three overlapping stitches. Bring each corner to the center of the plain side and catch it securely at the center point and to each other.

FIGURE 14-3

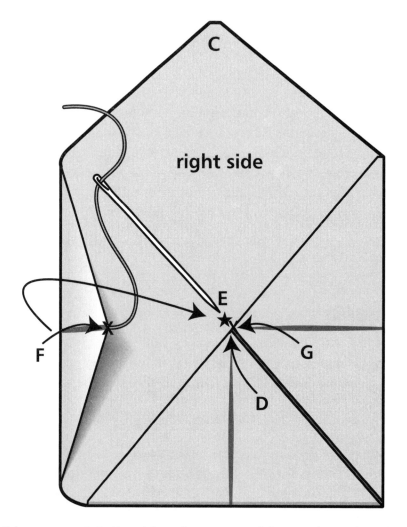

▲ Bring corners C, D, F, and G to the center E of the seamless side and stitch in place.

You now have a 3"-by-3" square with open folds crossing the diagonal. There are also less prominent folds crossing the length and width. The back looks as if four 1½" squares have been pieced together.

Combining Blocks and Adding Color

The background squares are put together a few at a time and the color squares are added. What you want to avoid is trying to stitch a color square into place several feet from the edge of your growing quilt. Work with small sections to add the color pieces, sew them together, and add the color pieces between the sections as you go.

Preparing the Background

Begin by pressing the background squares. You will want a sharp crease to guide you as you sew the squares together. Join four squares in a unit using the blind stitch. You can make several of these units before moving on to the next step or move back and forth between the two tasks. Later, you can work with larger units if you like or work in rows. And there's no need to stay with the system you start with; try something different if you get bored.

Color Squares

You will need lots of color squares. Cut them the way you did the squares for the Trip Around the World quilt in Chapter 12 and the Watercolor quilt in Chapter 13. If you want many squares from one fabric, cut the fabric in strips and then into squares either by pulling a thread and cutting along the line or using a rotary cutter and acrylic ruler. If you are cutting pieces from scraps of fabric, make a 2"-by-2" template and use it to cut the squares. The arrangement of the color squares is only important in that you probably don't want two similar squares next to each other. Dark, light, small, or large prints can all be used at random.

Each seam between the background squares is ready to accommodate one of your 2" color squares. Pin the square in place, on point like a diamond, centered between the loose folds that extend from the center to the corner of each background square.

FIGURE 14-4

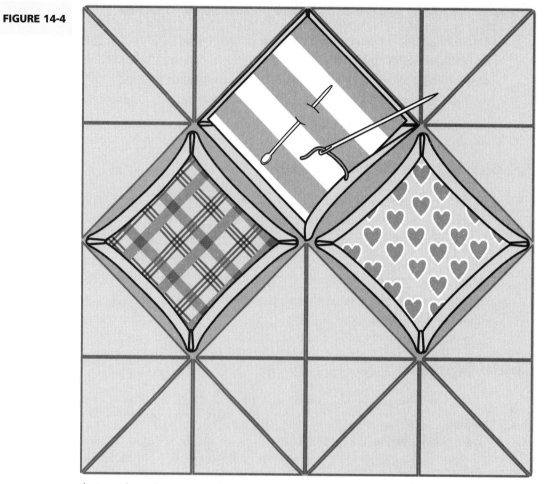

▲ Sew the print squares between the background squares, using the folds to cover the raw edges and frame the prints.

Fold the flap over the raw edge of the colored square and blind stitch it into place. The fold is on the diagonal of the background cloth and eases into place easily. You may discover you need to trim your color square slightly to keep the edges from folding back and showing under the "frame." At the corners, stitch the adjacent folds together for about 1/4".

Add three more color squares to your group of four background squares. Repeat the process with another four-square block; then sew the two blocks together. You will need to add two more color squares in the spaces created between the two blocks.

This quilt travels extremely well. Take a stack of background pieces with the seam allowances pressed and a collection of colored squares. If you don't have a travel iron, put your finished background pieces on a flat surface and cover them with a book and a fairly heavy object. The pieces will be flat enough to sew together by morning.

You're Almost Finished!

You have several different options for finishing the edges of your Cathedral Window quilt. One is to do nothing else. Though the triangles between the outside rows of colored squares look a little unfinished, that is the way you'll find most antique Cathedral Window quilts left.

If you'd like a smoother finish, sew a narrow strip of binding around the edge. Don't use anything wide enough to interfere with the outside rows of colored squares. Binding made from the background fabric is probably the best choice.

A third option is to sew half squares into the vacant triangles around the edge. Fold the colored squares in half on the diagonal, wrong sides together and press. Trim away all but 1/4" of one half, leaving a turned-under seam allowance. Sew the triangles in place as you did the squares, except blind stitch the diagonal along the edge of the quilt. These triangles can be leftover prints or all one color for a different look.

One Design, Several Uses

There are several possibilities for the Cathedral Window blocks besides making them into a quilt. And there is one sewing trick that is almost certainly intended to copy the look of this clever quilt.

Other Uses for Your Blocks

If you want to try the Cathedral Window technique, but have no interest in making a couple of thousand squares for your queen-size bed, here are a few ideas. Twenty-five background blocks (or sixteen or thirty-six) will make a charming pillow. Or make four large background blocks (beginning with 13" fabric squares to reduce to 6" finished blocks). Sew the four together with four inserts for a more dramatic pillow top.

ESSENTIAL

Try sewing six background squares together into a stuffed cube. Insert juvenile prints at each edge for an infant's toy. Expect it to be chewed on, however. Five or six of these cubes would make an unusual mobile to hang over a child's crib.

If you're looking for a challenge, begin with 5" of fabric to reduce to two. Make six into a cube and decorate it with Christmas prints for the tree or school colors to embellish a graduation present. How about making a pair with sewing prints to create a quilter's version of fuzzy dice? If you plan to hang them from your rearview mirror, avoid bright colors as they will fade rather quickly.

Sweatshirt Decoration

You can decorate the front of a sweatshirt to look like a Cathedral Window quilt. Choose a solid-color sweatshirt and a piece of print fabric that coordinates with it. Be sure the motif of the print is relatively small and the repeats are close together. Check it with a $1\frac{1}{2}$" transparent template to see how it will look.

Cut the print fabric $6\frac{1}{2}$" by $4\frac{1}{2}$". Turn *up* the edge $\frac{1}{4}$" and stitch. This puts the allowance on the right side of the fabric since that part of the fabric will be against the sweatshirt.

Sew the fabric to the inside of the front of the sweatshirt, right side of the print fabric against the inside of the sweatshirt. Sew close to the edges and in lines that divide the print fabric into 2" squares. It might be wise to stitch two lines close to each other rather than just one. It won't matter if the squares are slightly less than 2".

Cut crossing lines, horizontal and vertical, in each of these squares through the sweatshirt fabric only. Be very careful that you don't cut through to the print fabric. The cut sweatshirt fabric will curl up, giving the appearance of a Cathedral Window quilt. You can vary the size of the squares or even the number of squares to fit different sizes of sweatshirts. (E)

Chapter 15
A Crazy Quilt Vest

Crazy quilts are made from odd shapes of fabric put together seemingly at random. They are great quilts for puzzle fans. Crazy quilts are seldom done as full-sized quilts, but even throw-sized quilts are usually done in manageable blocks, which are then sewn together. To get some experience with this kind of quilting, try making a crazy quilt vest.

Cut the Vest Pieces

FIGURE 15-1 shows a simple pattern for a vest. You can enlarge it or buy your own pattern. The only specification is to choose a vest that is flat, without any darts or shaping seams on the front. These would have to be done after the scraps have been added and the bulk of the extra layers of fabric would make it difficult to flatten these seams.

FIGURE 15-1

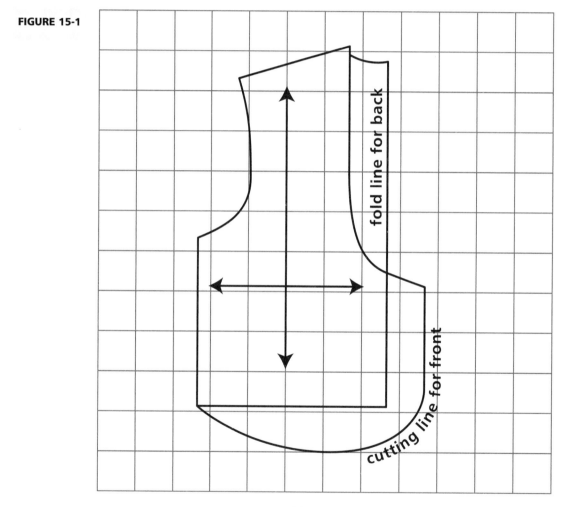

▲ Vest pattern.

Enlarging the Pattern

If you decide to use the pattern provided, the first thing you will need to do is determine how much you will need to enlarge it. Take a chest measurement and a measurement from a normal shoulder seam to the waist of the person for whom you are making the vest. With a yardstick, draw perpendicular lines on a large piece of paper or poster board. These lines correspond to the crossing lines shown in the drawing.

The vertical line should be the length to the waist plus $1^1/_4$". The horizontal line should be one-fourth of the bust measurement plus $^5/_8$". The reason for these seemingly odd numbers is the seam allowances. In most clothing construction, $^5/_8$" is allowed for the seams. This amount is added twice to the vertical measurement for the shoulder seam and for the seam at the bottom. It is added only once to the horizontal line for the side seam. The back piece is cut along a fold in the fabric and the center back will not need a seam allowance.

If you have an appropriate vest, you can decorate it instead of making a new one. The only difficult part will be turning under the edge around the front and along the side and shoulder seams. You might check garage sales for vests that are likely candidates.

Using these two lines on your pattern paper, draw the center back line, the bottom of the back piece, and the line for the side seam. These lines are all straight and at right angles from each other.

Use the grid on **FIGURE 15-1** to help you draw the curved lines of the pattern. You can draw the grid lines in the appropriate proportions on your pattern paper or use the grid lines in the pattern to help you measure proportions for the curve of the arms and neck. Cut the pattern out all in one piece.

Cutting from the Pattern

You will need to cut two back pieces, one for the vest itself and one for the lining. These can be of the same fabric. You will need two front pieces, a left and a right, of the lining fabric, and two of a lightweight fabric to serve as the backing for the crazy quilt scraps.

Cut the back pieces first. Put the center back line along a fold in your fabric. Make sure the fold is straight with the grain. Cut out around the pattern starting at the top. When you get to the bottom, cut along the straight line through the pattern for about 2" or 3". This will not damage the pattern for cutting out the front pieces but will give you a guide to finish cutting the back.

Remove the pattern and, with the help of the yardstick, mark and cut the rest of the straight line across the bottom. Repeat the process for the back lining piece.

To cut the front pieces, fold or stack the fabric so you can cut the right and left sides at the same time. Be sure both pieces of fabric are straight with the grain and either the right or the wrong sides are together. If both pieces of fabric are right-side down, for example, you will get two left front pieces.

This time, cut around the pattern, cutting away the upper part of the center back that extends outside the front curve. This piece of your pattern can be taped back into place if you want to use the pattern again. Cut a pair of lining pieces and a pair of backing pieces.

Fit the Pattern

Your vest pieces may need a bit of trimming or resizing at this point. Begin with the shoulder seams. The back and front pieces should be the same length $5/8$" from the cut edge. It doesn't matter if they are the same length along the edge. It is the stitching line that matters. Trim the larger piece at the neck edge. Whatever correction you make with one set of shoulder seams, be sure you do the same thing to the other three so the sides will look the same and the lining will fit.

FACT

The term *crazy quilt* is not intended to suggest the quilter is insane. The term comes from a little-used meaning of *craze:* to break up or shatter or produce cracks on a surface. The quilt reminded the early quilters of the crazed surface of old crockery, perhaps.

Sew the lining pieces together at the side seams, right sides together. Do not sew the shoulder seams, but pin them together at the stitching line.

Try the lining on its future owner as if it were the finished vest. Remember the front, armholes, and the bottom edge will be $5/8''$ smaller than they are now.

If the vest is small, the side seams can be resewn to as little as $1/4''$. This will add a total of $1^1/2''$ around the vest. If it is too large, the side seam can be taken in. The front can also be trimmed, if necessary.

If you do any trimming, remember to do the same thing on the outside vest pieces. Remove the pins from the shoulder seams and set the lining and the back piece aside. It's time to decorate the front.

Arrange the Scraps

Collect small scraps of cloth that you want to use on your vest. Your vision of the vest has already influenced your choices for the back and for the lining. Keep this vision in mind as you go through your scraps.

Trim the Pieces

In all likelihood, the first crazy quilt was designed by a homemaker who wanted to use every bit of her scraps. You will be able to salvage more of your odd-shaped scraps with this type of quilting than if you were to cut them into squares, but you will still need to do some trimming.

Curves are difficult to piece together on a crazy quilt and should be trimmed to straight lines. These lines don't have to meet at right angles, however, so little is lost.

Also decide on the minimum and maximum sizes for your vest. Each exposed edge will need to be turned under $1/4''$ and must overlap the pieces below it by at least that much as well. If your pieces are too small, this will be difficult to accomplish. Turn under one edge of a piece and place a second piece over the other end to get a feel for what you are willing to work with. Larger pieces can simply be cut in half.

Lay Out the Scraps

Beginning at the bottom of one of the backing pieces, lay out the scraps, overlapping them a little like shingles as you work your way upward. Don't worry if the pieces hang over the edges of the vest; be more concerned that the pieces are overlapping sufficiently.

Arrange and rearrange the pieces, considering color, value, size of motif, and size of the pieces themselves. You may want to trim some pieces that seem to overshadow the others.

ALERT!

Don't try to match the sides exactly. Crazy quilts are all about an organized randomness. Besides, it will be impossible to get them the same, and if you tried, the little differences would look more out of place than all your larger, intended differences.

You can work on your left and right fronts one at a time or do them simultaneously. When they are both done, place them side by side to see if they have the same look even though they don't look the same. In other words, be sure all the largest or the darkest pieces didn't end up on one side.

Save the extra pieces for the moment. They may be called into service later if you discover a miscalculation as you sew.

Hold the Scraps in Place

When you've decided on the placement of your pieces, you will need to hold them in place. No matter how careful you've been about allowing for the seams, there will almost certainly be some adjustment necessary as you go. If you baste the pieces into place now, you'll need to remove stitches to make even the slightest adjustment. Also the basting stitches can interfere when you need to turn the edges under.

Pin basting will leave lots of sharp points to scratch you as you sew. Safety pins are an excellent alternative. Begin at the bottom again and pin each piece in place. Test each piece by turning under the edge and being certain that neither the raw edge of the scrap below it nor the backing fabric is exposed. Don't forget the sides of the scraps as well as the bottom edge.

FACT

Some quilters always use safety pins instead of basting. They get the large, 1½"-size pins and pin through their quilt's layers every few inches. They are easier to remove than basting stitches and hold the layers just as securely. However, the pins can leave holes in the fabric or, worse yet, rust, as well as get in the way of the quilting hoop.

Blind Stitch in Place

Beginning near the bottom, turn a raw edge under ¼" and blind stitch it in place. The blind stitch is described in Chapter 6, where it is used to close the edges of the turned quilt. The primary difference between it and other stitches is that the thread is almost entirely hidden in the fabric. The needle goes into one piece of fabric exactly opposite the spot where it exited the other. The stitch works the same here, even though you are working on a flat surface and an edge rather than two turned edges.

Be sure the stitches go through both the lower scrap and the backing. Otherwise the scraps won't be held in place. A table (with something to protect the surface from needle scratches) might be better for this step than working the "quilt" on your lap.

If you discover a piece is too small or has shifted out of place and is going to expose the backing, remove the pin and move the piece. If this creates a problem above as well, work in another scrap. Once the scraps are all stitched in place, flip the vest front over and trim away any excess fabric that extends beyond the edge of the backing.

Decorate with Embroidery

How much decorating you do on the vest will depend on your vision and the fabrics you've chosen. Traditionally, crazy quilts were decorated with rows of fancy stitches, often in several colors, accenting the lines between each scrap. Other figures were embroidered in as well, flowers in particular, but also animals. A spider on its web was supposed to bring good luck to the quilter. Names and dates were embroidered prominently on the cover.

If you are making a throw, sew the blocks together and baste to a backing fabric to cover the seams before you do the embroidery. The embroidery stitches will serve as the quilting stitches to hold the layers together. Generally, no batting is used in crazy quilts.

Buttonhole Stitch

Even if your vest is made from simple cotton scraps and you plan to wear it with jeans, it ought to have a little decorative stitching to give it a finished look. A great stitch to start with is the buttonhole stitch. This is the same stitch seamstresses used to line buttonholes before sewing machines took over the task, except you'll be taking larger stitches much farther apart.

FIGURE 15-2

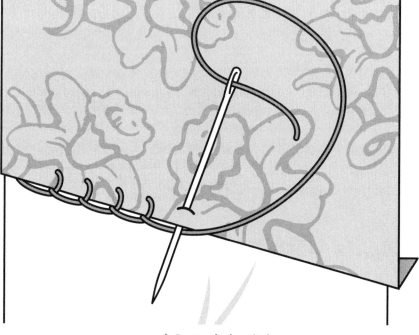

▲ Buttonhole stitch.

Refer to **FIGURE 15-2** and follow these steps:

1. Using two strands of embroidery floss, begin along the outside edge at the point where one scrap overlaps another.
2. Pull the thread from the back through the lower scrap only.
3. Insert the needle into the upper fabric and out just below the fold.
4. Catch the loop of thread under the needle before you pull it out.
5. Repeat these two steps, creating a line right along the fold with perpendicular stitches above it.

If you angle the needle slightly toward the last stitch instead of exactly perpendicular to the fold, the stitches will actually be straighter. This is true because the stitch you see is the thread that curved around the needle rather than what followed the needle through the stitch. You can take all your stitches the same size, vary the size according to the size of the motif on the scrap, or even alternate a short and long stitch in a row of stitching.

Technically you could stitch your scraps down with this embroidery stitch and skip the blind stitch. However, it is difficult to hold the scraps in place, turn the edge under, and keep the embroidery stitches straight all at once. Until you are experienced with these tasks, don't try to combine them.

Fancier Stitching

Perhaps your crazy quilt vest cries out for fancier embroidery. There are books available with diagrams of many embroidery stitches, or you can make up your own. Stitches that travel along the edges of the scraps, giving the appearance of holding them in place, are the most effective. Simple straight stitches might suit a folk art–style vest, while feathery stitches might complement more Victorian fabrics. Stitches that mimic a series of plant vines would look great on earth tones.

If your vest needs some trimming but you don't enjoy embroidery, consider adding ribbon or lace between some of the pieces or an occasional button just for decoration.

Assemble the Vest

Once the decorating is complete on the front pieces, it's time to sew the vest together. Begin by sewing the two front pieces to the back along the side seams, right sides together. Take the same size seams you decided on for the lining. Trim the allowances of the front to approximately $1/2$" and the allowance of the back to approximately $1/4$". By trimming them to different lengths, they will look smoother on the finished quilt. If you had to alter them to $1/4$", don't be concerned; simply press them toward the back. Do not sew the shoulder seams yet.

Sew the Lining to the Vest

With right sides together, pin the lining to the vest. Match the side seams at the bottom and at the underarm. Stitch a $5/8$" seam down the front and across the back at the waist. If you are concerned about your fabric stretching, stop in the center of the back and stitch down the other front and across to overlap with your earlier stitches. Stitch around the armholes in the same way and across the back of the neck. The shoulder seams are left alone at this point.

Clip the inward curves around the neck and armholes the way you did the curves on the Drunkard's Path pieces in Chapter 10. Clip to a thread or two of the stitching. Also cut small *V*s into the allowances in the outward curves on the front pieces. To be sure you've clipped enough, press the allowance of the lining back over the seam as you clip. If sections of the allowance overlap or crease, cut more *V*s. If the allowance will not lie flat, cut more straight clips.

Pressing one allowance away from the other also makes it easier to trim the allowances separately, which is the next step. The allowances should be trimmed to different depths to make a smoother transition from the thickness at the edge of the vest (two layers each: lining, backing, and cover scraps) and the thickness of the cover and lining beyond the allowances. If the allowances are trimmed to the same depth, they will create a ridge around the edge of the finished vest.

Shoulder Seams

Through one of the shoulder seam openings, turn the entire vest right-side out. Press the edges, as you did the baby quilt in Chapter 6, being sure the seams are opened out completely.

With right sides together, sew the shoulder seams of the vest itself. Be sure you don't catch the lining in the seam. Trim the seam allowances to different lengths and press toward the back.

ALERT!

There are other ways to assemble a vest. If you have a favorite way or wish to follow the directions with a vest pattern, by all means do so. However, you might want to give this method a try. See if it isn't faster and easier than the others.

Tuck the seam allowances of the front lining pieces into the back along with the outside vest pieces. Turn the allowance on the back lining piece under and blind stitch it into place.

Buttons

Your vest is finished now unless you want to add buttons and buttonholes. The vertical line on the pattern (see **FIGURE 15-1**) that indicates the center back is also the center front line of the front piece. This can serve as a guide for the placement of buttonholes or you can place them according to how the vest fits. Use the directions with your sewing machine for use of the buttonhole attachment. Be sure to take into account the added thickness of the overlapping scraps or your buttonholes may be too small for your buttons.

Don't discount the decorative quality of buttons even if you never intend to button your vest. They come in all shapes and sizes and you're sure to find some that are the perfect finish for your vest.

String Piecing

A related technique that at first glance can be mistaken for crazy quilting is string piecing. The idea is the same in both cases: to use up the smaller scraps.

FIGURE 15-3

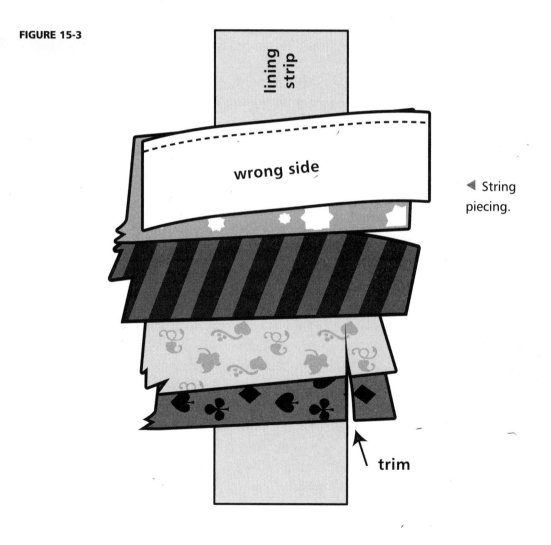

◀ String piecing.

String piecing seems to have been invented by slave women who sewed their owner's quilts and clothes but had no blankets for their own families. By saving the smallest scraps, which would have been thrown away, and the long strips of fabric trimmed from quilt backing, they were able to piece together their own quilts.

In spite of its sad history, this clever technique can make very charming quilts. Begin with strips of backing the length of your desired quilt and varying in width, whatever you choose.

Collect fabric scraps that are, at least for the most part, wider than your strips. Sew the first scrap on one end of the strip. This scrap is placed the same way you placed the first scrap of the crazy quilt but can be sewn on by a machine close to the outside edge. Place the second scrap on top of this piece, right sides together, raw edges in line, and stitch. This is very similar to the way you pieced the Log Cabin potholder in Chapter 5, except the pieces aren't square.

Open the piece out and press. If a piece doesn't cover the whole width of the fabric strip, angle another piece over the gap and stitch it in place. Continue in this manner, being sure you do not leave any raw edges exposed.

Trim away the pieces that extend beyond the strips. Sew the strips together and press the seam allowances open. Assemble with backing and batting. To quilt, you can stitch in the ditch—that is, machine stitch directly on the seams between the strips. This is usually done on the machine, but you can do it by hand if you so choose. You can use any all-over pattern of quilting if you prefer. (E)

Chapter 16

One-Patch Quilts

One-Patch quilts are made from pieces that are all the same size and shape. Equilateral triangles can be used as One-Patch patterns, as can thimble shapes. If every patch in the quilt is from a different fabric, it is known as a charm quilt. Yet another example is the Double Axe Bit described in this chapter.

Size and Supplies

Use the chart in Chapter 7 to determine the size of your quilt and the amount of batting and backing you will need. Determining the amount of cover fabrics you will need is a bit trickier.

FIGURE 16-1

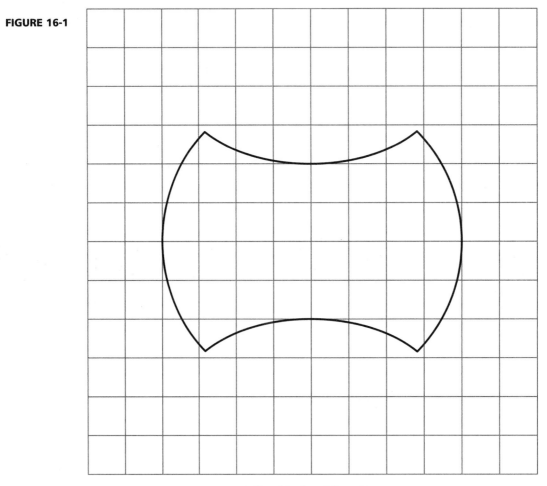

▲ Double Axe Bit pattern.

If you are using scraps, you can cut out more patches as you go along. But if you choose to make your One-Patch of only a few fabrics, you will need to do some figuring. If you enlarge the pattern to 6" across, which is a common size, the narrow part of the patch will be only $2\frac{1}{2}$". Since the patches alternate directions across your quilt, you can figure the average length of the patches to be just under $4\frac{1}{2}$", 5" when you add the seam allowances. Use this to determine the number of patches for your size quilt and divide by the number of fabrics you want to use.

How much fabric you need will depend on how you place the patches as you cut them out. As a close approximation, figure the yardage required to cover the whole quilt, divided by the number of fabrics you are using, then add at least $\frac{1}{2}$ yard of each fabric for the waste that is inevitable because of the shape of the pieces and the seam allowances. For a queen- or king-size bed, adding a full yard would be safer.

While it is normally best to avoid stripes while quilting, they work well in this pattern. In fact, if you cut only stripes, all in the lengthwise direction, you would have a very interesting quilt cover as the stripes alternate directions with the pieces.

Make a Template and Cut the Pieces

Because of the curves, the patches will need to be cut from a template made to mark the stitching line the way the Drunkard's Path pieces in Chapter 10 were. It is important that they are cut accurately. Otherwise they won't fit together properly and your quilt won't lie flat.

Start with a Circle

You can enlarge the pattern from **FIGURE 16-1**, but it is better to start with a circle. Use a protractor or perfectly round object to make a circle on paper. A 6" salad plate might be ideal. This circle will be the size of your patch on the long side. Cut out the circle, fold it in half, and crease it. Now unfold it and fold it again the other way, matching the creases to divide the circle in exact fourths.

Draw a line from the point where one crease meets the circle to the point where the next crease meets the circle. Do the same on the opposite side of the circle. Fold the edge of the circle inward along these lines. Draw around the curve to create inward curves in two quarters that exactly match the outward curves in the other two. Cut away these pointed ovals, but save them. They will come in handy later if you want your quilt to have true scalloped edges.

Create Your Template

Copy your pattern to template material or glue it to cardboard and cut out the template. If you are making a full-sized quilt, you will probably want more than one template, especially if you are using cardboard.

ALERT!

If you are creating your own One-Patch pattern, be certain that your pieces are going to fit together exactly. To test it, draw around your template on a piece of paper and make certain that each side of your template will fit exactly with all the sides of the one you've drawn.

Draw around your template on the wrong side of your fabric. This will be your stitching line. Cut approximately 1/4" outside this line. If you are cutting more than one piece from the same fabric, remember to allow for both seam allowances between the pieces. If you alternate the pieces vertically and horizontally, you will be able to cut more pieces from a length of fabric.

Hand Piece

Hand stitch the inward curve of one patch to the outward curve of the next the way you did the pieces of the Drunkard's Path in Chapter 10, *except* you do not extend the stitching line from the end of the marking to the edge of the fabric. This is left unstitched to help the pieces lie flat where four curves join together.

Follow this procedure to stitch all the patches together. They can be joined in groups of four or in rows, at random or in an organized pattern. Because you are never crossing one seam with another, you don't have to worry about what order they are sewn together.

If you are not making a charm quilt and want to establish a pattern with a limited number of fabrics, it is probably better to work in groups or units that contain each of your design repeats. Lay out your fabrics to settle on your arrangement. Keep the layout for reference until you have a completed unit to follow.

Remember the pointed ovals you cut away when you made the Double Axe Bit pattern? You can make a template of one of these ovals and cut narrow pieces to sew to the inward curves around the outside edge of your quilt. This will create a true scalloped edge. If the axe-head shape is what you are after, you can leave it a waving curve instead.

Once the patches are all together, press the seams toward the inward curve as you did the seams in the Drunkard's Path. The difference here is that four seams will join in what will look like a pinwheel effect in the back.

FIGURE 16-2

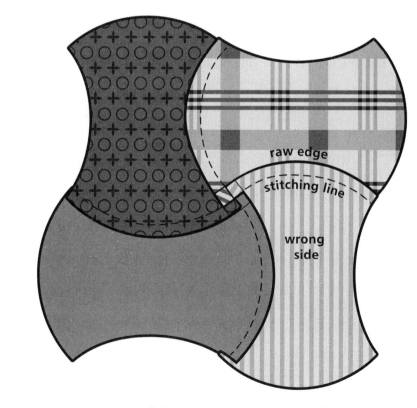

▲ Press all the seams toward the inward curves.

Because the seams were stitched only to that junction point, you will be able to press the allowances very flat and smooth. With a steam iron, press each junction thoroughly to be sure it will stay in place.

FACT

When young mothers made charm quilts, they often cut two of one particular fabric and hid those pieces among the others. In the days before television, convalescing children would make a game out of trying to find the matched pair.

Mark, Assemble, and Quilt

One-Patch quilts are usually quilted to accent the shape of the patch itself. Occasionally the way the patches fit together is more interesting than the shape, which is the case with the Double Axe Bit.

Mark to Complete the Circles

Your templates will be needed again to mark the quilting design for your quilt. On the right side of your cover, position the template over a patch so that the inward curves of the template are opposite the outward curves of the patch and the outward curves of the template extend into the neighboring patches. Mark around the template, essentially completing the circles.

Assemble

Layer the cover with the batting and backing. Be sure the batting and backing both extend a little beyond the edges of the cover. Pin; then baste the layers together.

If you are having trouble basting a full-sized quilt, fold or roll up about half of the quilt to give you better access to the center. Baste from the center outward about 12". You can have thread on several different needles while you are doing this. Smooth everything out again, roll the side that you started stitching, and baste for a while on the second half. Repeat this process, folding aside what you are not stitching on to give yourself access to the entire surface of the quilt.

If the layers were completely smooth when you put the pins in place but you find yourself adjusting the pins as you baste, you have probably pulled one layer out of position. Smooth everything out again. Flip the quilt over to see if it is smooth on the back. Take out any basting that you need to and begin again. It is very important that the layers be smooth before you start to quilt.

You can splice batting for a quilt the same way you spliced the batting in the blocks of the take-along quilt in Chapter 11. Be sure that your pieces of batting are the same weight. Overlap them slightly and cut through both layers to make them fit exactly, then whipstitch them together.

Quilt

Beginning in the center, quilt along all the marked lines and along each seam. The easiest way to do this is to follow a curving line of seams or markings outward from the center. When you come to the edge of your hoop or frame, park the needle and start back at the center with another piece of thread and another needle, following another curving line. When you are outlining the patches, stitch along the edge of the outward curve. This will let you avoid the seam allowances except at the very corners, and your stitches will be smaller as a result.

Quilt to about 2" from the outside edge. Remove the needles, but leave any quilting thread that remains on these unfinished lines. You will thread them back onto a needle to finish these rows of quilting later.

Keep one of your templates handy as you quilt. You may discover a need to re-mark a curve, especially on dark fabric, or there may be one you missed. Tailor's chalk is handy for a quick fix since you will have these few stitches done before it rubs away.

Turn Under to Bind

It would be possible to trim the sides straight and bind in any of the ways already described. If you've gone to the trouble of finishing the outside circles, however, you won't want to do that. Even if you haven't, you may want to extend the pattern established throughout the quilt clear to the edges. In these cases, you will need to turn the seam allowances under.

Begin by trimming the batting and the backing to match the curving edges of the cover. Be sure the pieces are smooth from the last quilting stitches outward.

Turn the quilt cover-side down. With the backing and batting held out of the way, clip the inward curves with straight cuts and clip the outward curves with *V*s just to the stitching line. If you have true scalloped edges and did not stitch beyond the marked stitching line, you will not need to clip the point where your seams meet the edge. Press the seam allowance under.

Turn the quilt cover-side up again. Trim the batting back another $1/4$" to match the turned-under cover. Clip the curves of the backing. You will need to clip the point between the scallops on this side. Press the seam allowance over the batting.

Overcast Stitch

Stitch all around the quilt with a tiny overcast stitch. This stitch is sometimes called a whipstitch, because it's a fast stitch. In this instance it's got to be tiny, which means it's not so fast.

QUESTION?

Why not use the blind stitch?
The blind stitch is perfect for straight edges, but since the curves have been clipped, you must loop the thread over the layers of the quilt. This loop will help hold the short threads at the clips inside while the blind stitch would actually drag them out.

FIGURE 16-3

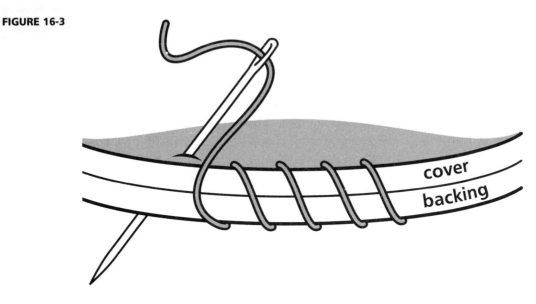

▲ Overcast stitch.

Refer to **FIGURE 16-3** and follow these steps:

1. Hold the layers tightly closed between the thumb and forefinger of your off hand.
2. Bury your knot in the seam allowance, bringing the needle out of the backing close to the edge but not on it.
3. Enter the quilt from the top, going all the way through the quilt to the backing, letting the needle angle a little as you stitch.
4. Repeat step 3, progressing forward with both the stitch inside the quilt and the loop on the outside.

Finishing

Once the edges are done, go back and finish the quilting. Don't forget the inward curve markings on the outside circles or the corresponding seams if you added the pointed ovals to your edge. Last, be sure to sign your quilt and enjoy it.

Using Rectangles

There are many examples of One-Patch quilts made from rectangles. Generally they are not charm quilts because—since the shape is so simple—the interest lies in the patterns created by the repeat of fabrics.

The Fence Rail is made up of several narrow strips that are sewn together into a square-shaped block. The same pattern of strips is repeated in each of the blocks. The blocks are then set in alternating directions, creating a zigzag effect across the quilt.

Patches that measure 6" by 3" make up the Brick Sidewalk. They are paired up to make 6" squares. The squares alternate direction the same as the Fence Rail does. The difference is the color. The "bricks" are made of five or six different colors repeated more at random, avoiding the zigzag effect of the Fence Rail.

Get Creative with Mosaics

Mosaics are quilts made from small hexagons. These can be done as charm quilts or the pieces can be arranged into six-pointed stars or other designs. Often the arrangement makes one think of paving stones or mosaic tiles, though they rarely form a picture. The most common Mosaic is Grandmother's Flower Garden.

FACT

Charm quilts were so called because of a superstition that there would be some sort of good luck or even romance associated with acquiring the fabric that would become the last patch. This was the case for single women, at least. If a married woman made a charm quilt, it might be called a Beggar quilt because she would beg scraps from her friends.

Piecing

The layout of Grandmother's Flower Garden is one yellow center hexagon surrounded by two or three rounds of hexagons representing flower petals. The flowers may be made from a round of solid color surrounded by a round or two of coordinating prints. They might be all the same or each a different color. Separating these flowers is a round or two of white or off-white hexagons meant to represent a path between the flowerbeds. The number of rounds used in each repeat is determined by the quilter's tastes and the size of the hexagon.

The yellow pieces don't necessarily need to be of the same fabric, and the flowers are generally from scraps as well. The neutral pieces should all be the same, however. You will need one-third to one-half as much fabric for it as you will for the backing, depending on your particular layout.

Sometimes stencils of common shapes—such as circles, squares, triangles, and hexagons—can be found in craft stores. Whether they are intended for quilters or artists, they are a great addition to a quilter's pattern library. You might use them for piece or appliqué patterns or even for quilting patterns.

The best way to make a perfect hexagon is to use a protractor to draw a circle the size you want your pieces to be. Without changing the size of the protractor, place the point on the circle and mark the distance of the radius on the circle on either side of the point. Move the point to one of these marks and repeat the process. You will divide the circle into six equal parts. Draw lines between these points to make a hexagon.

Make a template and cut your pieces the same way you did the Double Axe Bit. Piecing is easy, if a bit tedious, because you don't have to fight with a curve. Begin with a center flower and piece the rounds around it. If you are only using one round of white path, don't make the mistake of adding it to every flower. When the flowers are done, add path pieces and sew the flowers together.

Pressing

There is no perfect way to press the seams between the hexagons. You can start in the center and press everything outward or clip *V*s in every one of those points and press all the seams open. The choice is up to you and your level of perfectionism.

Quilting

Mosaics are nearly always quilted with a round of stitches inside each patch. Generally the stitches are $^1/_4$" away from the seam, which is nice because it's beyond the seam allowances.

It is not a good idea to quilt a hexagon inside each patch and move on to the next. As with the Axe Bit, it's better to progress in lines outward from the center. Stitch the bottom half of one hexagon; then make the $^1/_2$" move to the next hexagon and stitch the bottom half of it. When you come to the edge of your hoop or frame, park the needle and go back and work the top half of that row of hexagons.

Finishing

As with the Axe Bit, you can trim the edges straight if you want to, or turn under the outside seam allowances and overcast stitch them together. Since the edges are actually straight, you might try blind stitching them. When you are pressing under the points, you should fold one seam allowance over the other, as you did the corners on the Trip Around the World quilt in Chapter 12, rather than clipping them, since these places will be vulnerable to fraying if they are clipped. The inside valleys of the backing will need to be clipped, however, and perhaps the cover as well, depending on how the seams were pressed.

Don't forget to go back and quilt the last round of hexagons and sign your finished quilt.

Chapter 17

Stained Glass Wall Hanging

Stained Glass quilting is a form of appliqué in which bias tape is used to cover the raw edges of the appliquéd pieces. When the tape is black, the finished quilt resembles a stained glass window. This type of quilting is used most often in wall hangings.

Make a Pattern

The pattern in **FIGURE 17-1** is copied from a stained glass window made around 1915 and installed in a farmhouse in Kansas. You can enlarge the pattern using graph paper or your own grid as you did the quilting pattern for the center of the Rising Star pillow in Chapter 9. To make the torch the size of the actual window detail, make your grid using 1" squares. This will make a 10"-by-10" wall hanging.

FIGURE 17-1

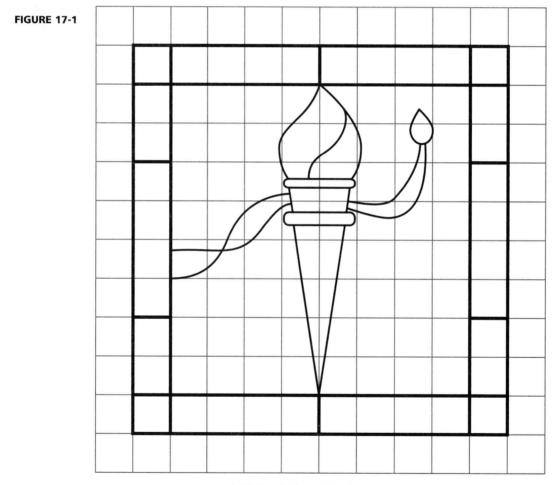

▲ Stained Glass Window pattern.

If you would rather create your own picture, keep the limitations of the bias tape in mind. The two oblong ovals below the flame are about the sharpest curves it's capable of. For example, if you want to create a dragonfly wall hanging to complement your Tiffany-style lamp, remember that the wing tips should not require too sharp a curve.

Sharp points are not difficult, but to keep from exposing a raw edge at the end of the binding, consider taking the tape out to the edge, as illustrated with the top of the flame and the bottom of the torch. Otherwise, tuck the tape under another piece, the way the ends of the accent ribbon behind the torch can tuck under a side accent. The tip of the teardrop shape at the end of the ribbon is zigzagged to hide the raw edge and protect it from unraveling.

ALERT!

Stained glass artists don't try to cut a shape or hole out of the center of a piece of glass. For your hanging to look authentic, your bias tape should extend to the sides somewhere or to the top and bottom if not in all four directions.

Draw your picture the size you want your finished hanging to be. Mark over every line with a narrow marker. This will give you a better idea of how the finished hanging will look, and it will also make tracing the pattern easier.

Supplies

Fabric for a Stained Glass quilt can be anything you want. Special fabrics printed with a marbled design can look like old-fashioned stained glass. These are excellent, especially for the background pieces.

Bright colors will look more like sunlight through colored glass and are also good choices. Since this will be a wall hanging and not require regular washings, you can use dry clean–only silks and satins for a glassy appearance, if you want.

Some additional supplies you will need are:

- Backing/binding fabric 5" longer and wider than your cover
- Low loft batting 2" larger than your cover
- Fusible interfacing the size of your cover
- Black double-fold, narrow bias tape
- $1/4$" double-sided fabric tape, optional
- Butcher paper or template material

QUESTION?

Why not use gray bias tape since lead in windows is gray?
When light is shining through a stained glass window, the lead looks black. Also, stitches will disappear completely in black because there are no shadows. No matter how well you match your thread to a gray tape, your stitches are going to show.

Cut the Pieces

Once you've made your pattern and collected your materials, you're ready to begin. You will need to make patterns or templates to cut your fabrics. But before you do that, you will need a copy of your original pattern on the interfacing.

The Interfacing

Place your pattern on a flat surface and lay your piece of fusible interfacing on top, smooth-side down. Trace the pattern details directly onto the fusible side. A fine-line permanent marker works best.

Butcher Paper

Next, trace the pattern onto the butcher paper. A light table may make it easier to see the pattern through the paper. Copy the entire pattern onto the paper side of the butcher paper. Label each separate area of the pattern on the butcher paper to make it easier to identify later. Cut the pieces apart and sort them by fabric color.

Iron the butcher paper patterns onto the right side of their respective fabrics, including the background. Cut out the pattern pieces along the edges of the patterns. There is no need to allow for seams except along the very outside edge.

Template or Paper Patterns

If you are not using butcher paper, you can make templates or cut your original picture out to pin directly to the fabric. Remember to keep the papers right-side up and cut from the right side rather than wrong side of the fabric.

Assemble

Take the pieces along with the interfacing to the ironing board. Remove the butcher paper and place the pieces on the corresponding sections of the interfacing. Press them in place, following the instructions that come with the interfacing for the iron setting and time.

Layer the unstitched cover with the batting and backing. The batting should extend 1" all around the cover, and the backing 1¹/₂" beyond that. Use a few safety pins to hold the layers together, keeping them away from the edges of the individual fabric pieces so they don't interfere with your sewing.

ALERT!

If you have cut accurately, the pieces should fit together without more than a sliver of space between them. It is important that they do since the binding that will hold them down is very narrow and can't cover up any but the tiniest mistakes.

Quilt with Bias Tape

The bias tape needs to cover all the raw edges of the fabric. Ideally, the ends of the tape will be covered by a crossing piece of tape, which will itself be covered, and so on until a piece of tape extends off the fabric to be covered when you bind the quilt. Before you start, take a few minutes to plan the order and placement of the bias tape.

Cut the first piece of bias tape to the appropriate length. Back it with the fabric tape. Follow the directions on the tape for use. Some will need to be ironed in place, while others will have a piece of backing paper to remove. Carefully place the bias tape so it covers the raw edges of both fabrics.

With the first piece of bias tape in place, cut the second and so on. With black thread, machine stitch over each piece of tape close to both edges. Both rows of stitches should be in the same direction on a particular piece of tape to keep from creating wrinkles. Zigzag over any ends that are exposed.

If you are not using double-sided fabric tape to hold the bias tape pieces in place, you should sew the first piece down before you cut and place the second piece. That way, the second piece can be placed to cover the raw edge of the first piece of bias tape.

Fabric glue is not recommended, because it is difficult to stitch through. If you don't stitch over the bias tape, your hanging is not quilted. If you don't care about the quilting, there is still the problem of the double-fold tape coming unfolded unless it is glued shut as well as glued down. Single-fold tape would be too wide for most wall hanging projects.

Double-sided fabric tape can make this project much easier, but it has its problems, too. It's difficult to get it lined up exactly with the bias tape. As a result, slivers of it might be visible. Once the bias tape is stitched down, try to carefully trim away any of the tape that is left.

Back-to-Front Binding

A method of binding a quilt not yet discussed is back-to-front binding. This can be used on any straight-edged quilt. It can include a wide border or can be as narrow as $1/4$" binding. When you are cutting the backing, simply allow twice the width of your desired border plus $1/2$" beyond all the sides of the cover. Allow enough batting to accommodate the desired border.

Trim and Fold

If you cut your backing and batting to the specifications given, you have allowed enough fabric and batting for the binding/border to be a little more than 1" wide. Be sure the batting extends an equal distance all around the quilt. Trim any excess.

Trim the backing so that it can fold over the batting and extend $1/2$" over the cover. The $1/2$" allows for $1/4$" seam allowance turned under and $1/4$" overlap on the edge of the cover.

Turn up the edge of the binding $1/4$" and press. Also, fold the backing over the batting and press to crease. Press the corners as extensions of the sides so the creases form a square at each corner. If you discover you are crimping the edge of the batting when you fold the backing down, trim it along the backing's crease line.

FACT

Stained glass manufacturing began in the Middle Ages, around the same time as quilting. Stained glass artists draw blueprints and make patterns before they cut their glass. Details are painted on the glass like embroidery on a quilt. Needle pokes and pin scratches heal more quickly than glass cuts, however.

Miter the Corners

For your border to give the appearance of a frame around your hanging, you will want to miter the corners. Because you are folding the binding from the back to the front rather than adding a separate piece, the technique is somewhat different from the mitered binding described in Chapter 7.

Begin somewhere in the middle of a side. Machine stitch the folded backing to the cover, close to the edge. Stop stitching at the crease line at the edge of the batting. Backstitch a couple of stitches, remove the border from the machine, and clip the threads.

FIGURE 17-2

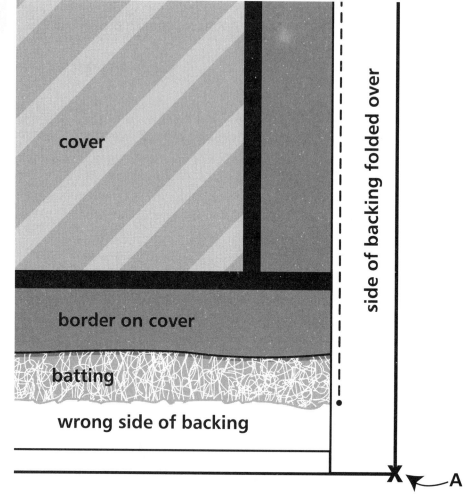

▲ Fold the backing to the front and stitch to the fold line.

The square defined by the two lines of creases is folded but is still loose. Open out this flap and match the corner marked by the "A" in **FIGURE 17-2** to the edge of the backing alongside the end of the stitching. The crease that extended from the first side should now line up with the edge of the batting on the second side.

Pin the binding at point "A," and trim away part of the triangle flap that extends above it. Do not trim too close to the fold line or loose threads will work their way out of your mitered corner.

FIGURE 17-3

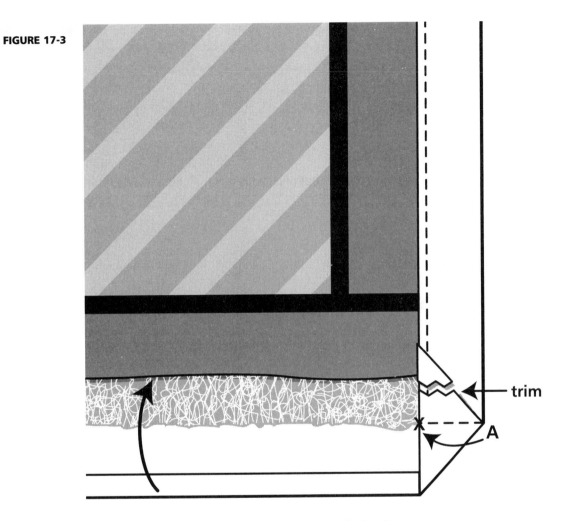

trim

A

▲ Fold up the corner and trim the excess.

Remove the pin and restore "A" to its position in **FIGURE 17-2**. Now, fold the corner up again, without opening out the trimmed flap. Line up point "A" with the stitching point as in **FIGURE 17-3**. This time the raw edges created by trimming away some of the fold will be tucked inside. Turn the backing up over the batting and sew the next side.

If you wish, you can sew both sides from batting edge to batting edge; then miter all the corners before you sew the top and bottom. This way you can fold all the corners in from the side instead of folding them in a clockwise formation around the hanging. The wider the border created by the folded backing, the more the direction of the corner fold is going to show.

Alternate Mitering Method

Another way to miter the corners is to fold the corner of the backing up before the sides are stitched. The entire corner square defined by the creases should lie over the batting. Point "A" should be in the same position it was in the other method, as shown in **FIGURE 17-3**.

FIGURE 17-4

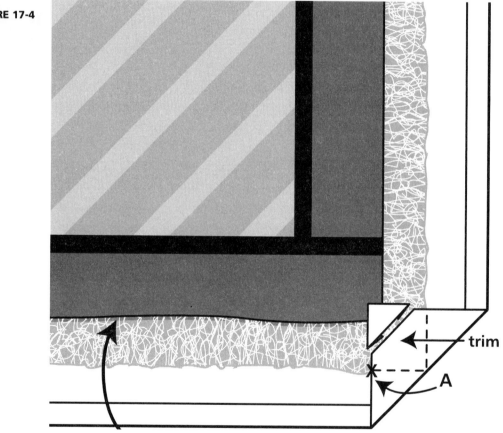

▲ An alternate method, easier to understand but harder to get a sharp point.

Trim away the tip of the corner that is above the cover. Turn the sides up and stitch close to the edge of the backing. The sides will fold up to form a mitered corner if the corner was folded up exactly.

This method is easier to understand and can work well with proper care. However, it is easy to have the side edges not quite meet, making the corner less than square. Overlapping edges are just as possible and nearly as messy looking.

With the first method, there is only one diagonal fold coming across the corner instead of two. If the corner is less than true, the one fold will still give the appearance of a mitered corner. With the two folds, they must meet exactly to give the same impression.

Unmitered Method

You can bind with the backing without mitering the corners. Window frames, after all, are usually not mitered. Rather than sewing around the quilt, sew the sides in place first, all the way to the edges of the backing. Then fold over the top and bottom to make the unmitered corners consistent.

You can use the unmitered method to fold the front to the back. Since this isn't going to be visible, it will be essentially a narrow hem. This is useful if you don't want anything interfering with the appearance of the border of the quilt.

Finishing Touches

Because of the interfacing, your wall hanging should hang easily from a dowel extended through loops sewn on the back as described in Chapter 8. Place the loops close enough together that your hanging won't sag. If it's quite large, a sleeve to hold the dowel as described in Chapter 13 would be better. Be sure the width of the sleeve is enough less than the hanging that it can balance on two nails without the nails showing.

ALERT!

Mitering the corner is not as complicated as it sounds. All you are doing is folding in one side, turning up the corner, and folding in the adjacent side. The steps in between are designed to help you trim away some of the excess bulk.

Additional Projects

While this technique is almost always used for wall hangings intended to resemble stained glass windows, you can use seam binding to cover the raw edges in other pieced or appliquéd projects.

Ring Bearer's Pillow

You can use this technique to make a ring bearer's pillow. Use fabric from the wedding dress or pieces of white satin. In place of the bias tape, use lace or silk ribbon. The pieces could form a heart, but you may have to box in the curves a bit since the ribbons aren't going to curve as well as bias tape. Attach the ribbons for the rings in the center, and back and stuff it like the pillow in Chapter 9.

Full-Sized Quilts

This same method can be used to appliqué quilts whether the desire is to look like a stained glass window or not. White bias tape between soft pastel fabrics is going to give a very different impression than black between bright colors. The possibilities are limited only by your imagination.

Because interfacing is too stiff for use in a bed quilt, you will need to vary the technique a little. Pin the pieces to a lining fabric instead of interfacing and zigzag along the raw edges, sewing down two adjacent pieces at once.

With something the size of a quilt, wider bias tape will not look out of place. Single-fold bias tape would be easier than double, and it is wide enough to cover the zigzag stitches. Be careful to avoid sharp curves in your pieces, though, as the wider tape will not curve as sharply.

Consider using the bias tape in straight lines only, between pieces of fabric to form a geometric design, or over whole cloth to make it appear to be divided. You could use white bias tape to form a trellislike hatchwork over the top of a flower print. Leave a few spaces in the trellis to make it appear that the flowers have wrapped around it.

Chapter 18

Sunbonnet Sue Baby Quilt

An old pattern still popular today is Sunbonnet Sue. There are probably hundreds of different versions of the little girl in the big hat. A fairly modern addition, Overall Sam, was designed to promote gender equality. This chapter offers the patterns for both quilts, allowing you to choose between them or try your hand at both.

Design Your Quilt

Before you get started, you will need to make some decisions about your quilt. The size you want for the finished quilt will determine the amount of backing and batting you will need. What you choose to do on the cover will determine the rest of your fabric needs.

FIGURE 18-1

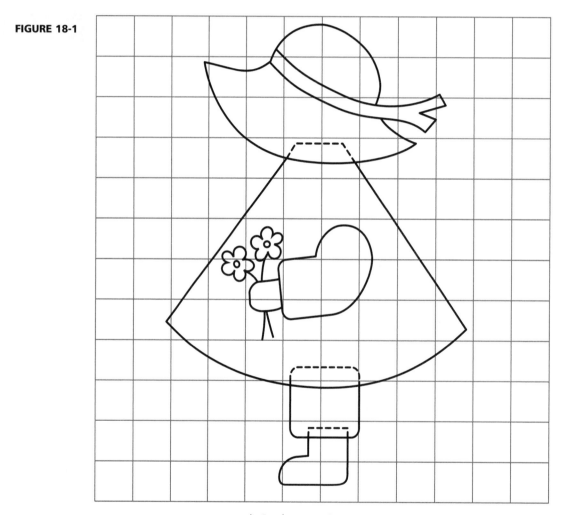

▲ Sunbonnet Sue pattern.

FIGURE 18-2

▲ Overall Sam pattern.

Reading the Patterns

The dotted lines on the patterns show where one piece is intended to overlap another. Sam's pockets and Sue's flowers are not made of different pieces of fabric, but are embroidered on.

The ribbon on Sue's hat can be made from the same fabric as the dress or from actual ribbon. Her sleeve is the same fabric as the dress, but turned so the motifs don't match. Her pantaloons can be made from hat material or from eyelet lace. If you wish, you can add an apron over

Sue's dress using a coordinating fabric or even lace over the dress fabric.

The crown of Sam's hat is made the same way as Sue's sleeve. His overall straps can be overall material or striped ribbons.

FACT

The earliest Sunbonnet Sues wore old-fashioned bonnets that took up half the picture. In some early patterns she didn't wear a dress; she wore bloomers. And Sam looked almost like her. There was a little difference in the shape of his hat, but his pants were baggy enough to closely resemble hers. Today, they could both be girls.

Size and Arrangement

You can make one large Sue or Sam in the center of your quilt or arrange as many as a dozen on blocks to form the cover. They can all match or be made from a variety of colorful scraps. They can be appliquéd on neutral-colored blocks, separated by panels, or appliquéd on different-colored blocks.

Do some sketching on graph paper to decide what you want to do; then enlarge the patterns to the appropriate size the way you did the quilting pattern in Chapter 9. The diagram of the completed block will be your guide not only for cutting out the appliqué pieces but also for placing them on the block. Darken all the piecing lines with a marking pen.

Trace the individual pattern pieces off of this picture. You won't be able to simply cut out a completed picture as you did the Stained Glass design in Chapter 17, because some pieces extend under others. Use these pattern pieces to make templates the way you did the Drunkard's Path templates in Chapter 10.

Pieces, Patterns, and Panels

This pattern is designed to be machine appliquéd by zigzag stitching around each piece. Because the zigzag stitch will prevent raveling, there is no need to turn under the raw edges and therefore no seam allowance is necessary. You can cut your fabric pieces the same size as your pattern pieces.

Cut the pieces from templates by drawing around them on your fabric. This is both the cutting line and the stitching line. Or you could pin your paper patterns directly on the fabric. If you are making several matching Sues or Sams, be aware that paper patterns wear out quickly.

Cut the blocks and panels by measure as you did the pieces in Chapter 5. Straighten your fabric and cut the pieces with a rotary cutter and an acrylic ruler or by pulling a thread and cutting along the line. Be sure to remember to allow for seam allowances in these pieces.

Appliqué and Embroidery

If you want to stuff the appliqué, you will need to do the detailing before it is appliquéd to the blocks. Otherwise your embroidery stitches or the stitches holding the sleeve, for example, will prevent the stuffing from puffing properly.

The thread you use to appliqué your pieces is going to be very visible on the finished quilt. Change thread to match each piece that is being stitched inside the appliqué and match the outside stitches to the block. Or stitch everything in a contrasting color to accent the stitches.

Hat Ribbon

Sue's ribbon needs to be sewn to the hat piece. The ends that extend beyond the hat will be sewn to the block when the hat is. Position the ribbon in the proper place, pin, and zigzag along both sides. If you are using ribbon instead of fabric, you can straight stitch it in place. In this case, you can leave the ends loose if you choose or add a bow to the finished block instead. Be sure to cut the ends of the ribbons on the diagonal to prevent them from fraying.

Sleeve and Hat Crown

The sleeve will need to be stitched next. The hand can either be embroidered or made from a small scrap of fabric. If it is fabric, it should extend under the sleeve and be sewn on the dress first. Find its placement by laying your dress fabric over the top of your original pattern drawing. You should be able to see the sleeve and hand positions through the fabric. If the fabric is too dark, hold one side of the dress in place and fold back the other to locate the position.

Zigzag around the hand and then around the sleeve. Your zigzag stitches should be close enough together that threads from the fabric won't poke out between them. The outside of the stitches should be just barely off the edge of the appliqué piece and the inside far enough in that the fabric won't fray and pull away from the stitches.

Sam's hat crown must be sewn on the brim in the same way.

Overall Straps

The overall straps need to be stitched onto the shirt. If the overall straps are ribbons, they can be straight stitched in place. Be sure that the ends will extend below the overalls. A diamond stitched onto the area where they overlap will lend a look of authenticity.

ALERT!

An embroidery hoop will make any embroidery stitches much easier, but, depending on the size of your dress or overalls piece, it may be difficult to use one. A solution might be to cut your piece a couple of inches outside the cutting line and trim it down to the cutting/stitching line once the embroidery's done.

Shirt and Overalls

To avoid a valley at the top of the overalls when you add stuffing, appliqué the overall and shirt pieces together now. Find their placement the way you did the sleeve and zigzag around the part of the overalls that overlaps the shirt. If you have chosen not to stuff your quilt, these pieces can be sewn onto the block separately.

Outline Stitch

Sam's pockets and Sue's flowers are important details to the quilt that are embroidered on. This needs to be done before the pieces are appliquéd to the quilt block. Two or three strands of embroidery floss are usually used for this type of embroidery, depending on the size of your appliqué.

Sam's pockets are embroidered on using the outline stitch. You can cut pocket "windows" in your template to help you mark their placement. This is particularly useful if you are making more than one Sam and want the pockets to look consistent. Otherwise, you can draw them freehand. Outline the marked pocket with short overlapping stitches as described in Chapter 8.

Sue is holding a bouquet of flowers. A hole in the dress template can help you place the centers of the flowers, and a slit can help you mark the stems. Draw them freehand if you want each of your Sues to be holding different bouquets. Use the outline stitch to define the stems of her flowers.

Daisy Stitch

The daisy stitch, sometimes called the lazy daisy, is one of the most common embroidery stitches and one of the easiest. You will use it to make flower petals and leaves.

Refer to **FIGURE 18-3** (on the following page) and follow these steps to make the daisy stitch:

1. Bring your embroidery floss up at the center of the flower.
2. Poke the needle back into the fabric at the same spot and out again at the desired length of a petal (Step 1, **FIGURE 18-3**).
3. Catch the floss under the needle and pull the needle through, being careful to leave the floss loose enough to give some width to the petal.
4. Insert the needle just beyond the loop and back out at the flower's center (Step 2, **FIGURE 18-3**).
5. Repeat the process for each petal of the flower.

FIGURE 18-3

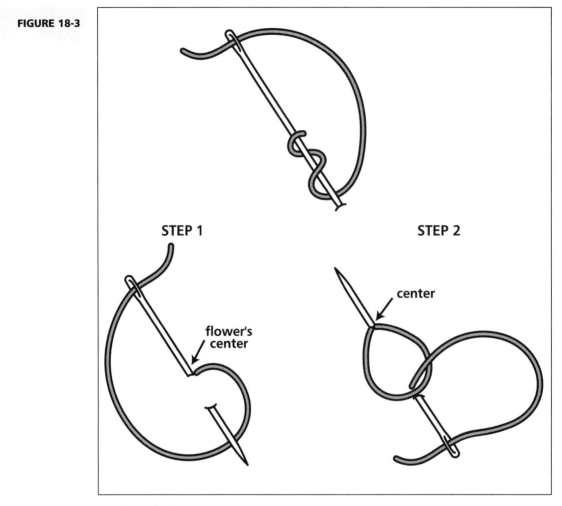

STEP 1

STEP 2

flower's
center

center

▲ Daisy stitch.

QUESTION?

What is the chain stitch?

One daisy stitch is the same as one link in the chain stitch. Instead of returning to the starting point (or center of the flower) after you've made one petal, make another daisy stitch out from the end. Try a row around the bottom of Sue's dress.

French Knot

The flower's center can be made with a French knot. These may take a little practice. Refer to **FIGURE 18-3** again and follow these steps:

1. Bring the needle and floss up through the flower's center.
2. Hold the floss with the off hand about 2" from the fabric.
3. With the needle close to the cloth, wrap the floss around the needle two or three times, depending on what size of knot you want.
4. Insert the tip of the needle back in the hole where it emerged.
5. Pull the floss until the loops are close to the fabric but not terribly tight.
6. Hold the loops in place gently while you pull the needle and floss through the loops and through the cloth.

If your knot pulls through the hole, you either wound the floss too tightly or you pulled too hard. If it unwinds and follows the thread through the hole, you didn't have it wound tightly enough. Give it another try.

Position the Pieces

When all the details have been stitched to the various pieces, you are ready to appliqué them to the blocks. Return to your original pattern. Crease it down and across the middle. Mark the outside ends of these crease lines with the marking pen.

Fold the block piece and press creases down and across the center of it. Place the block over the pattern picture, matching the creases to the marks on the patterns. The outline of Sue or Sam should show through the fabric.

Pin each piece down with enough straight pins or safety pins that the piece will not rotate out of position. If Sue or Sam is especially large, you may want to baste the pieces in place. No matter how careful you are, the piece is going to want to move out of place as you stitch around the curves. Your best bet is to run straight pins perpendicular to the outside edge every couple of inches around the piece you are preparing to stitch.

If you are using blocks too dark to see through, line up the creases by peeking underneath and pin the block to the pattern. Turn the pattern over and run pins through the pattern and the block at key points in the design. Turn the pattern back to the block side and pin the appliqué pieces in place through the block only. Remove the pattern from the back and you're ready to appliqué.

FACT

Sue and Sam can make nice pillows to complement the quilt or just on their own. You might want to use them for two sides of one pillow. Consider adding pigtails to the overalled child and making them two "sides" of the same girl. Pillow instructions are in Chapter 9.

Stitch the Pieces in Place

The pieces that extend under other pieces should be sewn first. Begin with Sue's shoes and work upward. Zigzag around the pieces the way you did the hand, sleeve, and hat crown.

Sam is a bit more difficult because his shoes and his shirt should be sewn on before the overalls. If you've already sewn the overalls to the shirt, this can now be treated as one piece. If you have not stitched the shirt to the overalls, stitch it in place first. Begin by taking just a few stitches on the shirt where it extends under the overalls. Stitch all the way around to where the other side of the shirt is under the overalls; take just a few stitches and stop. The overlap will show less if you do not stitch all the way across the bottom of the shirt. The same is true for the top of his shirt, which is under his hat, and the top of Sue's pantaloons. The smaller pieces like the shoes and the top of the dress are of less concern.

Stuff the Body and Hat

To give your appliquéd figures a three-dimensional look, you can add some cotton stuffing as you did in the puff quilt in Chapter 7. In the puff quilt, however, you stuffed the pieces before they were sewn shut. If you tried that with this pattern, it would be very difficult to get the pieces smooth on the block fabric and you would have puckers somewhere. Instead, you should use a technique borrowed from Italian trapunto.

On the back of the block, cut a slit ½" to 1" long through the block fabric only. Cut one slit behind Sue's dress and another behind her hat. Cut slits behind Sam's body and his hat.

Through these slits, insert a small amount of stuffing. A crochet hook can help you move the stuffing around under the appliquéd pieces as well as help force it though the slits. Turn to the front often to judge the amount of stuffing you want to have.

Don't worry about the cut in the fabric. The back of the block will be quilted against the batting and should never be under enough stress to tear.

This same appliqué technique is often used to decorate tote bags, shirts, jackets, and many other items. Draw your picture and make your template the same way as described for Sue and Sam. If you are making your own tote bag, stitch on your appliqué before you sew the tote together, for easier access.

You're Ready to Finish

With the appliqués sewn onto the blocks and stuffed, you're ready to finish the quilt. Lay the blocks out to determine their arrangement and piece them together as you did the blocks in Chapter 6.

Mark any quilting designs. Some suggestions include outlining Sue and Sam or echo stitching as described in Chapter 4. Panels or plain blocks can be quilted with a latticework or perhaps a larger version of the daisy shape. Butterflies or bugs are additional ideas.

Assemble the cover with the batting and the backing. You can bind by turning the quilt as you did the baby quilt in Chapter 6 if you intend to tie rather than quilt.

You can bind with commercial or your own binding tape. You could also purchase special blanket binding. Since it is wide, you need to allow extra batting around the quilt if this is your choice. Otherwise, it will cover too much of your outside blocks.

Storybook Quilts

Another type of baby quilt that has come in and out of popularity is the storybook quilt. These quilts are made from blocks of embroidered pictures.

Usually all the pictures in the quilt relate in some way. They may all be of the same cartoon or nursery rhyme character, for example, or taken together, they may tell a story.

A good place to find line drawings that turn easily into embroidery patterns is coloring books. Transfer the pictures to your quilt block with dressmaker's tracing paper or by using a light table.

You can embroider the pictures with just the outline stitch from Chapter 8 and the daisy stitch and French knot from this chapter, or you can look for more stitches in embroidery books.

Embroidered blocks aren't just used in children's quilts. Elaborately embroidered or cross-stitched blocks make lovely full-sized quilts.

FACT

The Quilt Maker's Gift by Jeff Brumbeau, illustrated by Gail de Marcken (New York: Scholastic Press, 2000), is a delightful children's book about a quilt maker who teaches a miserly king a lesson in generosity. It would make a great companion gift with a baby quilt, especially if you use fabric printed with de Marcken's illustrations available in some catalogs and specialty stores.

Quick Quilts

If you need a baby quilt in a hurry, machine appliqué a single large design in the center of the quilt. Cut out a simple shape like a heart or a butterfly. Pin it to your cover fabric. Put the layers together with lots of pins and machine appliqué around the design through all the layers. Bind it, add a few ties if you want, and it's done. It may not look very professional, but it can be done in an afternoon.

Chapter 19

Tea Time Placemats

Among the most beautiful and impressive quilts are those with hand-stitched appliqué. Some are incredibly intricate, with a single design covering the whole quilt. The difficulty is more a matter of scope than technique. Most are appliquéd on manageable blocks with the last pieces appliquéd on after the blocks are set. Practice on placemats and tackle the full-sized quilt when you're ready.

Choosing Fabric

FIGURE 19-1 shows a finished placemat. It features an appliquéd cup with an embroidered handle. It is hand quilted and finished with bias strips made from the same fabric as the "inside" of the cup.

FIGURE 19-1

▲ Tea Time placemat.

Cup Fabric

You might choose fabrics with small flowered motifs reminiscent of old china patterns. One-third yard should be enough for the side panels and cups on four placemats. Or you might want to make each placemat from different prints. Check your scrap bag and the remnant bins.

If antique china doesn't suit your décor, consider the two dominant colors in your dining room and work from there. Would blue-speckled ironstone fit better? Fiestaware? A stark white and black? Adjust the shape of your cup to suit your style.

You don't have to include the side panels, and the background doesn't need to be a neutral color, or even a solid. Avoid stripes and large motifs on the cups, however, since they will ruin the illusion of a curved surface.

The Contrasting Color

The inside of the cup requires a very small scrap of fabric. The binding, made from the same fabric, will require a bit more. As you consider your scraps, think in terms of the length of the bias of the particular scrap. One-inch strips cut on the bias will need to go all the way around your placemat.

FACT

Consider making a square runner for the center of the table, perhaps decorated with a teapot instead of cups. Depending on the size and shape of your table, you might want to put a small teapot in each corner. You could also make matching napkin rings, or even use the appliqué on a tea cozy.

One-fourth yard of new fabric will yield enough binding for all four placemats. Less fabric will require a great deal of piecing since the fabric needs to be cut on the bias. In other words, if you are buying new fabric, you will need to buy ¼ yard of fabric, even if you are using it for only one placemat. Consider making the bindings all the same, even if the cups are not.

Backing and Batting

The backing can be any quiltable fabric. The batting should be low loft for easy stitching and a flatter surface. Too much loft between rows of quilting can create an uneven surface that will make your dishes look unstable.

Enlarge the Pattern and Cut the Pieces

Based on **FIGURE 19-1**, consider your own needs and adjust the size of your project accordingly. The panels and background can easily be made larger or smaller.

Draw Your Picture

Draw a picture of your cup the size you want it to be, using the grid as a guide or by drawing your own type of cup. Darken the lines with a marking pen.

Trace the pattern pieces the way you did the Sunbonnet Sue pieces in Chapter 18. You will need to trace the pieces individually because they overlap one another in the drawing.

The saucer can be cut as a complete oval, the cup can extend behind the inside-of-the-cup piece. The inside piece could be under the cup, of course, but the points on the inside piece are going to be somewhat easier than the points at the top edge of the cup. For that reason, it is better to make the cup piece a straight line at the top and appliqué the inside-of-the-cup piece over it.

ALERT!

If the cup fabric is darker than the inside piece, it might be worth the extra effort to put the cup piece over the inside-of-the-cup piece. Having the dark fabric showing through the lighter will definitely ruin the illusion of a china cup.

Make the Templates

Turn the traced patterns into templates by gluing them to cardboard and cutting them out. Save your plastic template material for machine appliqué patterns. You will want to use your cardboard pattern pieces as a guide when you press the seam allowances the way you did the Cathedral Window background fabric in Chapter 14. Plastic template material will melt if you try to use it as a pressing guide.

Cut

Use the template to mark the stitching line on the wrong side of the fabric. Since you will embroider the handle, the cup itself, as shown in **FIGURE 19-1**, is symmetrical, so you don't have to worry about the right or wrong side of the template. Cut the pieces out approximately $1/4$" away from the markings as you did the Drunkard's Path pieces in Chapter 10.

Cut the background block and the side panels by measure. The backing and batting can be cut slightly larger than the expected measurement of the finished cover, or you can wait until the cover is set to cut these out.

Turn Under the Seam Allowances

All the edges of the appliqué pieces need to be turned under at the stitching line except what is covered by another piece. If the edges that are covered by other pieces are turned under, they will only increase the chances that the fabric line will be visible through the upper piece.

> **ESSENTIAL**
>
> Do not try to pin the seam allowances under. The crease from pressing will be enough to help you turn the edges under as you appliqué. A great many pins will only be in the way. If it helps, you can use one pin that you move along 1" or so ahead of your stitching.

Use your original picture to determine how much of the saucer will be behind the cup. Clip Vs in the seam allowance of the saucer $1/8$" or so inside the points where the saucer and cup edges meet. Clip Vs all around the saucer except the section that will go under the cup.

Position the cardboard template on the piece and, with a hot iron, press the seam allowance over it. Leave the seam allowance that will be under the cup flat or trim it at the stitching line. Press the seam allowances of the cup the same way.

The inside-the-cup piece will be pressed up all the way around as well, but the corners will require some extra trimming. Clip the whole corner of the fabric perpendicular to the point of the stitching line. Press up the allowances on each side using the template. The fabric in the allowance that extends beyond the template and onto the opposite allowances, needs to be trimmed away. Don't be alarmed that there's nothing to turn under at the point. The appliqué stitch will cover any visible raw edge, which should be just at one tiny point.

Pin the Pieces in Place

The appliqué pieces need to be positioned on the background block. You will want the cups to look consistent from one placemat to another, so you will need to go back to your original picture.

Begin by locating the center of your drawing. Fold it in half in both directions as you did the drawings of the stained glass window in Chapter 17 and Sunbonnet Sue in Chapter 18. Likewise, crease the horizontal and vertical centers of the background block.

Center the block over the drawing and locate the positions of the appliqué pieces. This is similar to positioning the overlapping pieces of Sunbonnet Sue in Chapter 18, except the clipped seam allowances make it a little more difficult. Tuck them under with your fingers long enough to locate their positions.

Pin the pieces in place with safety pins. Straight pins will scratch you too much while you try to sew, and the pieces are too small to bother basting.

Appliqué Stitch

The appliqué stitch is very much like the overcast stitch you used to finish the One-Patch in Chapter 16. The main differences are that you are sewing along a flat surface instead of an edge, and the stitches must be smaller than you might get away with along an edge.

Your thread should match your fabric as closely as possible to keep it from showing. Some quilters believe quilting thread is stronger and use it for appliqué, but the color choices are very limited. Invisibility is more important than strength in most cases.

FIGURE 19-2

▲ Appliqué stitch: Tuck the seam allowances under as you sew.

Refer to **FIGURE 19-2** and follow these steps:

1. Tuck the allowance under for 1" or 2" and hold or pin in place.
2. Bring the needle up through the backing fabric next to the appliquéd piece.
3. Insert the needle into the appliqué piece two or three threads beyond the fold and slightly to the left of the starting point.
4. Rock the needle so the point comes out through the background next to the appliqué piece and about $1/16$" from the starting point.
5. Repeat these steps, taking between twelve and eighteen stitches per inch.

It is perfectly fine to begin stitching on the appliqué and stitch into the block and out through the appliqué. Practice to discover which is more comfortable for you. With the stitches as tiny as they are, no one is going to be able to tell if you switch styles unless you leave a gap between your stitches when you do it.

FACT

All hand-stitched appliqué is done essentially the same, from big round flowers to tiny delicate leaves. A very challenging type of appliqué involves cutting snowflakes from folded paper, as mentioned as a possible quilting pattern in Chapter 9. Victorian women would use it as an appliqué pattern, clipping all the intricate curves and appliquéing it to a quilt block.

At the points, you will need to take a few extra stitches to be sure everything is tucked under and secured.

Satin Stitch

If you loved the appliqué stitch, you can cut a curved piece of fabric for the handle and appliqué it on. Or turn the sides under on a narrow strip of bias fabric and curve it into place. Either of these will more easily be done before the cup is appliquéd in place, because you can tuck the ends under it. If neither of these suggestions appeals to you, you can embroider in a handle with the satin stitch.

Return your block to the picture and mark the cup handle with a pencil. Two parallel curves will be easier to stitch on than one.

Divide your embroidery floss into two or three strands. An embroidery hoop is strongly recommended to help you keep the stitches even and smooth. Since no one else will ever see the back, you can knot the thread when you start.

FIGURE 19-3

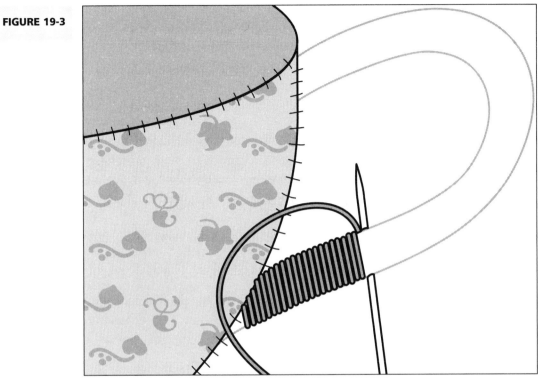

▲ Satin stitch.

Refer to **FIGURE 19-3** and follow these steps:

1. Bring the needle out close to the appliqué along one line that defines the area to be stitched.
2. Insert the needle on the line opposite and back out close to where the floss emerges from the cloth.
3. Pull the floss through tight enough that it isn't loose but not so tight that the cloth puckers between the two marked lines.
4. Repeat steps 2 and 3, keeping the top stitches straight and the bottom stitches slanted.
5. At the curve, put the inside stitches slightly closer together and the outside stitches slightly farther apart.
6. When you're finished, bury the tail by running the needle under about 1" or so of the stitches on the back.

The stitches should be close enough together that no fabric shows between them except perhaps a few teeny, tiny glimpses. Yet the stitches should not pile up on each other. The proximity of the stitches and their evenness should make the handle smooth, like satin.

ALERT!

While you are embroidering, you might want to run a curve of outline stitch around the cup to better define the line between it and the saucer. Choose a color that comes close to matching the fabric so it looks like a shadow where they meet, or use the same color you used on the handle's satin stitch.

Mark, Assemble, and Quilt

If you are adding side panels to the appliquéd block, sew them on before you mark your quilting design. Press the seams toward the darker fabric, and iron the block while you're at it—it's likely gotten wrinkled while you sewed.

Mark the Quilt Pattern

The easiest way to mark a hatchwork design is with an acrylic ruler that has a diagonal line painted on its surface. Line the painted line up with the seam of the panels and use the straight edge to help you draw the quilting line up to and beyond, but not through, the cup. Move the ruler until the marked line is under the 1" mark and draw the next line and so forth.

If you don't have an acrylic ruler, you might make an angle template out of cardboard or, better yet, plastic template material. Cut the angle in the template and line up the edge with the seam. Mark the template to help get the distances between the quilting lines the same.

You could also use a yardstick to draw a line exactly across the diagonal of the appliquéd block; then use the width of the yardstick to draw the rest of the lines.

The printed panels can be quilted in an extension of the hatchwork or they can be different. Consider a curving, feathery garland for old china patterns, or Southwest/Native American–inspired designs for more rustic prints.

Assemble and Quilt

Assemble the placemats with batting and backing and baste together. Quilt the stitches you've marked using a small hoop.

When you are done, trim the batting and backing if necessary. You might want to trim the corners into a curve. Making a pattern for the curve is a good idea so all the placemats (not to mention all the corners on any given one) will be the same.

FACT

One technique used in some of the more intricate appliquéd quilts is to cut a flower or other desired figure from a printed fabric and appliqué it onto the quilt along with all the shapes cut from solid-color fabrics. At first glance, the flower will look as if it has been pieced from many different fabrics.

Your Own Bias Binding

Commercial double-fold bias tape will work to bind the edges of your placemats, but the chances of getting an exact match to your inside-the-cup fabric are pretty slim. The best solution is to make your own binding. If you chose not to round off the corners, you can make grain-straight binding out of narrow strips of cloth and miter them as you sew them on as you did for the Puff Lap Robe in Chapter 7. If you rounded off the corners, however, the binding should be cut on the bias so it will stretch around the curves.

Cut the Binding

If you have 1/4 yard of fabric (minus a corner used for the inside-the-cup piece), begin by pulling threads and trimming both cut sides. Straighten the fabric if necessary.

Fold one selvaged edge up in line with one cut edge to form a right triangle of the folded section. Iron to crease the fold; then cut along the crease line. This is the bias of the fabric.

For the placemats, a very narrow binding is all that's needed. Cut 1" strips from the fabric along the bias cut. Four or five will be sufficient to go around the placemat.

Splicing the Binding

The ends of each of your binding strips look as if they have been cut on the diagonal when actually they are straight with the grain. This is exactly how you need them in order to piece the strips together.

Bring two strips together, not on top of each other, but looking as if they are forming a right angle. Line the two short edges up, not even at the points, but even along an imaginary line $\frac{1}{4}$" from the ends. This, of course, will be your stitching line.

When the strips are opened out, they will form a straight line. The seam, setting at a forty-five degree angle with the strip, will be smoother than one that is at a right angle across the strip because the bulk of the seam allowance will be spread out rather than all in one place.

ALERT!

As you sew the binding to the placemat, be careful not to stretch it. Your own bias binding will probably be of a looser weave than commercial binding and therefore will want to stretch more. If your strips are stretched the long way as you sew, they will become too narrow to turn over the edge.

If you are using scraps for the binding, cut as near to the bias as possible. Cut off the ends with the grain and piece as described earlier.

If you are cutting bias binding for a full-sized quilt, after folding one selvaged edge of your fabric up to the trimmed raw edge, fold the other selvaged edge down to the other raw edge, creating two parallel bias lines. Bring the two cut grain-straight edges together and offset them the width of your desired strips. Stitch $\frac{1}{4}$" from the edge. Cut the bias strips continuously around the loop of fabric, much like you did the grain-straight strips in Chapter 7.

Fold and Attach the Binding

Press the sides of the binding up using the pin guide described in Chapter 7. Press a few inches of the seam allowances on the binding up, position the pin over them, and press the rest of the allowances up using the pin guide to help you fold them. It should be slightly more than $1/2$" wide when it's completely folded.

Sew it in place the way you did the potholder in Chapter 5, except you won't want to leave a loop on your placemat. Trim the tip of the binding so it is straight with the strip and press $1/4$" to the wrong side. Begin near one corner of the bottom, sewing to the backing side. With the wrong side of the binding facing you, stitch the turned edge down as you sew along the pressed crease of the binding.

ESSENTIAL

It is possible, and somewhat of a time-saver, to stitch the binding on without first pressing the edges. However, you won't have the creases to use as guides and will have to turn the binding under as you stitch the second side.

When you've sewn the binding on all the way around, let about $1/2$" of binding overlap with what is already sewn down. Cut any remaining binding off at the end of your stitching.

When you turn the binding to the front, pay careful attention to the place where the beginning and end of your binding overlapped. Turn the outside fold of the bottom layer, which becomes the top layer when it's turned, over the overlapping binding to hide all the raw edges. Stitch the binding to the front as you did the potholder in Chapter 5. The binding should just cover the stitches left from the first round of sewing on the binding. (E)

Chapter 20
Dresden Plate Quilt

The Dresden Plate is a good example of a design that combines piecing and appliqué. Petal-shaped scraps are pieced together into a flowerlike ring that is then appliquéd to the block. The rings can be anywhere from around 10" to 18" in diameter. (The smaller ones are more difficult to do.)

The Pattern

The pattern consists of a circle broken into sixteen, or sometimes twelve, petals with a small circle in the center. **FIGURE 20-1** shows what an individual petal should look like. The circle in the center prevents you from having to piece sixteen points into an exact center.

FIGURE 20-1

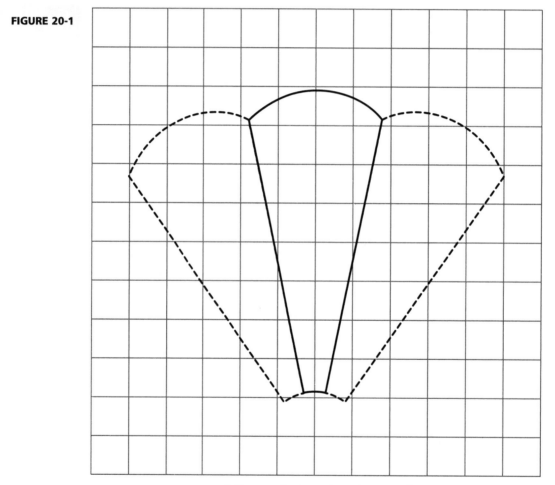

▲ Pattern for Dresden Plate petal.

The Petal Template

The most accurate way to produce a pattern is to begin with a circle the size you want your finished plate to be. Divide it in half, fourths, eighths, then sixteenths by folding. Cut one of the sixteenths pieces out as your pattern.

If you want twelve instead of sixteen petals, you have to divide a fourth of a circle into three equal parts. This may be the reason so many quilters choose sixteen instead. Cut one of the quarter sections of the circle out. Fold both ends over the center and over each other, adjusting until you've divided it into equal thirds. Crease both sides and cut one of them out as your pattern. Or you can use a protractor to divide your circle into sixths as described in the section on Grandmother's Flower Garden in Chapter 16 by marking off the distance of the radius on the circle itself. Cut out one-sixth of the circle and fold it to get a twelfth.

ALERT!

If you have any question about the accuracy of your template, draw a test circle by outlining your template on a piece of paper to be sure the petals are going to go together in a complete circle.

Fold your petal pattern in half the long way and round off the outside end. Folding will help you be sure you are making your petal end symmetrical. You may trim it to a point instead if you prefer. Neither seems to be more traditional than the other. Some Dresden Plate quilts actually have pointed petals at the four compass points while the rest are rounded. To do this, make two separate templates from your drawn circle.

The Center

Once you have your petal template, clip the inside point off. To determine how much you want to cut away, decide on the size of your center circle. These vary widely and can be whatever you want. Go back to your original circle to see what appeals to you.

Determine the radius (center to edge) of your desired inner circle. Cut that length off the end of your petal pattern. You don't need to allow for a seam since the pattern defines the stitching line. Also, don't worry about trying to cut off the end on a curve; cut straight across the end.

You do not need a pattern for the center circle. You can cut it by measure later. You will be stitching the plate appliqué over the center circle, not vice versa, so it can be a square.

Fabric and Layout

The petals of a Dresden Plate can be made from all different fabrics, from eight fabrics repeated twice to four repeated four times to two that alternate around the plate. Occasionally they are made all of one fabric. The plates on the quilt top can repeat the same color combinations or can all be different. Like a flower, the center is traditionally yellow, but it isn't always and can even vary from plate to plate.

The most common layout for the Dresden Plate quilt is to appliqué the plates on background blocks and alternate the appliquéd blocks with plain quilted blocks. All the blocks are from the same fabric, usually white, so it looks as if the plates were appliquéd to one single whole cloth.

If you are using coordinating fabrics instead of a wide variety of scraps, you might want to separate the appliquéd blocks with panels instead of more blocks to emphasize a particular fabric.

FACT

The Dresden Plate pattern was named for a type of porcelain produced near Dresden, Germany, beginning in 1710. The quilt pattern doesn't go back quite that far, of course, but it is a very old pattern with many variations.

To Hand or Machine Piece

Since the seams on the Dresden Plate are all straight, you can machine piece them if you choose. If you want to be more traditional, they are easy to hand piece and make handy take-along work. It is best to decide before you make your template. You can change your mind, but you can save yourself some trouble by deciding first.

If you plan to machine piece, add $1/4$" all around the pattern piece when you make the template. This will allow you to line up the edges of the pieces and stitch $1/4$" inside.

If you would rather hand piece the petals, make the template from the paper pattern and mark the stitching line on the fabric. Then cut the pieces $1/4$" or so outside this line.

If you mark your petals to hand piece and then decide to piece by machine, you can use straight pins to be sure you've lined up your stitching lines exactly. If you've marked your petals to machine piece and decide you'd rather piece by hand, line up the edges the same as you would for the machine and hand stitch as close to $1/4$" from that edge as possible. Keep a small ruler handy to check your distance occasionally.

Whichever way you decide, stop your stitches $1/4$" from the edge of the pieces or at the corner of the stitching line. This will make turning the edges under much easier.

Cut, Piece, and Appliqué

While the Dresden Plate appears to be complicated, the most difficult part is making the pattern. Everything else is done one simple—though somewhat time-consuming—step at a time.

The Plate

Cut the petals for your plate with your template and stitch them together either by hand or machine. Be alert if you have a particular arrangement of fabrics in mind, as it is easy to forget which side you are adding on as you piece around the circle. If you are machine piecing, you can pin all the pieces in your plate together at the wide end and the center before you start to sew. The narrow end can be pinned just before you sew each seam. The center is too small to accommodate sixteen pins all at once.

Press all the seams in one direction, clockwise or counterclockwise. Trim the top seam allowance on these seams slightly shorter than the bottom one. This will help prevent any dark fabric from showing through a lighter one, since you can't press toward dark colors with this pattern.

Clip the curves and press the allowances under as illustrated in **FIGURE 20-2**. Press the seam allowance under at the plate's center as well. If you used a heat-proof template, you can slip it into the space between the seams and use it to help press the allowances.

FIGURE 20-2

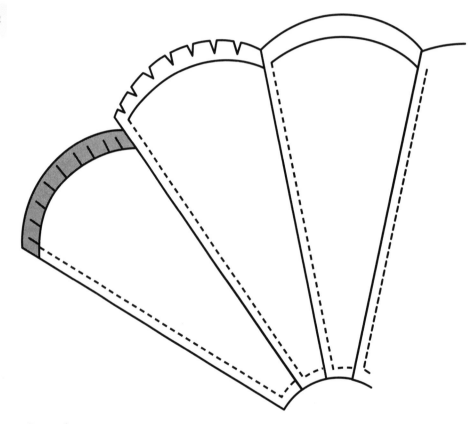

▲ Press the seams in one direction. Clip and turn the seam allowances under on the curves.

Press creases in the block across the center horizontally and vertically. Use these lines to center your pieced plate by lining up the creases on the block with the seams on the plate. Pin the plate in place with several safety pins and hand-appliqué around the outside edge as you did the teacups in Chapter 19.

FIGURE 20-3

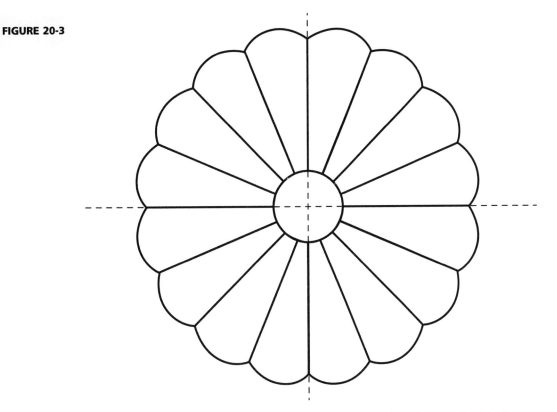

▲ Align the seams with the fold lines to center the plate on the block.

FACT

A variation of the Dresden Plate includes what looks like a second ring of usually green petals peeking out between the first round. These are made from semicircles slightly larger than the tips of the regular petals, appliquéd beneath the plate.

The Center

Believe it or not, it is easier to make a sixteen-sided figure look like a perfect circle than it is to clip and turn under the seam allowance of an actual circle. For this reason you will reverse appliqué, or appliqué through a hole, rather than appliquéing the center circle on top.

The hole that you will be appliquéing through is created by the center cutout of the plate appliqué. Measure the diameter of this circle and add 1/2". Cut squares of your yellow center fabric (or whatever fabric you have chosen for this center) by measure. Unless your center fabric is much darker than the petals, you don't need to cut out circles.

Slip your center fabric square under the edges of the hole and pin it in place. Be sure that it is centered enough that its raw edges will be covered by the plate. Appliqué the inner "circle" to the block through the center fabric.

Set and Mark the Quilt Designs

The most common quilt design for a Dresden Plate quilt is to repeat the outline of the Dresden Plate on the plain blocks. Sometimes the design is fancier, but it is still generally contained within each block. In other words, the quilting does not cross into the panels or onto other blocks. If you've chosen a quilt design that is complete within the blocks, you can mark the design before you set the quilt.

Go back to your original circle and your pattern without the seam allowance to mark a Dresden Plate outline on the plain block. Draw a square around the outside of this outline, at least 1/2" inside the raw edge of the block. Mark another quilting line inside the corner, paralleling the outside square and the curve of the circle. In other words, mark a sort of echo-stitch row shaped nearly like a triangle to fill in the corner. Mark the same outside square and near-triangles on the appliquéd blocks.

This is a great quilt to make as a take-along quilt as described in Chapter 11. When the quilting designs are contained in the individual blocks anyway, they might as well be quilted separately. Be sure to keep the quilting stitches 1" from the raw edges if you are going to join the blocks using the traditional method.

The problem with true echo stitches around the plates and the quilted plate outlines is what happens at the seams between the blocks. Your echo stitches will not meet up exactly and the effect of them ending on either side of the seam can be jarring.

Set the quilt in your planned arrangement and assemble with the batting and the backing. If your quilt pattern flows from one block to the next, set the cover before you mark the design; then assemble.

Quilt and Finish

Quilt along the marked lines, beginning near the quilt's center and working outward. Outline the Dresden Plates on the block just outside the appliqué. Define each of the petals by stitching close to the seams on the side that doesn't have the seam allowances under it. Quilt around the inner circle on the center insert.

Bind the quilt using any of the methods described previously. The center color fabric might be ideal for binding the quilt.

FACT

The Dresden Plate is sometimes called the Friendship Ring because quilters often traded scraps with friends. If a member of a quilting group was moving away, the others might each make a block using the same Dresden Plate pattern and present it as a going-away present.

Additional Piece and Appliqué Patterns

The Dresden Plate is just one of many patterns that combine piecing and appliqué. Now that you know the techniques common to all of them, you shouldn't be afraid to tackle any of them.

More Petal Patterns

The Dahlia patterns are very similar to the Dresden Plate except the pieces are shaped more like petals and they overlap. The center might have to be a circle rather than reverse appliqué. Sometimes a stem emerges from under one petal and disappears at the edge of the block.

Fans

Any of the fan patterns are made like the Dresden Plate except they form only part of a circle. The pattern is made the same way as the Dresden Plate except you'll need a larger circle to begin with, and you'll only use one-fourth or one-third of the circle to make the fan.

Often there is a solid-color accent that encompasses the outside edge of the fan. This is either appliquéd under or over the fan "blades" and prevents the need to round or point them. If this is not included, the blades are usually pointed.

The inside tip of the fan can be made from the points of the fan blades but is more often a semicircle. The curved edge is appliquéd under the blades, while the two straight sides are appliquéd to the block along with the rest of the fan.

Baskets, Flowers, and Bees

Whether the basket is filled with fruit or flowers, the many basket patterns nearly always call for a pieced basket while the contents are appliquéd. Sometimes the basket is pieced, usually with triangles, and appliquéd onto the block. Other times, the pieced basket forms part of the block itself. Sometimes the basket is empty and the only appliqué is the arching handle that makes up the top half of the block.

QUESTION?

What is a medallion quilt?
A medallion quilt has a large appliqué design in the center, which is surrounded by a border, normally elaborately pieced. This is surrounded by wider panels of more appliqué and yet another pieced border, and so on to the edges of the quilt.

Most basket patterns are done on the diagonal. The blocks are sewn together set on point like diamonds with triangles around the outside edge so the baskets are upright on the quilt. The blocks are cut on the grain of the fabric like any other blocks, but the outside triangles are cut with the long side on the grain. This helps to keep the quilt square. If the outside triangles were cut with the two short sides on the grain, the outside edge of the quilt would all be on the bias and would stretch when you bind it.

The Honey Bee is a dressed up Nine-Patch. Nine $1\frac{1}{2}$" patches are pieced into the center of an 11" block. The corners are appliquéd with teardrop shapes with points toward the corners of the Nine-Patch. On either side of each teardrop is an elongated circle or petal shape. The pieces all together reminded someone of four honey bees flying toward the center of the Nine-Patch.

Double Wedding Ring

One of the most popular quilts during the Great Depression is actually one of the most difficult to piece and appliqué. The Double Wedding Ring consists of small scraps that are pieced together to form interlocking circles. The arrangement of the circles is similar to the interlocking circles created by the quilting stitches in the Double Axe Head quilt in Chapter 16. The rings can be anywhere from 12" to 24" across and are composed of thirty-two, forty-eight, or sometimes even more pieces.

The individual pieces are generally thimble shaped except at the junctions where the circles overlap, which are squares or diamonds. All the thimble pieces are the same shape and fit together to form the arch of the circle. Occasionally the arches are made up of two sizes of triangles, in which case it is called an Indian Wedding Ring quilt.

It is tricky to figure out exactly what shape that thimble or the triangle pieces need to be. The place to start is to draw the large circle with the smaller circle inside to define the ring. Divide that ring into fourths, indicating where the rings cross. Draw in the squares on either end of the quarter-ring; then set about dividing up what is left into equal parts— six, eight, or however many pieces you want to use.

The more or less football-like shape that is the overlap of two quarter circles is worked as a single unit. These units are fitted together and appliquéd onto the background. To save some frustration, however, it might be well to invest in an actual pattern. Look online, in quilting magazines, and in books for pattern offers.

FACT

You can make pieced shapes either for a hanging or quilt blocks like those suggested in Chapter 8. Add appliqué details for the shapes that aren't easy to piece to make a combination pieced and appliquéd quilt.

Mirror Image Quilting

A new technique that is reminiscent of the traditional flowers and fans, but with a new twist, is mirror image or kaleidoscope quilting. The basic idea is to cut several usually diamond-shaped pieces exactly alike from a print fabric and lay them out with the matching points together, creating a kaleidoscope effect.

Fabrics

The best fabrics for this technique are large-scale prints with lots of colors and different shapes to provide the necessary contrast. Novelty prints are often the most fun.

Yardage requirements are going to depend on the closeness of the motif repeats in the fabric and the number of identical pieces you need for your pattern. Count the repeats on the length of fabric and buy one or two more to be safe.

You will need background fabric, perhaps something that matches the background of the print. Panels and borders are often made from a coordinating fabric with a smaller motif than the mirror image fabric. Solid accents are very effective as well since the print fabric is often too bold to complement another print.

Patterns

Any quilt pattern where several pieces converge, such as six- or eight-pointed stars, pinwheels, or fans, can be used for mirror image quilting. You can make your pattern the same way you did the Dresden Plate except stop with six or eight divisions. If you try to make the pieces smaller, the prints will blend together and mask the mirror effect.

You can leave the outside ends of your pieces as a circle if you wish. Your finished circle can then be appliquéd to the background block. This will look the most like a kaleidoscope, especially if the outside edge shows some background in the print fabric that matches the block.

More often, all the pieces are turned into triangles or diamonds. After you divide your circle to make your pattern, point the outside half of the wedge to match the inside half. With this shape, you can piece the block around your star, rather than appliqué the star to the block.

When you've decided on your pattern, make a template out of clear template material that includes the seam allowance. Do this by tracing your pattern on the template material, then adding $1/4$" all around the edge before cutting it out. An acrylic ruler is handy for this process.

Consider putting squares from another part of your fabric between the outer points of your star. These squares should all be the same, or at least similar.

Choosing the Location in the Motif

There are special mirrors designed to help you see what your star or other shape will look like when it is finished. Remember that the mirror inverts every other reflection so it isn't a true picture of your finished star, but it can help you isolate what you're cutting from the print around it.

It is possible to do without the mirror, however. Slide your template over the print, paying close attention to the contrast from the point that will be the center outward. Covering the $1/4$" seam allowance with masking tape can be helpful. Fold a motif and lay it next to another to help you visualize the finished star. If you are having trouble, cut a hole the size and shape of your pattern (without the seam allowances) in the center of a large piece of cardboard. This will block out what won't be in your piece.

If you are making a quilt with several different stars from the same fabric, make all your choices before you begin to cut the first one to be sure your choices don't interfere with each other.

Cutting the Pieces

Once you have located the design you want to repeat, use a pencil to trace the main lines of the fabric motif onto the template. This will make it possible to cut them all exactly alike.

Mark the fabric around the template and cut it out, being careful not to cut through any more fabric than necessary. If you have a rotary cutter, cut directly around the template. Be careful that you don't cut the template itself. Cut all the pieces for one star. Erase the pencil marks on the template and move it to another location for the next star.

ALERT!

Accuracy in cutting and piecing becomes even more important than usual with this quilt. Be sure your fabric is well pressed, your pattern is precise, and your pencil and scissors are both sharp.

Piecing the Star

To give your star the full kaleidoscope effect, you will need to piece to the point, something you were able to avoid with the Dresden Plate by reverse appliquéing a center.

The template will show you where the finished circle will be at the intersection of the two seam allowances. Find this point on your pieces and begin your stitching there. Move forward a couple of stitches, backstitch over these stitches, and then stitch the rest of the seam the way you did the roof section of the Schoolhouse in Chapter 10. Stop stitching 1/4" from the outside edge.

The next piece will be stitched on, beginning at the same spot and so on. Press all the seam allowances in one direction. Add the other pieces to complete the blocks, or turn under the outside edge and appliqué to the block.

Once your cover is together, mark it with your quilting design. It's probably better not to have an overall quilting design that would have you stitching on one piece of your star differently than on another. Follow a detail of the fabric motif around the star. Outside the star you might want to create a pattern borrowed from the theme of the fabric. Ⓔ

Chapter 21

Antique Replica Quilting

You can do a few little things to make your quilt look antique, or you can choose an era and try to copy it in pattern, fabric, and quilting stitches. Since you are not trying to pass your quilt off as an antique, the fact that your quilt is in perfect condition will enhance, rather than detract from, its value to you.

Planning Your Quilt

Whether you have a particular antique quilt you would like to replicate, or an era you would like to represent, your first step might be to do a little research into the period. The availability of certain fabrics was often influenced by the politics of the day. But remember, too, the fabric used in a quilt could logically be several years old.

It's often difficult to determine the exact age of a particular quilt pattern. The name often offers a clue but can be deceiving. For example, the pattern called the Underground Railroad did not, as some people assume, contain a map or any other code connected with the slaves' flight to freedom. It dates to colonial times as Jacob's Ladder and was renamed in western Kentucky after the Civil War to commemorate the Underground Railroad. The name change may have come about because the song "Climbing Jacob's Ladder" might have had some coded messages related to which verses were sung.

Appendix B lists several books that have pictures of old quilts. You might look for these and others in your local library. Check out antique quilts offered locally or online. Museums might be another source of patterns. If you bring a pad and pencil with you, you might be able to sketch a quilt's design and make your own pattern.

FACT

Every work of historical fiction reflects the attitudes and sensibilities of the time it is written at least as much as the time it is set. Your quilt is, in essence, a work of historical fiction. Of necessity, it will reflect our modern idea of pleasing color combinations and graceful stitchery no matter how much you try to make it look like an earlier time.

The quilting stitches were much denser in earlier quilts than today. A basic rule is the earlier the era you are trying to imitate, the more intricate your quilting stitches should be.

The section on the history of quilting in Chapter 1, along with this chapter, can help you design a replica quilt that is reasonably authentic. However, since this is your quilt, your own impressions of the era and your own vision should be your best guide.

Colonial Era

Few quilts still exist from this early era, and the ones that do were probably the best quilts that were saved from common use. Some standard patterns are known to go back this far and much is known about the fabrics that were available during this time.

Fabrics

The basic quilting fabric available in the early 1700s was referred to as wash goods and consisted of cotton and linen. Most wash goods were dyed a solid color, but gingham, called Scotch cloth, was available, as were other woven stripes. Spotted lawn, a nearly sheer polka-dot fabric, was popular for dresses and would have found its way into quilts of the time.

A printed cotton imported from India through England was calico. The glazed, thinner version was called chintz. The prints were dyed with blocks cut in relief, one block for each color. Small floral or nonrepresentational designs with fairly close repeats were the norm. Modern calicoes often have larger or more cluttered prints than those of this age. Choose small single-design motifs for your replica quilt. Homespun was also common, which would have had a somewhat coarser weave, and home-dyed fabrics were very much in use.

Perhaps because of the shortage of prints, bright colors were favored and often used in what we might consider poor combinations, for example, purple and red together. However, some of the odd colors found in these early quilts might have been caused by a dyeing accident. Solid colors, gingham, stripes, plaids, polka-dots, and a limited number of small-print fabrics will give an impression of the era.

QUESTION?

Why are small-print fabrics called calicoes?
Calico entered our language in 1578. From *callicoe* to *calicoe* and, finally, *calico,* it gets its name from Calicut, India, from which the cloth was imported. It was in use long before the westward-migrating pioneers who are most closely associated with it began to use it.

Patterns

The Nine-Patch described in Chapter 6 and its many variations have always been popular. The blocks can be made to include more colors by splitting the corner patches into two triangles. Another common variation was to make a fairly large-scale Nine-Patch in which the corner squares or the center square was made up of a smaller Nine-Patch.

The Simple Star pattern goes back to the 1700s. It is designed like the Rising Star in Chapter 9 except that it is only one star. Generally, the center square matched the eight points. The early version of this quilt had many different-colored stars scattered across the cover.

Appliquéd quilts were also popular, often featuring a rose design made with only two or three colors, as were combination appliqué and embroidery quilts.

Early American Era

Following the Revolution, there were many new textile factories. Domestic cotton was increasingly used. The new copperplate method of dyeing fabric made prints more attainable. Most were two-color prints, since running the fabric under a second copperplate to produce a third color was not practical.

Pioneers in the late 1700s and early 1800s continued to make and dye homespun cloth. Dyeing recipes have survived from these days but are so full of terms whose meaning has been forgotten, as well as mysterious ingredients, that they aren't practical for use today. Around 1810 "painted cambric" was available in the East. This fabric was painted with elaborate designs, often pillar or column prints. It might have had wide floral stripes with a neutral background separated by a narrower stripe with a simpler flower on a solid background. These stripes ran the length of the fabric, similar to what would now be called wallpaper prints.

About the same time, more colors became available, though dyes were still made from animal (insect), vegetable, or mineral ingredients. Reds were a Turkey red or crimson and blues were shades of indigo or Prussian blue. There was an abundance of brown shades. Green could be produced only by mixing blue and yellow. As a result, most greens were bluish-green or yellowish-green. The green in prints sometimes had a one-sided halo of blue or yellow that indicated a miss by the second block.

Around 1825, in sophisticated circles, soft grays and lavenders became the style. Quilts remained brighter than the clothing, however, with leftover dress fabric being home dyed to brighten it up.

Patterns from this era include the Log Cabin, described in Chapter 5, and its cousin the Fence Rail. Grandmother's Flower Garden, described in Chapter 16, was first seen in the early 1800s.

Some quilting shops and catalogs offer antique replica fabrics from different eras. These take the guesswork out of choosing your fabric since they are actually designed to match fabrics found in dated quilts or garments. This might be the place to start to plan your replica quilt.

Victorian Age

A little of the Victorian Age, which spanned from 1832 to 1901, has already been discussed in Chapter 1 and also in Chapter 15. Though the United States was greatly influenced by the Victorian style, there were other factors that contributed to the popularity of other quilt patterns and styles.

Victorian Influence

The Victorian Age saw a greater use of velvets and satins in the quilts. The crazy quilt was only one of the examples. Puff quilts, like that described in Chapter 7, were often made from silk, as were other pieced patterns.

Quilts were still needed for everyday use, of course, and these remained primarily cotton. An abundance of fabrics in each quilt and more intricate appliqué designs were evident. Quilting stitches became more fanciful as well. Pineapples, birds, plants, butterflies, and other representations were used, but ostrich feathers or plumes were probably the most popular.

To make a Victorian quilt, you might choose an allover appliqué pattern with an abundance of flowers. Use cutouts of prints for some of the appliqué. Quilt around nearly every detail of the appliqué and fill in the spaces with more stitching. Stitch the border with ostrich feathers.

Pioneers

From before the Revolutionary War until the West was settled, people were setting out into unknown territory. With each of these stages, the lifestyle, quilts included, bore more resemblance to the early colonial settlers' than it did to that of the contemporary inhabitants of the established cities and farms they left behind.

Once they were settled, however, the women would sometimes go to great lengths to obtain magazines. Once they were aware of the latest styles, they would do their best to copy them. Victoria had her influence, although somewhat belatedly, even on the frontier.

Many of the old quilt patterns have pioneer names, but it is difficult to tell if the pattern reminded the quilter of a current aspect of her life or was named to commemorate something of an earlier time. However, if the pattern and its name suit you, try not to obsess on the pattern's exact date of origin.

FACT

Between 1840 and 1880, French Provincial prints made to look like Indian calicoes were imported. They were often characterized by a white halo around the figures made by the wax that protected the area from the background dye before the figures were stamped on. These fabrics, called French Indiennes, are still manufactured in France and still have the halo. Unfortunately they cost between $45 and $75 per meter. American reproductions are more reasonably priced.

Civil War Era

During the Civil War, fabric became very expensive. Northern women did not want to give support to the South by buying cotton. Southern women found themselves paying $20 to $25 for a yard of calico, which had formerly cost only 25 cents. Unbleached muslin was the cheapest cloth available. Women missed their calicoes and sometimes splatter painted the cloth with dyes.

Because cloth was so valuable and blankets were necessary, quilts were still made, often with political themes. Any fabrics from the previous several years would still be in the quilter's scrap bag and similar fabrics would be appropriate for a replica quilt.

ALERT!

For authenticity, sign your replica quilt in permanent ink. Prior to 1835, the permanent ink that was available would rot cloth. Once fabric ink was invented, quilts were more often signed in ink than with embroidery. Set the ink by pressing it with a vinegar-dampened cloth to be certain it won't run.

The same quilt patterns continued to be popular, with modifications to include more scraps. The Dresden Plate and the Double Wedding Ring quilts, described in Chapter 20, were occasionally made during this era, though they reached their greatest popularity later. In the North, stars seemed to be the thing. Small stars were worked into corners between Nine-Patches. Stars lined the top of Flying Geese quilts, representing the North Star and freedom. Stars found their way into the corners of nearly any type of quilt.

After the war, the Log Cabin quilt, described in Chapter 5, became very popular in the North. Perhaps it was to honor the fallen Log Cabin president.

You might consider making a Sanitary Commission quilt. (The Sanitary Commission was established in 1861 to organize the multitudinous relief and soldiers' aid societies that were operating independently at the beginning of the Civil War.) As blankets were in short supply for soldiers during the war, the commission requested that aid societies send very narrow quilts, approximately 7' by 4' (Nine-Patch or Four-Patch seemed to be favorite patterns) to cover, as well as cheer, sick and wounded soldiers recovering in hospitals. This size quilt might be just the thing to leave folded on the couch for Sunday afternoon naps.

Post–Civil War Era

In 1860, synthetic dyes were invented and soon came into common use. This increased the number and intensity of colors that were available in fabrics.

During the war, women who owned sewing machines quit using them because they used twice as much thread as hand sewing. After the war, they were happy to show them off and began machine quilting their quilts. Contrasting colors were often used to draw attention to the stitching. Since the machines were not adept at curves, quilting stitches followed the straight piecing lines or were done as diagonal hatchworks. If you make up your replica quilt entirely on the machine, you might have difficulty convincing your friends of its historical accuracy, however.

About the same time, blankets and comforters were being manufactured and the old patchwork quilts began to look quaint. Plain quilts were still considered worthwhile and many a woman flipped her patchwork quilts over to keep her bedroom looking stylish.

Arts and Crafts Era

As mentioned in Chapter 10, the Arts and Crafts movement was a response to the overly elaborate Victorian Age. It is identified with the end of the nineteenth century and the beginning of the twentieth. Two-tone quilts like the Robbing Peter to Pay Paul quilts were very popular, as were earlier patterns that could be made up in two colors. Solids were considered more favorable than prints, though tiny prints were acceptable. Most quilts of this era were pieced, to make good use of the sewing machines. Hand quilting fell more and more out of favor as more women entered the workplace.

FACT

In *Old Patchwork Quilts and the Women Who Made Them* (Philadelphia & London: J. B. Lippincott Co., 1929), Ruth E. Finley suggests that rather than competing with men for jobs, women had their work taken away from them by men and their factories: "There are economic reasons … for the dust that gathered on quilting frames."

To look typical of a turn-of-the-century quilt, yours should be red or blue on white with comparatively simple quilting. Perhaps you could outline the pieces and mimic the design again on the open spaces.

Depression Era

The Great Depression of the 1930s saw a revival of scrap bag quilting. Grandmother's Flower Garden and the Double Wedding Ring quilts became very popular. Many of the old patterns were revived and often renamed. Quilts of this era were more likely to have quotations or wise sayings embroidered on them.

Bright fabrics were more popular than ever, perhaps because the rest of life was so difficult. Flour sacks were also used for home sewing and for quilting. Flour sack fabric has a noticeable weave and a slightly faded look to the colors. These can sometimes be found in antique stores or estate sales. Also look for flour sack replicas in quilting shops and catalogs.

A lot of men and most women found it difficult to get a job. As a result, hand quilting came back into vogue.

To make a quilt look like one made in this era, choose any pattern that uses small pieces. Do not try to make the fabrics coordinate with one another. The more different prints in your quilt, the better. Machine or hand piece, depending on the requirements of the pattern. Embroider some brief witticism on one of the blocks and hand quilt.

More Recent Times

Perhaps you would like to commemorate someone's birthday or anniversary by making a quilt typical of some more recent era. Pictures of the time will show you what people were wearing and give you some hint of the prints available, and, by the mid-fifties, the colors to a certain extent, as well. Clothing displays in museums might give you some inspiration.

Since the best synthetic dyes were produced in Germany during the first half of the twentieth century, they were in short supply during World War II. Quilts, however, were often made out of older cloth.

ALERT!

The 1970s marked the lowest time for quilting. Cotton prints actually became difficult to find because of the popularity of double knits. For this era, forget about making a replica and choose a pattern or print that commemorates the event in some other way.

Color combinations that were popular in certain decades, such as pink and gray in the 1950s and orange and yellow in the 1960s, are less difficult to discover. If you're too young to remember, you should know someone you can ask.

Tea Dye

Some quilters want their era quilts to look old. They do this by staining the quilt with tea. This adds an aged look to the light colors and tones down the brighter ones.

Begin by boiling approximately one gallon of water and four tea bags for a few minutes; then let it cool. Test a few small pieces of your background fabric to see how long you'll want to soak your fabric. Remove a piece in ten minutes and another in fifteen, and so on. Place the pieces on paper towels that have been labeled with the times. Wait until they have dried to judge the amount of stain in each one.

Add a cup of vinegar to your gallon of tea to help set the color, and submerge the fabric in the tea. Overcrowding your pot will prevent the fabric from staining entirely, but you don't want a perfectly even stain.

You might want to set the blocks of your quilt first, then dye the whole cover. It is possible that more tea will soak into the seams and be less likely to rinse away. On a pattern like the Dresden Plate, which is supposed to look like the plates were appliquéd to whole cloth, it might be better to stain the blocks before they are set. You can stain the background fabric before you cut the blocks, but the appliqué would need to be stained at some point as well.

Remember to stain the backing and the binding as well. After it has soaked for the desired length of time, let it dry; then iron it. Assemble your quilt in the usual way. Ⓔ

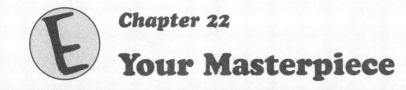

Chapter 22

Your Masterpiece

Now that you have completed a quilt (or perhaps several quilts), there are a few things you should know in order to get the most enjoyment out of your masterpiece. And if you do own antique quilts, you need to know how to preserve them.

Quilt Diary

If you are the proud owner of an antique quilt, or one not quite old enough to bear the title, you probably wish you knew more about the quilt and the person who made it. Do your part now to help the next generation by documenting in a quilt diary what you know about your antique and/or your new masterpiece.

Your Quilt

Your quilt diary can be as simple as a loose-leaf notebook, something easy to add to that can hold both photos and lined pages. A must is a picture of your finished quilt. One showing you working on it would be nice as well.

On the page facing the photos, record the quilt's title (if you've given it one), the name of the pattern, and perhaps the source of the pattern. Include your name, the date you finished the quilt, the date you started it (if you want), and your address when you made it. This is not intended to take the place of signing your quilt.

FACT

Most quilters cannot make money selling their quilts. They simply aren't valuable enough to pay for the hours of work. On average, depending on the region, new quilts sell for $200 to $500, perhaps more in large cities. Hand versus machine quilting is the main difference in the cost. A quilter would be lucky to make fifty cents an hour.

Include any difficulties you had and how you overcame them as well as any other information that will help the next generations better appreciate the quilt. If you want a quilt to go to a particular person once you are gone, include that here as well.

If you wish, you can include a pocket for the templates or patterns you used. This might be a good way to keep everything together and to make it easy to find the pattern if you decide to use it again.

Gift Quilts

Don't forget to include the quilts you give away in your diary. Even baby quilts should be recorded. A picture with the recipient would be nice. Be sure to include the recipient's name, relationship to you, and the occasion in your quilt's story. Make a copy of the page and present it along with the quilt.

Antique Quilts

Take pictures now of your antique quilts and date the pictures. Record what you know about them. Information will be missing, of course, making it all the more important that some record be made before everything is forgotten. Check quilt pattern books to see if you can identify a standard pattern. Interview family members, if you can, to find out what they know about the quilt and/or its maker.

If it is an antique quilt that you bought, see if you can find a textile historian who can help you identify the approximate date of the quilt. You may even discover some clues about where the quilter lived by the materials or the style of the quilt.

Laundering

Laundering a quilt seems to be one of the most worrisome problems for quilters. They imagine opening their washer to find their carefully constructed quilt reduced to rags. As a result, quilts are allowed to collect dirt and oils until they are imbedded in the fibers and impossible to get out. Dirt will break down these fibers, shortening the life of your quilt.

Dry Cleaning

Some quilters recommend that quilts always be dry cleaned. There may be a little of "what you don't know won't hurt you" in this attitude. You drop the quilt off at the cleaners and they magically get it cleaned. (And on very rare occasions lose it!)

The primary advantage to dry cleaning is that it is a way to clean fabrics that cannot be washed without shrinking or water spotting. If you used washable fabrics and preshrunk them before you made your quilt, you don't have to worry about either of these problems with your quilt. Furthermore, the chemicals used in dry cleaning can shorten the life of your quilt if not actually ruin it outright.

Talk to your dry cleaners to see what process is used and be sure you feel comfortable with it before you turn your quilt over to them. It would be best if they specialize in quilts.

QUESTION?

Should a quilt be ironed?
Probably not. Ironing compresses the batting. It's also a great deal of work with very limited benefit unless you have a quilt that has been wrinkled in storage. A better idea is to put your wrinkled quilt in a dryer with a couple of damp towels and let them tumble dry.

Machine Washing

Depending on the size and weight of your quilt, machine washing is probably the best way to launder your quilt. Baby quilts and twin-bed quilts will be no problem for your washing machine. Be sure you use a minimal amount of soap, the gentlest cycle, and cold water unless you're washing a soiled baby quilt. Pretreat any stains and be sure that the stain is removed before drying your quilt.

Tumble dry on a moderate setting for the softest, fluffiest results. Line dry if you prefer. Be sure to wipe the line and hang your quilt cover-side down to prevent the sun from fading it. Avoid extremely windy days.

Larger quilts may be too bulky to fit in your washer. See if the washers at a commercial laundry are larger. Commercial dryers are often too hot to give your quilt the best care. If you can adjust the heat setting, you might try them; otherwise, plan on hanging your quilt to dry when you get home.

Antique quilts and very intricate appliqué quilts should not be machine washed. The agitation could make the pieces pull away from the seams.

Hand Washing

Hand washing your quilt is the gentlest way to handle the washing dilemma, especially for antiques. For a really large quilt, you may have to resort to the bathtub. Be careful not to use too much soap, as it can be difficult to rinse out. Without the benefit of the spin cycle, your quilt will soak up several pounds of water. Squeeze out as much as possible; don't ring.

> There are special soaps made for quilts. They are low sudsing and very mild. Look for them at your fabric store or in quilting catalogs.

Plan on your quilt taking awhile to dry. Be sure to dry it in a light, airy place. You don't want to compound your dirt problem by encouraging mildew.

Home Dry Cleaning

It is best to keep washing to a minimum on the more fragile quilts. Some quilters spot wash their quilts only.

You can clean dust off your quilt by covering the upholstery attachment of your vacuum cleaner with a piece of women's hose. Spread your quilt on the floor and weigh it down at the corners. Carefully vacuum the surface of the quilt. Remember to flip it over and clean the other side.

Displaying

Your masterpiece is something to be proud of, and you want to show it off. In general, the best place to do this is on a bed. This is what your quilt was designed for, after all. If you have an antique quilt and no seldom-used bed to spread it on, you have a few other choices.

Quilt racks are available at most furniture stores. They are freestanding racks designed to hold a quilt or, in some cases, more than one. The quilt is folded, usually twice in one direction, and hung over the rack. There are some, however, that are extra long and require little, if any, folding.

This is a fairly harmless way to display your quilt. An antique quilt should be refolded occasionally to prevent the creases from becoming permanent and eventually cracking. Since the quilt is not protected from dust, it should be vacuumed whenever it is refolded.

Lots of Options to Choose From

A recent innovation is a quilt display case. This is a glass-front cabinet with a quilt rack inside. The quilt is still folded but at least it is protected from dust.

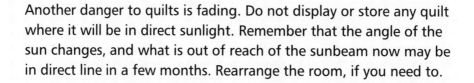

ALERT!

Another danger to quilts is fading. Do not display or store any quilt where it will be in direct sunlight. Remember that the angle of the sun changes, and what is out of reach of the sunbeam now may be in direct line in a few months. Rearrange the room, if you need to.

There are also wall racks. These are fastened to the wall and the quilt is draped over the rod. Some even have decorative shelves above them and can be very attractive. Be aware that part of the quilt will most likely be directly against the wall. Acid in the paint or wood might stain the quilt or mildew might be allowed to grow. Again, the quilt is probably still going to be folded.

Quilt Hangers

Quilts that are made to be wall hangings should have some means to hang them stitched onto the back. Wall hangings are generally smaller than a full-sized quilt and therefore lighter weight. They are not especially difficult to hang. For suggestions, see the section on hanging the Christmas tree hanging in Chapter 8 and the Watercolor quilt in Chapter 13.

A full-sized quilt hanging on a wall like a tapestry can be a very dramatic accent to a room, but there are a few problems. You can sew a sleeve onto the back, through the backing only, and hang the quilt from a rod. If the rod is wood, make sure it is treated so the acid won't damage the cloth. If the rod is metal, be certain that it will not rust and stain the quilt.

You will probably hesitate to sew anything to an antique quilt, however. A better choice is one of several styles of quilt hangers. The quilt is held between two flat pieces of wood, which are pressed together with peglike screws. Be sure the hanger you choose makes your quilt hang a few inches away from the wall.

The end of the quilt that is held between the boards is compressed considerably and the weight of the quilt itself is going to pull on the fibers and stitches near the top. Rotate the quilt every few months to minimize damage. Your quilt will also be subject to dust and should be cleaned when it is rotated. The style of hanger that has a shelf built in might protect the quilt a little more from dust.

Storing

As with displaying, the best place to store a quilt is on a bed. This isn't always possible if you are a prolific quilter. You may have some out-of-season quilts or simply too many to use at once. With the exception of antique quilts that are too fragile to use, you should consider any quilt storage as short term.

You wouldn't make a dress, then store it away to be admired every ten years or so but never worn. Yet that is how some people treat their quilts. Your quilt will mean more to the next generation if they have memories to connect with it. Catching a glimpse of it twice during their childhood doesn't count.

Flat Storage

Flat storage is by far the best way to store your quilt. If you have a little-used guest bed, spread your quilts out on it, one on top of another. Ten high might be a maximum, or the one on the bottom will become compressed. Cover the top with a sheet to protect them from dust. This way the only time they are folded for storage is when the guest room is in use.

Folded Storage

For short-term storage, quilts can be folded and stored as you would any other linens. An old pillowcase or sheet will protect your quilt from any acid in the shelves. Do not store quilts in cardboard or pasteboard boxes unless they are thoroughly lined with acid-free tissue, as the boxes will discolor your quilt. Plastic bags are not a good idea because of the possibility of molds and mildew.

Avoid basements because of the humidity, which will also promote mildew. The extreme heat in attics will dry out the fibers of a quilt, making them brittle. Where you're comfortable is the best place for your quilt. Under your bed might be a solution if your storage is limited.

If your folded storage threatens to become long term, refold the quilts regularly. You might consider using old white or very light-colored towels or acid-free tissue inside the first fold to keep it from being so sharp. Fold the backing to the inside to protect the cover from this fold.

Rolled Storage

Some quilters prefer to roll their quilts to avoid the problem of creases. Use a roll of some kind to prevent the end where you start rolling from becoming severely crimped. Cardboard rolls should be covered with tissue or white cloth before the quilt is rolled around it. See if your favorite fabric store will give you the centers from bolts of cloth.

If you really don't want to fold your quilt, you may be able to fasten several fabric bolts together and roll your quilt onto them. Under the bed is probably the only practical place to put this long roll. Roll the quilt the short way and store it under the bed the long way.

Unless you can get carpet rolls or other unusually long rolls, you will have to fold your quilt at least once before you roll it, so it will still have to be refolded periodically. Again, towels inside that first crease might be helpful.

Antiques

Though antique quilts require special care, if you are lucky enough to have one, you probably feel it is worth it. Time, especially women's time, was valued differently in the past than it is today, and early quilters put in more time on their quilts than most quilters are willing to today. As a result, antique quilts are often more intricately made than modern ones.

Buying

A quilt's greatest value is its history. Owning something that was made by an ancestor or family friend is inspiring. But this means that it is worth far more to family members than to outsiders. Like all antiques, quilts are only worth what someone is willing to pay for them. As a result, antique quilts often sell for far less than one would suspect. Imagine the disappointment of the seller who, having caught a glimpse of the treasured quilt twice in Grandmother's cedar chest, has greatly inflated its value in his mind. Check the online auction sites for an idea of the going rates.

The danger of buying online is you don't get a chance to really look over a quilt to check for damage. A certain amount of wear is to be expected and can add to a quilt's charm, but holes or frayed seams are only going to get worse. It's better if you can really look over a quilt, front and back.

Watch for estate auctions in your area that advertise quilts. These quilts, however, may be more expensive, because you may be bidding against dealers with connections to interior decorators who can inflate the value. Be sure you've checked around and determined what you want to spend before you jump into the bidding.

Restoring

There is a fine line between mending a quilt and refurbishing one. The first is necessary maintenance. If your restoring goes too far, you may destroy any historical and antique value your quilt has.

Things to consider are: what you have at present, what you can realistically do for the quilt, and what value it will have to you when you are done. A fifty-year-old machine-pieced tied quilt with disintegrating batting has no real antique value the way it is. Yet, if it was pieced by an ancestor, it has value to you. Do you store it away? Or attempt a renovation?

FACT

There are valuable quilts. These are either quilts of some specific historic value, very old quilts in excellent condition, or modern quilts that are so exquisitely done as to be considered works of art.

A tied quilt can be taken apart and reassembled with fresh batting. There will be holes left from the ties on both the cover and the backing. It will not be possible to match these holes with new ties, but you can match the ones on the cover.

But suppose you have a 100-year-old hand-quilted quilt with the same problem. In this case, mend any loose seams, replace any quilting stitches that have broken, and let it go at that.

Quilt Shows and Contests

Quilt shows range from small church or quilting club fund-raisers to elaborate conventions sponsored by national or international quilting organizations or manufacturers of quilting supplies. Attending even the smallest of these affairs can be both inspiring and humbling. A list of a few annual shows is in Appendix B.

Quilts occasionally disappear from quilt shows. If you are considering entering a quilt in a contest or show, no matter how small, be sure there is some sort of security present. At the very least, you should be given a receipt when you drop off your quilt so no one else can claim your quilt at the end of the show.

Some shows carry their own insurance. Be sure that this is more than nominal coverage. It should be for full replacement value or you should have your quilt insured.

Your homeowner's insurance may not cover your quilt. Even if it does, it may not be covered once it leaves your home or car. You may need a rider for your quilt. This will require that your quilt be appraised. Have it reappraised every few years to be sure you're sufficiently covered.

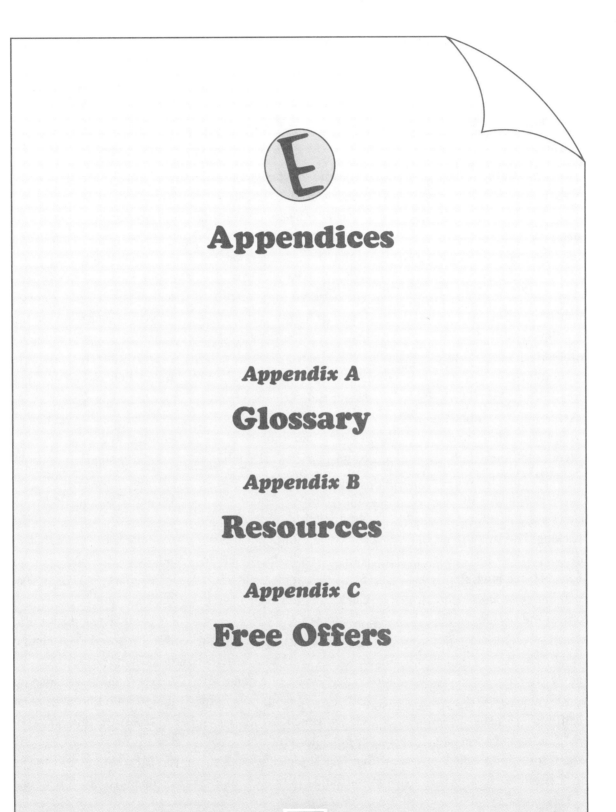

E

Appendices

Appendix A

Glossary

Appendix B

Resources

Appendix C

Free Offers

Appendix A

Glossary

all-over pattern: A quilt cover that consists of one large picture.

appliqué: (v) The act of sewing one piece of cloth onto another for decorative purposes. (n) The piece of cloth that is appliquéd on.

appliquéd quilt: A quilt decorated with shapes of cloth sewn on top of the cover.

appliqué stitch: A tiny stitch that holds an appliqué piece in place while holding the seam allowance under.

assemble: Put the layers of a quilt (cover, batting, and backing) together.

backing: The bottom layer of a quilt, sometimes called lining.

back-to-front binding: A way of finishing the edge of a quilt by turning the backing to the front and sewing it down like binding.

baste: To sew pieces in place with temporary stitches.

batting: The insulating layer of a quilt, usually cotton or polyester, sometimes called filling or padding.

betweens needles: Are short, fine needles used for quilting.

bias: The diagonal direction on a piece of cloth.

bind: To finish the outside edge of a quilt whether using binding or some other method.

binding: Narrow strips of cloth sewn on the outside edge of a quilt to cover the raw edges of the layers.

bleed: When the dye from a dark fabric stains adjoining fabrics, it is said to bleed.

blend fabric: A fabric that has a fabric content that is a blend of cotton and polyester.

blind stitch: The tiny hidden stitches done on the outside of a seam when it is impossible to get inside to machine stitch.

block: An individual section of a quilt cover.

block pattern: A drawing on a grid that is used as a pattern for a single block of a quilt.

bolt: Unit of cloth bought by the retailer, which the shopper's yardage is cut from.

border: The pieces of cloth that surround the outside of a

quilt cover that are different from the rest of the cover.

broadcloth: A plain-weave fabric with a semiglossy finish.

butcher paper: A white paper with a coating of plastic on one side used for quilt patterns because the plastic will adhere temporarily to the fabric.

chain piecing: A shortcut for joining quilt pieces in which one pair of pieces is seamed following another without stopping to cut the threads.

chain stitch: A decorative embroidery stitch that resem-bles a chain and is made by a series of daisy stitches.

colorfast: Fabric that will not fade when washed.

comforter: Another name for a tied quilt.

cover: The top layer of a quilt, often decorated, sometimes called the quilt top or face.

crazy quilt: Victorian quilt made with odd shapes of fabric.

crosswise threads: The threads of a woven fabric that run from selvage to selvage.

daisy stitch: A decorative

embroidery stitch that looks like the petal of a flower.

echo stitch: A quilting stitch that outlines a figure, then repeats that same outline in consecutive rows outward from that figure.

fat quarter: One-half yard of fabric cut in half lengthwise.

finishing strip: A strip of fabric used to cover what would otherwise be exposed seam allowances.

friendship quilts: Quilts given as gifts with blocks made by several different quilters.

lap quilting: Quilting with a hoop held or balanced on one's lap.

lengthwise threads: The threads in a woven fabric that run the entire length of the bolt.

medallion quilt: An appliquéd and pieced quilt with a center design surrounded by several rows of decorative borders.

miter: Made to look like a mitered joint or a joint where two pieces of wood are joined at an angle.

mosaic quilt: Quilt made from many small, usually hexagonal, pieces.

nap: Texture on the surface of a fabric.

One-Patch quilt: A quilt made from pieces that are all the same shape and size.

on point: Square pieces or blocks turned to appear as diamonds on a quilt.

outline stitch: A decorative embroidery stitch that makes a straight or curved line, sometimes called a stem stitch.

overcast stitch: Stitches done on the outside that include a loop of thread wrapping over the edges of the pieces.

panel: A piece of cloth separating the blocks on a quilt cover.

patchwork: Anything made with pieces of different fabrics.

pattern: The guide to making a quilt as well as the design itself.

piece: (v) To sew pieces of cloth together that are treated as whole cloth. (n) The individual units of a quilt pattern.

pieced quilt: A type of quilt made from pieces of cloth sewn together.

piping: Fabric-covered cord used as trim.

plain quilt: A quilt cover made from whole cloth and decorated only with the quilting stitches.

quilt: (v) To stitch layers of cloth together. (n) Generally a bed covering or wall hanging made from layers of cloth. Other objects are referred to as quilted.

quilting bee: A gathering of quilters where they help each other with their quilts.

quilting stitch: Tiny in-and-out stitches through the layers of a quilt done in a rocking motion.

reverse appliqué: Appliquéing a fabric through a hole in the fabric on top of it.

rotary cutter: A cutter with a circular blade, similar to a pizza cutter, designed especially for cutting fabric.

running stitch: A stitch in which the needle weaves in and out of the fabric several times before being pulled all the way through.

satin stitch: A decorative embroidery stitch made with parallel stitches very close together.

scrap quilt: A quilt made from pieces of leftover fabric.

selvage: The tightly woven edges of a length of fabric.

set (color): To treat fabric so the dye will be colorfast or ink will not run.

set (quilt): To sew the

blocks of a quilt cover together.

sharps needles: Are long needles used for most sewing.

stem stitch: Another name for the outline stitch.

stitch in the ditch: A row of quilting stitches, either by hand or machine, that runs directly on a seam.

straight with the grain: In line with the lengthwise or crosswise threads of a fabric.

string piecing: A technique of sewing small scraps of fabric to a lining strip.

template: A shape cut the size and shape of a desired quilt piece used to mark stitching or cutting lines on a piece of fabric.

tied quilt: A quilt in which the layers are tied together instead of quilted, sometimes called a comforter.

trapunto: Italian quilting form that includes strings or stuffing under the surface.

whipstitch: Fast, loose stitches similar to the overcast stitch.

yard goods: Fabric sold by the yard or fraction of a yard.

Appendix B

Resources

Books

Austin, Mary Leman, editor. *Twentieth Century's Best American Quilts* (Golden, CO: Primedia Special Interest Publications, 1999). This soft-cover magazine-size book features full-color photos of incredible quilts with a brief story of each.

Brackman, Barbara. *Quilts from the Civil War* (Lafayette, CA: C&T Publishing, 1997). The history of quilts of the Civil War era along with color photos of antique and modern replica quilts as well as instructions.

Brightbill, Dorothy. *Quilting as a Hobby* (New York: Sterling Publishing Company, 1963). General directions for quilting along with some mostly black-and-white photos.

Daniel, Nancy Brenan. *Learn To Do Hand Quilting in Just One Day* (San Marcos, CA: American School of Needlework, Inc.; ASN Publishing, 1996). This soft-cover magazine-size book offers patterns for a few wall hangings with the emphasis on hand quilting, for which it provides complete, detailed instruction.

Finley, Ruth E. *Old Patchwork Quilts and the Women Who Made Them* (Philadelphia & London: J. B. Lippincott Company, 1929). Interesting photos and many quilt block illustrations make this book valuable for anyone making period quilts.

Hall, Carrie A., and Kretsinger, Rose G. *The Romance of the Patchwork Quilt in America* (New York: Bonanza Books, 1935). Ms. Hall collected more than 800 pieced and appliquéd blocks, most of which are included in black-and-white photo groupings along with discussion of their origins.

Hassel, Carla J. *You Can Be a Super Quilter* (Radnor, PA: Wallace-Homestead Book Co., 1980). This is a very detailed, step-by-step instruction of every phase of basic quilting presented in a stern teacher's voice.

Havig, Bettina. *Carrie Hall Blocks* (Paducah, KY: American Quilter's Society, 1999). This book contains color photographs of most of Ms. Hall's collection discussed in her book, *Romance of the Patchwork Quilt*. The collection is now in the Spencer Museum of Art, University of Kansas, in Lawrence.

Lewis, Alfred Allan. *Mountain Artisans Quilting Book* (New York: Macmillan Publishing Co., Inc., 1973). This book contains mostly black-and-white but some color photos, some history of and instructions for quilting. However, it is mostly an account of the Mountain Artisans organization of Appalachia and the members' attempting to provide for themselves and their families by selling quilts.

Linsley, Leslie. *America's Favorite Quilts* (New York: Delacorte Press, 1983). This book contains detailed directions for twenty-six quilts.

Lithgow, Marilyn. *Quiltmaking and Quiltmakers* (New York: Funk & Wagnalls, 1974). This book contains some quilting history and general instructions for quilt making.

Magaret, Pat Maixner, and Slusser, Donna Ingram. *Watercolor Quilts* (Bothell, WA: The Patchwork Place, Inc., 1993). This soft-cover magazine-size book offers full color and detailed descriptions of every phase of this type of quilting.

McKim, Ruby Short. *One Hundred and One Patchwork Patterns* (New York: Dover Publications, Inc., 1962). This is a revised version of a book first published in 1931 by McKim Studios. Ms. McKim was recently inducted into the Quilters Hall of Fame for her work in preserving quilt patterns.

McMurtry, Rosemary, editor. *McCall's How to Quilt It!* (New York: McCall's Pattern Co., 1953). Most types of quilting, along with some complete instructions, are covered in this soft-cover magazine-size book.

Meredith Corporation. *501 Quilt Block: A Treasury of Patterns for Patchwork and Appliqué* (Des Moines: Better Homes and Gardens, 1994). This large book features a block pattern and a color photo along with a brief description of 501 patterns.

Pellman, Rachel T. *Tips for Quilters* (Intercourse, PA: Good Books, 1993). Quilters offer advice on everything related to quilting. The paperback book is organized by topic, making it a great quick reference book.

Safford, Carleton L., and Bishop, Robert. *America's Quilts and Coverlets* (New York: Weathervane Books, 1974). A historian's look at quilts, tapestries, and other textiles. Quilting is spoken of almost exclusively in the past tense.

Webster, Marie D. *Quilts: Their Story and How to Make Them* (Marion, IN: Doubleday, Page & Company, 1915). A view of nineteenth-century quilts from early in the twentieth century. A good source of patterns for period quilts.

Wiss, Audrey, and Wiss, Douglas. *Folk Quilts and How to Recreate Them* (Pittstown, NY: The Main Street Press, 1983). History and instructions for thirty old patterns are provided along with mostly black-and-white photos.

Magazines

American Patchwork Quilting Magazine
P.O. Box 37445
Boone, IA 50037-0445
✆ (800) 677-4876

Art/Quilt Magazine
P.O. Box 630927
Houston, TX 77263-0927
✆ (800) 399-3532
🖥 ArtQuiltMg@aol.com

McCall's Quick Quilts, McCall's Quilting, and McCall's Vintage Quilts
P.O. Box 56730
Boulder, CO 80322
✆ (800) 944-0736
🖥 mcq@primediasi.com
✐ www.mccallsquilting.com

Miniature Quilts, Quilting Today, and Traditional Quiltworks
P.O. Box 10615
Riverton, NJ 08076-0615
🖥 Chitra@epix.net
✐ www.QuiltTownUSA.com

New Zealand Quilter
P.O. Box 14-567
Kilbirnie, Wellington, New Zealand
🖥 Nzquilter@exra.co.nz
✐ www.nzquilter.com

Professional Quilter, The
22412 Rolling Hill Lane
Laytonville, MD 20882
✐ www.professionalquilter.com

Quilter's Newsletter Magazine
Box 59021
Boulder, CO 80322-9021
✆ (800) 477-6089 or ✆ (303) 604-1464
✎ (303) 604-7455
🖥 qnw@neodata.com
✐ www.quiltersnewsletter.com

Quilt It for Kids
741 Corporate Circle, Suite A
Golden, CO 80401
✆ (800) 590-3465; outside the U.S. ✆ (720) 836-1123; ✎ (303) 277-0370

Quilt Magazine
1115 Broadway
New York, NY 10010
✐ www.quiltmag.com

Quiltmaker
P.O. Box 58360
Boulder, CO 80322-8360
✆ (800) 477-6089; outside the U.S. and Canada
✆ (303) 604-1464; ✎ (303) 277-0370

Organizations

Alliance for American Quilts is dedicated to the preservation, documentation, and study of quilts. It established The Center for the Quilt and maintains three Web sites for quilt enthusiasts: *www.quiltalliance.org*, *www.quiltcenter.org*, and *www.quilting.about.com*.

International Quilt Association

(*www.quilts.org*) endeavors to promote understanding and appreciation of quilt making. It sponsors the International Quilt Festival and Quilt Expo.

National Quilting Association

(*www.nqaquilts.org*) was founded in 1970 and is the oldest organization of its kind in the United States. It has sponsored the National Quilting Association Annual Quilt Show since 1970 as well as seminars on the history and preservation of quilts.

Quilters Hall of Fame will send information if you send a self-addressed stamped envelope to T.Q.H.F., P.O. Box 681, Marion, IN 46952.

Annual Quilt Shows

International Quilt Festival

7660 Woodway, Suite 550
Houston, TX 77063
(713) 781-6864; (713) 781-8182
shows@quilts.com
www.quilts.com

Montana Cowgirl Quilt Retreat

Nine Quarter Circle Ranch
5000 Taylor Fork Road
Gallatin Gateway, MT 59730
(406) 995-4276

National Quilting Association Annual Quilt Show

P.O. Box 393
Ellicott City, MD 21041-0393
(410) 461-5733; (410) 461-3693
nqa@erols.com
www.nqaquilts.com

Quilt Odyssey

Send $1 for information.
15004 Burnt Mill Road
Shippensburg, PA 17257
(717) 423-5148
www.quiltodyssey.com

Rockome Gardens Quilt Celebration

125 N Co. Rd 425 E
Arcola, IL 61910
(217) 268-4106
www.rockome.com

Threads of Discovery

Appliqué Society's Annual Meeting and
Quilt Show
Box 218394
Columbus, OH 43221-8394
www.theappliquesociety.org

Waterloo County and Area Quilt Festival
Ontario, Canada
☎ (888) 804-7909 or ☎ (519) 699-5628
✍ www.quiltcapitalfestival.com

World Quilt Show
c/o Mancuso, Inc., Dept. QN
P.O. Box 667
New Hope, PA 18938
✍ www.worldquilt.com

Other Web Sites Worth Visiting

Original Sewing & Quilt Expo has a traveling exhibit: ✍ www.sewingexpo.com.

Planet Patchwork calls itself "the ultimate address in quilting": ✍ www.planetpatchwork.com.

Quilt Festivals by Mancuso: ✍ www.quiltfest.com.

Women Folk has extensive quilt history and quilt book reviews: ✍ www.womenfolk.com.

World Wide Quilting Page has help and information for quilters: ✍ www.quilt.com.

Appendix C

Free Offers

American Professional Quilting Systems
Free video of hand-guided quilting machines.
8033 University Avenue, Suite F
Des Moines, IA 50325
☎ (800) 426-7233 or ☎ (515) 267-1113
📠 (515) 267-8414
🖳 apqs@netins.net
✍ www.apqs.com

Art in a Pinch
Free brochure of hangers for quilts and rugs.
6549 Keystone Rd., Dept. MCC
Milaca, MN 56353
☎ (888) 369-4500; 📠 (320) 983-2151
✍ www.artinapinch.net

Country Heritage Tours
Catalog of tours designed for quilters.
P.O. Box 59
Amherst, NH 03031
☎ (800) 346-9820 or ☎ (603) 673-0640
✍ www.countryheritagetours.com

Creative Curves
Brochure of quilting books. Please send SASE.
Virginia A. Walton
3825 Camino Capistrano NE
Albuquerque, NM 87111
📠 (505) 294-1979
✍ Info@creativecurves.com
✍ www.creativecurves.com

Easy Quilt Kits
Free catalog of available quilt kits.
99 Nahanton Avenue
Milton, MA 02186
✎ (800) 939-KITS

Edward R. Hamilton, Bookseller
Free catalog of books for needlecrafters.
6445 Oak
Falls Village, CT 06031-5005
✎ (800) 677-3483
✎ www.erhbooks.com

Feathered Star Productions, Inc.
Free catalog of quilting books, fabric, and
products.
✎ (888) 377-7827
✎ www.MarshaMcCloskey.com

Fletcher Farm School for the Arts & Crafts
Free catalog of courses for a "learning vacation."
611 Route 1035
Ludlow, VT 05149
✎ (802) 228-8770
✎ www.fletcherfarm.com

Gammill Quilting Machine Co.
Free demonstration video, fact sheet, and price
list of their quilting machines.
1452 West Gibson Street
West Plains, MO 65775
✎ (800) 659-8224 or ✎ (417) 256-5919;
✎ (417) 256-5757
🖳 gammill@townsqr.com
✎ www.gammill.net

Gone to Pieces
Free brochure of their Block of the Month Club
and quilters' tools.
8374 SR 305
Garrettsville, OH 44231
✎ 800-205-7204
✎ www.gonetopieces.net

The Grace Company
Free brochures of their quilting hoops and
frames.
P.O. Box 27823
Salt Lake City, UT 84127
✎ (800) 264-0644
✎ www.graceframe.com

Hancock's of Paducah
Free catalog of the latest fabric for quilters.
3841 Hinkleville Road
Paducah, KY 42001
✎ (800) 845-8723
outside the U.S. ✎ (270) 443-4410
🖳 hanpad@sunsix.infi.net
✎ www.Hancocks-Paducah.com

Hinterberg Design, Inc.
Free brochure of their Homestead Quilting
Hoops and Frames.
2805 East Progress Drive
West Bend, WI 53095
✎ (800) 443-5800
✎ www.hinterberg.com

Jasmine Heirlooms
Free brochure of their quilt frames and hoops.
1308 Water Street
Kerrville, TX 78028
✆ (800) 736-7326 or ✆ (830) 257-5442
✆ (830) 896-9502
⌨ jasmine@jasmineheirlooms.com
✐ www.jasmineheirlooms.com

Keepsake Quilting
Free 128-page color catalog of fabrics, books, patterns, and quilting supplies.
Dept. MQ
Rt. 25B, P.O. Box 1618
Center Harbor, NH 03226-1618
✆ (800) 865-9458
✐ www.keepsakequilting.com

Lorie's Little Quilts
Free catalog of quilt patterns, kits, and oak quilt hangers.
241 Country Rd. 120
Carthage, MO 64836
✆ (888) 419-5618
✐ www.LoriesLittleQuilts.com

Main Street Cotton Shop
Free catalog of quilting fabrics and books.
141 E. 2nd Street
Redwood Falls, MN 56283
✆ (800) 624-4001
✐ www.mainstreetcottonshop.com

Newark Dressmaker Supply
Free catalog of quilting, sewing, and other craft products.
Dept. 630
P.O. Box 20730
Lehigh Valley, PA 18002-0730
✐ www.newarkdress.com

Pieceable Dry Goods
Free catalog of fabrics, quilt kits, books, patterns, and other handwork supplies.
5215 W. Clearwater, #106
Kennewick, WA 99336
✆ (888) 735-6080

Pieces of the Past
Free catalog of quilting products.
P.O. Box 1537
Pelham, AL 35124
✆ (877) 784-5833 or ✆ (205) 663-6782
✆ (205) 621-9093
✐ www.PiecesofthePast.com

Pigeon River Mercantile
Free brochure of their Block of the Month Quilts.
Dept. 341, Box 531
Pigeon, MI 48755-0531
✆ (888) 453-4554
✐ www.quiltinpigeon.com

Quiltwork Patches
Free catalog of quilting products
209SW 2nd Street, Box 724-MJ
Corvallis, OR 97339
✆ (541) 752-4820

Index

THE EVERYTHING KNITTING BOOK

By Jane Eldershaw

*T*he Everything® Knitting Book is a simple—and comprehensive—guide to get you started. From blankets and sweaters to hats and scarves, this book takes you step by step through the creative process, helping you choose the right yarn, find the appropriate needle, pick a pattern, learn a variety of stitches, devise original patterns, decorate knitted garments, and knit with more sophisticated materials, such as lace. Packed with clear line art and featuring a magnificent eight-page color insert, *The Everything® Knitting Book* is a must-have for knitters of all levels.

Trade paperback
$14.95 ($22.95 CAN)
1-58062-727-7, 304 pages

OTHER *EVERYTHING*® BOOKS BY ADAMS MEDIA CORPORATION

HISTORY

Everything® **American History Book**
Everything® **Civil War Book**
Everything® **Irish History & Heritage Book**
Everything® **Mafia Book**
Everything® **World War II Book**

HOBBIES & GAMES

Everything® **Bridge Book**
Everything® **Candlemaking Book**
Everything® **Casino Gambling Book**
Everything® **Chess Basics Book**
Everything® **Collectibles Book**
Everything® **Crossword and Puzzle Book**
Everything® **Digital Photography Book**
Everything® **Family Tree Book**
Everything® **Games Book**
Everything® **Knitting Book**
Everything® **Magic Book**
Everything® **Motorcycle Book**
Everything® **Online Genealogy Book**
Everything® **Photography Book**
Everything® **Pool & Billiards Book**
Everything® **Quilting Book**
Everything® **Scrapbooking Book**
Everything® **Soapmaking Book**

HOME IMPROVEMENT

Everything® **Feng Shui Book**
Everything® **Gardening Book**
Everything® **Home Decorating Book**
Everything® **Landscaping Book**
Everything® **Lawn Care Book**
Everything® **Organize Your Home Book**

KIDS' STORY BOOKS

Everything® **Bedtime Story Book**
Everything® **Bible Stories Book**
Everything® **Fairy Tales Book**
Everything® **Mother Goose Book**

KIDS' EVERYTHING® BOOKS

All titles are $6.95
Everything® **Kids' Baseball Book, 2nd Ed.** ($10.95 CAN)
Everything® **Kids' Bugs Book** ($10.95 CAN)
Everything® **Kids' Christmas Puzzle & Activity Book** ($10.95 CAN)
Everything® **Kids' Cookbook** ($10.95 CAN)
Everything® **Kids' Halloween Puzzle & Activity Book** ($10.95 CAN)
Everything® **Kids' Joke Book** ($10.95 CAN)
Everything® **Kids' Math Puzzles Book** ($10.95 CAN)
Everything® **Kids' Mazes Book** ($10.95 CAN)
Everything® **Kids' Money Book** ($11.95 CAN)
Everything® **Kids' Monsters Book** ($10.95 CAN)
Everything® **Kids' Nature Book** ($11.95 CAN)
Everything® **Kids' Puzzle Book** ($10.95 CAN)
Everything® **Kids' Science Experiments Book,** ($10.95 CAN)
Everything® **Kids' Soccer Book** ($10.95 CAN)
Everything® **Kids' Travel Activity Book** ($10.95 CAN)

LANGUAGE

Everything® **Learning French Book**
Everything® **Learning German Book**
Everything® **Learning Italian Book**
Everything® **Learning Latin Book**
Everything® **Learning Spanish Book**
Everything® **Sign Language Book**

MUSIC

Everything® **Drums Book (with CD), $19.95** ($31.95 CAN)
Everything® **Guitar Book**
Everything® **Playing Piano and Keyboards Book**

Everything® **Rock & Blues Guitar Book (with CD), $19.95** ($31.95 CAN)
Everything® **Songwriting Book**

NEW AGE

Everything® **Astrology Book**
Everything® **Divining the Future Book**
Everything® **Dreams Book**
Everything® **Ghost Book**
Everything® **Meditation Book**
Everything® **Numerology Book**
Everything® **Palmistry Book**
Everything® **Psychic Book**
Everything® **Spells & Charms Book**
Everything® **Tarot Book**
Everything® **Wicca and Witchcraft Book**

PARENTING

Everything® **Baby Names Book**
Everything® **Baby Shower Book**
Everything® **Baby's First Food Book**
Everything® **Baby's First Year Book**
Everything® **Breastfeeding Book**
Everything® **Father-to-Be Book**
Everything® **Get Ready for Baby Book**
Everything® **Homeschooling Book**
Everything® **Parent's Guide to Positive Discipline**
Everything® **Potty Training Book, $9.95** ($15.95 CAN)
Everything® **Pregnancy Book, 2nd Ed.**
Everything® **Pregnancy Fitness Book**
Everything® **Pregnancy Organizer, $15.00** ($22.95 CAN)
Everything® **Toddler Book**
Everything® **Tween Book**

PERSONAL FINANCE

Everything® **Budgeting Book**
Everything® **Get Out of Debt Book**
Everything® **Get Rich Book**
Everything® **Homebuying Book, 2nd Ed.**
Everything® **Homeselling Book**

All Everything® books are priced at $12.95 or $14.95, unless otherwise stated. Prices subject to change without notice.
Canadian prices range from $11.95–$31.95, and are subject to change without notice.

Everything® **Investing Book**
Everything® **Money Book**
Everything® **Mutual Funds Book**
Everything® **Online Investing Book**
Everything® **Personal Finance Book**
Everything® **Personal Finance in Your 20s & 30s Book**
Everything® **Wills & Estate Planning Book**

PETS

Everything® **Cat Book**
Everything® **Dog Book**
Everything® **Dog Training and Tricks Book**
Everything® **Horse Book**
Everything® **Puppy Book**
Everything® **Tropical Fish Book**

REFERENCE

Everything® **Astronomy Book**
Everything® **Car Care Book**
Everything® **Christmas Book, $15.00** ($21.95 CAN)
Everything® **Classical Mythology Book**
Everything® **Einstein Book**
Everything® **Etiquette Book**
Everything® **Great Thinkers Book**
Everything® **Philosophy Book**
Everything® **Shakespeare Book**
Everything® **Tall Tales, Legends, & Other Outrageous Lies Book**
Everything® **Toasts Book**
Everything® **Trivia Book**
Everything® **Weather Book**

RELIGION

Everything® **Angels Book**
Everything® **Buddhism Book**
Everything® **Catholicism Book**
Everything® **Jewish History & Heritage Book**
Everything® **Judaism Book**

Everything® **Prayer Book**
Everything® **Saints Book**
Everything® **Understanding Islam Book**
Everything® **World's Religions Book**
Everything® **Zen Book**

SCHOOL & CAREERS

Everything® **After College Book**
Everything® **College Survival Book**
Everything® **Cover Letter Book**
Everything® **Get-a-Job Book**
Everything® **Hot Careers Book**
Everything® **Job Interview Book**
Everything® **Online Job Search Book**
Everything® **Resume Book, 2nd Ed.**
Everything® **Study Book**

SELF-HELP

Everything® **Dating Book**
Everything® **Divorce Book**
Everything® **Great Marriage Book**
Everything® **Great Sex Book**
Everything® **Romance Book**
Everything® **Self-Esteem Book**
Everything® **Success Book**

SPORTS & FITNESS

Everything® **Bicycle Book**
Everything® **Body Shaping Book**
Everything® **Fishing Book**
Everything® **Fly-Fishing Book**
Everything® **Golf Book**
Everything® **Golf Instruction Book**
Everything® **Pilates Book**
Everything® **Running Book**
Everything® **Sailing Book, 2nd Ed.**
Everything® **T'ai Chi and QiGong Book**
Everything® **Total Fitness Book**
Everything® **Weight Training Book**
Everything® **Yoga Book**

TRAVEL

Everything® **Guide to Las Vegas**

Everything® **Guide to New England**
Everything® **Guide to New York City**
Everything® **Guide to Washington D.C.**
Everything® **Travel Guide to The Disneyland Resort®, California Adventure®, Universal Studios®, and the Anaheim Area**
Everything® **Travel Guide to the Walt Disney World Resort®, Universal Studios®, and Greater Orlando, 3rd Ed.**

WEDDINGS

Everything® **Bachelorette Party Book**
Everything® **Bridesmaid Book**
Everything® **Creative Wedding Ideas Book**
Everything® **Jewish Wedding Book**
Everything® **Wedding Book, 2nd Ed.**
Everything® **Wedding Checklist, $7.95** ($11.95 CAN)
Everything® **Wedding Etiquette Book, $7.95** ($11.95 CAN)
Everything® **Wedding Organizer, $15.00** ($22.95 CAN)
Everything® **Wedding Shower Book, $7.95** ($12.95 CAN)
Everything® **Wedding Vows Book, $7.95** ($11.95 CAN)
Everything® **Weddings on a Budget Book, $9.95** ($15.95 CAN)

WRITING

Everything® **Creative Writing Book**
Everything® **Get Published Book**
Everything® **Grammar and Style Book**
Everything® **Grant Writing Book**
Everything® **Guide to Writing Children's Books**
Everything® **Screenwriting Book**
Everything® **Writing Well Book**

Available wherever books are sold!
To order, call 800-872-5627, or visit us at everything.com